P9-AQY-329

NOTES ON THE IROQUOIS:

OR, CONTRIBUTIONS TO THE

STATISTICS, ABORIGINAL HISTORY, ANTIQUITIES AND GENERAL ETHNOLOGY

OF

WESTERN NEW-YORK.

By HENRY R. SCHOOLCRAFT,

Hon. Mem. of the Royal Society of Northern Antiquaries, Copenhagen; Hon. Mem. of the Royal Geographical Society of London; Vice-President of the American Ethnological Scociety at New-York; Member of the American Philosophical, of the American Antiquarian, and of the American Geological Societies; Hon. Mem. of the New-York Historical, of the Georgia Historical, and of the Rhode-Island Historical Societies, &c., &c., &c.

NEW-YORK:
BARTLETT & WELFORD,
ASTOR HOUSE.
....
1846.

KRAUS REPRINT CO.
Millwood, New York
1975

Library of Congress Cataloging in Publication Data

Schoolcraft, Henry Rowe, 1793-1864.
Notes on the Iroquois.

Reprint of the 1846 ed. published by Bartlett & Welford, New York.
1. Iroquois Indians. I. Title.
E99.I7S3 1975 974.7'004'97 75-8790
ISBN 0-527-03226-3

Printed in U.S.A.

SENATE DOCUMENT, TWENTY-FOUR.

In giving a more permanent form to the original edition of this document, a more convenient reference title has been prefixed to it.

The aboriginal nation, whose statistics and history, past and present, are brought into discussion in the following report, stand out prominently in the foreground of our own history. They have sustained themselves, for more than three centuries and a half, against the intruding and progressive races of Europe. During the period of the planting of the colonies, their military exploits gave them a name and a reputation which are coeval with Europe. These events are intermingled, more or less, with the history of each of the colonies, and impart to them much of their interest. But while we have made an extaordinary progress in population and resources, and gone far to build up a nationality, and commenced a national literature, very little, if any, progress has been made in clearing up and narrowing the boundaries of historical mystery, which shroud the INDIAN PERIOD prior to 1492. This forms, indeed, the true period of American Ethnology.

It was a desideratum in American statistics, that a complete census of one of these primary stocks, who had lived in our neighborhood all this time, and still preserved their nationality, should be taken. This task New-York executed in 1845. It appeared desirable to the agent appointed to carry the act of the legislature, embracing this feature, into effect, that the opportunity should not be lost of making some notes of the kind here indicated ; and it is in this feature, indeed, if any thing, in the report now presented, that it aspires to the character of research, though it be intended only to shadow forth outlines to be filled up hereafter.

New-York, Feb. 7, 1846.

MEMORANDUM OF PAPERS.

APPENDIX.

STATE OF NEW-YORK.

No. 24.

IN SENATE,

January 22, 1846.

COMMUNICATION

From the Secretary of State, transmitting the report of Mr. Schoolcraft, one of the agents appointed to take the census or enumeration of the Indians, &c.

SECRETARY'S OFFICE,
Albany, January 17th, 1846.

Hon. A. GARDINER,
President of the Senate:

SIR:

In compliance with the resolution of the Senate of the 15th instant, I transmit herewith a report of one of the agents appointed to take the census or enumeration of the Indians residing upon several of the reservations in the State, and an abstract of all the census returns, taken pursuant to the fifteenth section of the act chapter 140 of the laws of 1845, and of the statistical information required by the act, and also a report relating "to their past and present condition."

I am, very respectfully,
Your obedient servant,
N. S. BENTON.

REPORT

Of Mr. Schoolcraft, to the Secretary of State, transmitting the census returns in relation to the Indians.

CENSUS OF THE IROQUOIS.

New-York, October 31*st*, 1845.

SIR :

In conformity with your instructions of the 25th June last, I proceeded to the several Iroquois reservations therein named, and I have the honor herewith to transmit to you the census returns for each reservation, numbered from I to VIII, and distinguished by the popular name of each tribe, or canton.

I. The question of the original generic name, by which these tribes were denoted, the relation they bear to the other aboriginal stocks of America, and the probable era of their arrival, and location within the present boundaries of this State, is one, which was naturally suggested, by the statistical inquiries entrusted to me. Difficult and uncertain as any thing brought forward on these subjects must necessarily be, it was yet desirable, in giving a view of the present and former condition of the people, that the matter should be glanced at. For, although nothing very satisfactory might be stated, it was still conceived to be well to give some answer to the intelligent inquirer, to the end, that it might, at least, be perceived the subject had not escaped notice.

A tropical climate, ample means of subsistence, and their consequence, a concentrated and fixed population, raised the ancient inhabitantsof Mexico, and some other leading nations on the continent, to a state of ease and semi-civilization, which have commanded the surprise and admiration of historians. But it may be said, in truth, that, in their fine physical type, and in their energy of character, and love of independence, no people, among the aboriginal race, have ever exceeded, if any has ever equalled, the Iroquois.

Discoveries made in the settlement of New-York, west of the DE O WAIN STA, or Stainwix Summit, have led to the belief, that there has been an ancient period of occupation of that fertile and expanded portion of the State, which terminated prior to the arrival of the Iroquois. Evidences have not been wanting to denote, that a higher degree of civilization than any of these tribes possessed, had, at a remote period, begun to develope itself in that quarter. But, hitherto, the notices and examinations of the antiquities referred to, although highly creditable to the observers, and abounding in interest, have served rather to entangle, than reveal, the archæological mystery which envelops them. Some of these antiquarian traits, not appearing to the first settlers to be invested with the importance, as industrial or military vestiges, now attached to them, have been nearly or quite obliterated by the plough. The spade of the builder and excavator has overturned others; and at the rate of increase, which has marked our numbers and industry, since the close of the revolutionary war, little or nothing of this kind will remain, in a perfect state, very long.

To gratify the moral interest belonging to the subject, by full and elaborate plans and descriptions, would require time and means, very different from any at my command the past season; but the topic was one which admitted of incidental attention, while awaiting decisions and obviating objections which some of the tribes urged to the general principles and policy of the census. And while the subject of a full archaeological and ethnological survey of the State is left as the appropriate theme of future research, facts and traditions, bearing on these subjects, were obtained and minuted down, at various points.

In availing myself of the liberty extended to me in this particular, by your instructions, I have, in fact, improved every possible means of information. Notes and sketches were taken down from the lips of both white and red men, wherever the matter itself and the trustworthiness of the individual appeared to justify them. Many of the ancient forts, barrows and general places of ancient sepulchre were visited, and of some of them, accurate plans, diagrams or sketches made on the spot, or obtained from other hands. A general interest was manifested in the subject by the citizens of western New-York, wherever it was introduced, and a most ready and obliging disposition evinced, on all hands, to promote the inquiry.

The result of these examinations, and collections made by the wayside, it is my intention to report in the form of *Historical and Ethnological Minutes*, which will be engrossed without loss of time from my original notes. These minutes, when properly arranged and copied, will constitute a document supplementary to the report here offered. It is not to be inferred, however, that they will exhibit a compact and full digest of Iroquois history. Attention has rather been given to the lapses in their history, and to the supplying of data for its future construction. Little more has ever been thought of. This part of my investigations will be communicated, therefore, as a contribution to the historical materials of the State, touching its aborigines. Satisfied that the New-York public regard the subject with decided approbation, and well aware of the munificence which has marked the State policy, with regard to the acquisition of historical documents from abroad, I may, I trust, be permitted to indulge the hope, that the Legislature will likewise extend its countenance to this portion of the labor which, as the State Marshal under the act, I have performed.

II. The present being the first time* that a formal and full census of a nation or tribe of Indians has been called for, with their industrial efforts, by any American or European government exercising authority on this continent, the principles and policy of the measure presented a novel question to the Iroquois, and led to extended discussions. As these discussions, in which the speakers evinced no little aptitude, bring out some characteristic traits of the people, it may be pertinent, and not out of place here, briefly to advert to them.

---

* It forms no contradiction to the precise terms of this remark, that the Legislature of Virginia directed the numbering of the Powhattanic tribes, within its boundaries, in 1788. Vide Jefferson's Notes on Virginia.

As a general fact, the policy of a census, and its beneficial bearings on society, were not understood or admitted.* It seemed to these ancient cantons to be an infringement on that independence of condition which they still claim and ardently cherish. In truth, of all subjects upon which these people have been called on to think and act, during our proximity to them of two or three centuries, that of political economy is decidedly the most foreign and least known to them, or appreciated by them, and the census movement was, consequently, the theme of no small number of suspicions and cavils and objections. Without any certain or generally fixed grounds of objection, it was yet the object of a fixed but changing opposition. If I might judge, from the scope of remarks made both in and out of council, they regarded it as the introduction of a Saxon feature into their institutions, which like a lever, by some process not apparent to them, was designed, in its ultimate effects, to uplift and overturn them. And no small degree of pith and irony was put forth against it by the eloquent respondents who stood in the official attitude of their ancient orators. Everywhere, the tribes exalted the question into one of national moment. Grave and dignified sachems assembled in formal councils, and indulged in long and fluent harrangues to their people, as if the very foundations of their ancient confederacy were about to be overturned by an innovating spirit of political arithmetic and utilitarianism. When their true views were made known, however, after many days and adjourned councils, I found there was less objection to the mere numbering of their tribes and families, than the [to them] scrutinizing demand, which the act called for, into their agricultural products, and the results of their industry. Pride also had some weight in the matter. "We have but little," said one of the chiefs, in a speech in council, "to exhibit. Those who have yielded their assent, have their barns well stored, and need not blush when you call."

Another topic mixed itself with the consideration of the census, and made some of the chiefs distrustful of it. I allude to the long disturbed state of their land question, and the treaty of compromise

* To this remark, the Tuscaroras, who met the subject at once, in a frank and confidential manner, and the Onondagas, who appeared to be governed therein by the counsels of a single educated chief, form exceptions.

which has recently been made with the Ogden Company, by which the reversionary right to the fee simple of two of their reservations has been modified. In this compromise, the Tonewandas, a considerable sub-tribe or departmental band of Senecas, did not unite; yet the reservation which they occupy is one of the tracts to be given up. They opposed the census, from the mere fear of committing themselves on this prior question, in some way, not very well understood by them, and certainly not well made out by their speakers. It is known that, for many years, the general question of ceding their reservations, under the provisions of an early treaty of the State with the Six Nations, had divided the Senecas into two parties. A discussion which has extended through nearly half a century, in which Red Jacket had exhibited all his eloquence, had sharpened the national acumen in negotiation, and produced a peculiar sensitiveness, and suspicion of motive, whenever, in later times, the slightest question of interest or policy has been introduced into their councils. This spirit evinced itself in the very outset of my visit, on announcing to certain bands the requirements of the census act. Some of them were, moreover, strongly disposed to view it as the preliminary step, on the part of the Legislature, to taxation. To be taxed, is an idea which the Iroquois regard with horror. They had themselves, in ancient days, put nations under tribute, and understood very well the import of a State tax upon their property.

"Why," said the Tonewanda chief, Deonehogawa, (called John Blacksmith,) "why is this census asked for, at this time, when we are in a straitened position with respect to our reservation? Or if it is important to you or us, why was it not called for before? If you do not wish to obtain facts about our lands and cattle, to tax us, what is the object of the census? What is to be done with the information after you take it to Governor Wright, at Skenectati?"*

Hoeyanehqui, or Sky-carrier, a Buffalo chief, in answer to a question as to their views of the abstract right of the State to tax the tribes, evaded a direct issue, but assuming the ground of policy, com-

* The Aborigines are very tenacious of their geographical names. This ancient name of the seat of government I found to be used, on every occasion, among the Senecas, when it was necessary to allude to Albany. Its transference on the conquest of the province, in 1664, to the banks of the Mohawk, in lieu of the aboriginal name of *Onigarawantel*, never received, at least, their sanction.

pared the Iroquois to a sick man, and said, "that he did not believe the State would oppress one thus weak."

Kaweaka, a Tuscarora chief of intelligence, speaking the English language very well, in which he is called William Mount-Pleasant, gave a proof, in yielding to the measure promptly, that he had not failed to profit by the use of letters. "We know our own rights. Should the legislature attempt to tax us, our protection is in the Constitution of the United States, which forbids it." This is the first appeal, it is thought, ever made by an Iroquois to this instrument. The clause referred to relates, however, wholly to representation in Congress, [Vide Art. 1, Sec. II, 2d.] from the privileges of which it excludes "Indians not taxed," clearly implying that such persons might be represented in that body if "taxed." Civilization and taxation appear to be inseparable.

III. Having detailed the steps taken in procuring the census, it only remains to subjoin a few remarks, which I beg leave to add, on the general features of the statistics and the results of their agriculture upon their condition and prospects.

The printed queries being prepared exclusively for a population in a high state of prosperity and progress, embrace many items for which there was no occasion, among psuedo hunters, herdsmen, or incipient agriculturists. Neither privileged to vote, nor subject to taxation, nor military service, or covered by the common school system, or bearing any of the charactaristic tests of citizenship, the questions designed to bring out this class of facts remained mere blanks. Others required to institute comparisons between a civilized and quasi savage state, were left by the tenor of your instructions, to my own discretion. I should have been, I am free to confess, happy to have extended these comparative views, much more fully than I have, going further into their vital statistics, their succedaneous modes of employment and subsistence, some parts of their lexicography, besides that affecting the names of places, and a few kindred topics, had not the legislature omitted to make provision for the expenses incidental to such extended labors, and the department to which I applied giving me little encouragement that the oversight would be remedied. I have, however, proceeded to render the comparative tables effectual, and, I trust, satisfactory, and to this end, I have assumed obligations of a very limited pecuniary character, and incurred others for travel and some few kindred objects, which I trust the Legislature, with whom alone the subject rests, will meet.

It cannot be said that the Iroquois cantons of New-York have, as yet, any productive commerce, arts or manufactures. They are, to some extent, producers ; furnish a few mechanics, and give employment to, and own a few lumber mills ; but it is believed, while some of the bands, and at least one of the entire catons, namely, the Tuscaroras, raise more grain and stock, than is sufficient for their own full subsistence, the average of the agricultural products of the whole people is not more, at the most favorable view, than is necessary for their annual subsistence. If so, they add nothing to the productive industry of the State. But it is gratifying to know that they are at least able to live upon their own means ; and their condition and improvement is (certainly within the era of the temperance movement among them,) decidedly progressive and encouraging. They have reached the point in industrial progress, where it is only necessary to go forward. Numbers of families are eminently entitled to the epithet of good practical farmers, and are living, year in and year out, in the midst of agricultural affluence. That the proportion of individuals, thus advanced, is as considerable as the census columns denote it to be, is among the favorable features of the inquiry. There would appear to be no inaptitude for mechanical ingenuity, but hitherto, the proportion of their actual number who have embraced the arts, is, comparatively, very limited, not exceeding, at most, two or three to a tribe, and the effort has hitherto been confined to silversmiths,* blacksmiths, carpenters and coopers. A single instance of a wheelwright and fancy wagon maker occurs.

Viewed in its extremes, society, in the Iroquois cantons, still exhibits no unequivocal vestiges of the tie which bound them to the hunter state ; and even, among the more advanced classes, there is too much dependence on means of living which mark either the absolute barbaric state, or the first grade of civilization. Hunters they are, indeed, no longer ; yet it was desirable to ascertain how much of

* The Iroquois, in adopting our costume, have transferred their ancient love of silver amulets, frontlets, and other barbaric ornaments, to their guns and tomahawks, which are frequently richly inlaid with the shining metal, worked with great skill into the richest devices. They also fashion beautiful ear rings of silver for their women.

their present means of subsistence was derived from the chase. This will be found to be denoted in appropriate columns. It is gratifying to observe, that the amount is so small, nor is it less so, to the cause of Indian civilization, to remark, that the uncertain and scanty reward of time and labor which the chase affords, is less and less relied on, in the precise ratio that the bands and neighborhoods advance in agriculture and the arts. In cases where the cultivation of English grains and the raising of stock have thoroughly enlisted attention, the chase has long ceased to attract its ancient votaries, and in these instances, which embrace some entire bands, or chieftaincies, it has become precisely what it is, in civilized communities, where game yet exists, *an amusement*, and not a means of reward.

That delusive means of Indian subsistence, which is based on the receipt of money annuities from the government, still calls together annually, and sometimes oftener, the collective male population of these tribes, at an expense of time, and means, which is wholly disproportioned, both to the amount actually received, and the not unimportant incidental risques, *moral* and *physical*, incurred by the assemblage. I have denoted both the gross sum of these annuities, and the distributive share to heads of families, obtained from the office of the local government agent at Buffalo. These are believed to be authentic in amount. Estimated at the highest rate which can be taken, the sum, per capita, of these annuities, will not, on an average of crops and prices, for a series of years, equal the cash value of seven bushels of wheat—a product, which, as a means of actual subsistence to the Indian family, would be of double or treble value. But this is far from being the worst effect of both the general and *per capita* cash distribution. Time and health are not only sacrificed to obtain the pittance, but he is fortunate who does not expend the amount in the outward or return journey from the council house, or in the purchase of some showy but valueless articles, while attending there.

A still further evil, flowing from these annual gatherings for the payment of Indian annuities, is the stimulus which it produces in assembling at such places traders and speculating dealers of various kinds, who are versed in this species of traffic, and who well know the weak points of the native character, and how best to profit by them. In effect, few of the annuitants reach their homes with a dime. Most of them have expended all, and lost their time in addition. Health is not unfrequently sacrificed by living on articles, or in a manner not customary at home. The intemperate are confirmed in intemperance; and the idle, foppish and gay, are only more enamoured of idleness, foppishness and pleasure. That such a system, introduced at an early day, when it was policy for governments on this continent, *foreign* and *domestic*, to throw out a boon before wandering, hostile, and savage tribes, to display their munificence, and effect temporary interests, should have been continued to the present day, is only to be accounted for, from the accumulated duties, perpetually advancing jurisdiction, and still imperfectly organized state of that sub-department of the government, which exercises its, in some respects, anomalous administrative functions, under the name of the Indian Bureau. So far as the Iroquois are affected by the policy adverted to, their interests demand an immediate consideration of the subject on enlarged principles. It behooves them to meditate whether, as a people, now semi-civilized, and exercising, in their internal polity, the powers of an independent government, some more beneficial appropriation of the fund could not be made. Perhaps nothing would better serve to advance and exalt them, as a people, than the application of these annuities to constitute a confederate school fund, under some compact or arrangement with the State, by which the latter should stipulate to extend the frame-work of the common school system over their reservations.

Horticulture, to some extent, and in a limited sense, was always an incident to the hunter state among these tribes, so far, at least, as we are acquainted with their history. They brought the zea maize with them, we must concede, on their early migration to the banks of the Mohawk, and the Onondaga, Oneida, Cayuga and Seneca basins; for this grain is conceded, on all hands, to be a tropical, or at least a southern plant, and if so, it reveals the general *course* of their migration. It is of indigenous origin, and was not known to Europe before the discovery. We learned the mode of cultivation from them, and not they from us. This grain became the basis of their fixity of population, in the 14th or 15th centuries, and capacity to undertake military enterprises. It was certainly cultivated in large fields, in their chief locations, and gave them a title to agriculturists; but it is equally certain that they had a kind of bean, perhaps the same called *frijoles* by the early Spaniards, and some species of *cucurbita*. These were cultivated in gardens.

The tables will show a general and considerable advance, on any probable assumed basis, of the cultivation of corn. We cannot consider this species of cultivation, however, as any characteristic evidence of advance in agriculture, while the more general introduction of it, and the harvesting of large fields of it, by separate families, is undoubtedly to be considered so. Taking the item of corn as the test, another and an important result will be perceived. In proportion as the cereales are cultivated, the average quantity of corn is diminished; and these are the very cases where, at the same time, the degree of civilization is most apparent in other things.

The condition of herdsmen is deemed by theorists and historians to be the first step in the progress from the hunter state. But we are in want of all evidence to show that there ever was, in America, a pastoral state. In the first place, the tribes had tamed no quadruped, even in the tropics, but the lama. The bison was never under any subjection, nor a fleece ever gathered, so far as history tells us, from the Big-horn or Rocky Mountain sheep. The horse, the domestic cow, the hog and the common sheep, were brought over after the discovery; and the Iroquois, like most of their western brethren, have been very slow, all advantages considered, in raising them. They have, in fact, had no pastoral state, and they have only become herdsmen at the time that they took hold of the plough. The number of domestic animals now on their reservations, as shown by the tables, bears a full proportion to their other industrial field labors. It will be seen, that while horses, neat cattle and hogs are generally raised, sheep come in, at more mature periods of advance, and are found only on the largest and best cultivated farms. Sheep, therefore, like the cereales, become a test of their advance. With this stage, we generally find, too, the field esculents, as turneps, peas, &c. and also buckwheat. I have indicated, as a further proof of their advance as herdsmen and graziers, the number of acres of meadow cut. The Iroquois cultivate no flax. They probably raise no rye, from the fact that their lands are better adapted to wheat and corn.

The potato was certainly indigenous. Sir Walter Raleigh, in his efforts at colonizations, had it brought from Virginia, under the original name of *openawg*.* But none of the North American tribes are known to have cultivated it. They dug it up, like other indigenous edible roots from the forest. But it has long been introduced into their villages and spread over the northern latitudes, far beyond the present limit of the zea maize. Its cultivation is so easy and so similar to that of their favorite corn, and its yield so great, that it is remarkable it should not have received more general attention from all the tribes. With the Iroquois, the lists will denote that, in most cases, it is a mere item of horticulture, most families not planting over half an acre, often not more than a quarter of an acre, and yet more frequently, none at all.

The apple is the Iroquois banana. From the earliest introduction of this fruit into New-York and New-France, from the genial plains of Holland and Normandy, these tribes appear to have been captivated by its taste, and they lost no time in transferring it, by sowing the seed, to the sites of their ancient castles. No one can read the accounts of the destruction of the extensive orchards of the apple, which were cut down, on Gen. Sullivan's inroad into the Genesee country in 1779, without regretting that the purposes of war should have required this barbaric act. The census will show that this taste remains as strong in 1845, as it was 66 years ago.

Adverse to agricultural labor, and always confounding it with slavery, or some form of servitude, at least, deeming it derogatory, the first effort of the Iroquois to advance from their original corn-field and garden of beans and vines is connected with the letting out of their spare lands to white men who were cast on the frontiers, to cultivate, receiving for it some low remuneration in kind or otherwise, by way of rent. This system, it is true, increased a little their means of subsistence, but nourished their native pride and indolence. It seems to have been particularly a practice of the Iroquois, and it has been continued and incorporated into their present agricultural system. I have taken pains to indicate, in every family, the amount of land thus let, and the actual or estimated value received for it. These receipts, I was informed, low as they are in amount, are generally paid in kind, or in such manner as often to diminish their value and effect, in contributing to the proper sustenance of the family.

---

* By the Algonquins of the present day, this plant is called, in the plural, *opineeg*. The inflection in *eeg* denotes the plural.

I have been equally careful to ascertain the number of families who cultivated no lands, and insert them in the tables. The division of real property among this people appears to fall under the ordinary rules of acquisition in other societies. But it is not to be inferred in all cases, that the individual returned as without land has absolutely no right to any, or having this right, has either forfeited or alienated it, although the laws of the tribe respecting property, permit one Iroquois to convey his property in fee to another. It is only to be inferred, in every case, that they are non-cultivators. In a few cases the persons thus marked are mechanics, and rely for support on their skill. In the valley of the Alleghany, some of them are pilots in conducting rafts of lumber or arks down that stream. It would have relieved the industrial means of this band of the Senecas, extended as they are for forty miles along both banks of this river, could the amount received for this species of pilotage have been ascertained, together with the avails derived from several saw-mills owned by them, and from the lumber trade of that river generally. But these questions would have remained a blank in other tribes.

Not a few persons amongst the Onondagas and Tuscaroras, and the Tonewandas and other bands of Senecas, living in or contiguous to the principal wheat growing counties, labor during the harvest season as reapers and cradlers, for skill and ability in which occupations they bear a high reputation, and receive good wages in cash. There are a few engaged some parts of the year, as mariners on the lakes. It will be sufficient to denote these varied forms of incipient labor and strength of muscle and personal energy among these tribes, which it was, however, impracticable to bring into the tables.

Individual character vindicates its claims to wealth and distinction among these tribes in as marked a manner as among any people in the world. Industry, capacity and integrity, are strongly marked on the character and manners of numbers in each of the tribes. The art of speaking, and a facility in grasping objects of thought, and in the transaction of business, separate and distinguish persons as fully as physical traits do their faces. And it is to be observed that these intellectual traits run very much in certain families. That there are numbers, on the contrary, who are drones in the political hive, who do not labor, or labor very little; others who are intemperate; others who neither work nor own land, or would long remain proprietors of them, were new divisions and appropriations made, and all of whom are a burden and draw-back upon the industrious and producing classes, it requires little observation to show. Admitting what reforms teaching and example may accomplish among these, it is yet certain that of this number there are many who do not assimilate, or appear to constitute material for assimilation, in tastes and habits with the mass, nor appear likely to incorporate with them in any practical shape where they now reside, in their advances in agriculture, government and morals. The hunter habit in these persons is yet strong, but having nothing to stimulate it, they appear loth to embrace other modes of subsistence. Others stand aloof from labor, or at least all active and efficient labor, from a restless desire of change, or ambition to do something else than plough and raise stock; or from ill-luck, penury, or other motives. The proportion of the population who thus stand still and do not advance in civil polity, are a strong draw-back on the rest. It is conceived to be a pertinent question whether this class of the population would not find a better theatre for their progress and development by migrating to the west, where the general government still possess unappropriated territory at their disposal. It is believed by many that their migration would result in benefit to both parties. The question is one which has been often discussed by them in council, and is not yet, I should judge, fully settled. A point of approach for the Iroquois has already been formed in the Indian territory by the Senecas and Shawnees from Sandusky in Ohio, who, at the last accounts (vide President's Message to Congress, 1844,) number in the aggregate 336 souls. They are located on the Neosho river, (a branch of the Arkansas,) west of the western boundary of the State of Arkansas, where the reports of the government agents represent them as raising horses, cattle and other stock, and being producers of grain. In any view, the subject of the several classes of persons represented in the accompanying tables, as semi-hunters and non-cultivators, or individuals without lands, is one entitled to attention. They should not be permitted to live within the boundaries of the State without lands. The State should cherish all who choose to remain as vestiges of a once powerful race, to whose wisdom and bravery we owe the preservation of the domain. It would be unjust to expect the industrious and forehanded Iroquois to redivide their lands with the poor, and, to some extent, thriftless numbers of the cantons; while it may, at the same time be observed, that it would be very difficult, if not impossible, to provide by legislation, suitable guards against their deterioration and depopulation in their present locations without destroying wholly the fabric of their confederation, chieftainships and laws.

IV. Whether the Iroquois have advanced in population since they have laid aside the character of warriors and hunters, and adopted agriculture as their only means of support, we have no accurate data for determining. That their ancient population was overrated, and *very much* overrated, at all periods of our history, there can be little question. We may dismiss many of these rude conjectures, of the elder writers, as entitled to little notice, particularly that of La Houton, who estimates each canton at 14,000 souls. Still, after making every abatement for this tendency in the earlier authors to exaggerate their actual numbers, it could have been no small population, which, at one time, attacked the island of Montreal with twelve hundred armed warriors, and at another (1683) marched a thousand men against the Ottagamies.*

Smith puts the whole number of fighting men, in 1756, with a moderation which is remarkable, compared to others who had touched the subject, at about twelve hundred. Giving to each warrior a home population of *five*, which is found to hold good, in modern days, in the great area of the west, we should have an aggregate of 6,000—a result, which is, probably, too low. Douglass, four years afterwards, gives us data for raising this estimate to 7,500. Col. Bouquet, still four years later, raises this latter estimate by 250. It must be evident that their perpetual wars had a tendency to keep down their numbers, notwithstanding their policy of aiding their natural increase by the adoption and incorporation into the cantons, in full independence, of prisoners and captives.

Mr. Jefferson estimates the population of the Powhatanic confederacy or group of tribes, at one individual to the square mile.† Gov. Clinton, who ably handled the subject in a discourse in 1811, estimates that, if this rule be applied to the domain of the Iroquois in New-York, an aggregate of not less than 30,000 would be produced;‡ but he does not pass his opinion upon an estimate made so completely without reliable data.

---

* Colden's Five Nations. † Notes on Virginia. ‡ Coll. N. Y. Hist. Soc. vol. 2.

At a conference with the five cantons at Albany, in 1677, the number of warriors was carefully made out at 2,150, giving, on the preceding mode of computation, a population of 10,750, and this was the strength of the confederacy reported by an agent of the Governor of Virginia, who had been specially despatched to the conference for the purpose of obtaining this fact. Either, then, in the subsequent estimates of 1756, '60, and '64, the population had been underrated, or there had, on the assumption of the truth of the above enumeration, which is moderate, been a decline in the population of 3,000 souls in a period of eighty-seven years. That there was a constant tendency to decline, and that the cantons were aware of this, and made efforts to keep it up, by the policy of their conquests, is apparent, and has before been indicated.

During the American revolution, which broke out but eleven years after the expedition and estimate of Bouquet, when he had put the Iroquois at 1,550 fighting men, it is estimated that the British government had in their interest and service 1,580 warriors, of this confederacy. The highest number noticed of the friendly Oneidas and a few others, who sided with us in that contest, is 230 warriors, raising the number of armed men engaged in the war, to 1,810, and the gross population in 1776 to 9,050 souls. This estimate, which appears to have been carefully made, from authentic documents, is the utmost that could well be claimed. It was made at the era when danger prompted the pen of either party in the war to exhibit the military strength of this confederacy, in its utmost power; and we may rest here, as a safe point of comparison, or, at least, we cannot admit a higher population.

By the census returns herewith submitted, the aggregate population of the three full, and four fragmentary cantons, namely, the Oneidas and Cayugas, &c. still residing within the State, are denoted to be as follows, namely:

Senecas,	2,441
Onondagas,	398
Tuscaroras,	281
Oneidas,	210
Cayugas,	123
Mohawks,	20
St. Regis Canton,	360

By a statement submitted to Congress, on the 3d of December, 1844,* the number of Oneidas, settled in Wisconsin, is put at 722; the number of Senecas, who have removed from Ohio into the Indian territory west of the Mississippi, at 125, and the number of mixed Senecas and Shawnees, at the same general location, at 211. Deducting one-half of the latter, for Shawnees, and there is to be added to the preceding census, in order to show the natural increase of the Iroquois, 953 souls. The number of the St. Regis tribe, who are based, as a tribe, on the Praying Indians of Colden,—a band of Catholic Mohawks originally located at Caughnawaga is shewn by the present year's census to be 360. There are, at the village of Cornplanter, within the bounds of Pennsylvania, as numbered by me, the present year, 51 Senecas. Supposing that the Mohawks and Cayugas who fled to Canada *at* and *after* the revolutionary war, and who are now settled at Brantford on Grand river, Canada West, have merely held their own, in point of numbers, and deducting the number of Cayugas, namely, 144, found among the Senecas of Cattaragus, and herewith separately returned, and taking Dalton's estimate of the Mohawks and Cayugas in 1776, namely, 300 warriors for each tribe, there is to be added, to the census, to accomplish the same comparative view, two thousand eight hundred and fifty souls. From this estimate, there must be deducted, for a manifest error, in the original estimates of Dalton, in putting the Cayugas on the same footing of strength with the Mohawks, not less than 150 warriors or 750 souls, leaving the Canadian Iroquois at 2,106—say 2,000 souls.

Adding these items to the returns of the present census, and the rather extraordinary result will appear, that there is now existing in the United States and Canada a population of 6,942 Iroquois, that is to say, but 2,108 less than the estimated number, and that number placed as high as it well could be, at the era of the revolution in 1776. Of this number, 4,836 inhabit the United States, and 3,843 the State of New-York. I cannot, however, submit this result without expressing the opinion, that the Iroquois population has been *lower*, between the era of the revolutionary war and the present time, than the census now denotes; and that for some years past, and since they have been well lodged and clothed and subsisted by their own labor, and been exempted from the diseases and casualties incident to

* Vide Doc. No. 2, Ho. of Reps., 28th Congress, 2d Session.

savage life, and the empire of the forest, their population has recovered and IS NOW ON THE INCREASE.

I have thus brought to a close, so far as relates to their population and industrial efforts, the inquiry committed to me respecting this nation. It would perhaps have gratified statistical curiosity and philosophical theory, to have exhibited fuller data on the subject of their longevity and vital statistics generally, but it may be considered in the light of an achievement to have accomplished thus much. The general result indicates five, with a large fraction, as the average number of the Iroquois family. Throughout each canton, the number of females predominates over the males. This is a fact which has been long known to hold good with respect to wandering, predatory and warlike tribes, but was not anticipated among peaceful, agricultural communities. But few years, however, have supervened since they dropped the hatchet and took hold of the plough; and in this time, it is apparent that the proportion of males to females has approached nearer to an equilibrium. The effects on vitality of agricultural labor and a cessation from war, are likewise favorable, so far as we can judge, compared with the known results among the sparse, ill fed, warring and errating hunters of the western forests and prairies. The average number of the Iroquois family is not higher than the common average of the hunter state. The number of children borne by each female is a considerable fraction over four. Of a population of 312 Tuscaroras, five have reached to and passed the age of 80, or over 1¾ per cent. Among the Senecas and Cayugas of Cattaraugus, the per centage is 1½, with a smaller fraction, 12 persons in 808 having passed that limit. Local causes have diminished this to one per cent nearly on the Buffalo reservation. On the contrary, it is found to be increased in the valley of the Alleghany to full two per cent. The ruling chief of that tribe, TEN WON NY AHS, of Teonegono, commonly called *Blacksnake*, is now in his ninety-sixth year, and is active and hale, and capable of performing journies to the annual assemblies of his people at Buffalo.

I should have not fulfilled the principal object in view, without directing some attention to the effects of the labors of past years in the introduction, into the Iroquois cantons, of education, letters and Christianity. So much of this branch of the inquiry as admits of arithmetical notice, will appear, either under the ordinary heads of the census, or the additional columns which have been prepared under the headings of "statistics of occupation and of morality." The residue, comprising some remarks on the schools and churches, the present state of Iroquois society and manners, and the general condition and prospects of the cantons, will be included in the supplementary report and documents. I shall also defer to the same time, a particular notice of their annuities, and the extent of their ancient domain, and the periods of its cession to the State or general government.

In closing this report, it may be well to notice the fact that there are yet remaining in the State, some vestiges of the Algonquin race, who, under various distinctive names, occupied the southern portion of the State at the era of its discovery and colonization. As the language of the census act refers to such Indians only as live on the "reservations," I have not felt it to be within the scope of my appointment to search out and visit these scattered individuals, although I should have been gratified to make this inquiry. It is believed that they are comprised by about twenty of the Shinecock tribe, who yet haunt the inlets and more desolate portions of Long island, and by a very few lingering members of the ancient Mohegans, who under the soubriquet of Stockbridges, yet remain in Oneida county. The bulk of this people, so long the object of missionary care, migrated to the banks of Fox river and Winnebago lake, in Wiscon sin, about 1822. They were followed to that portion of the west, about the same time, or soon after, by the small consolidated band of Nanticokes, Narragansetts, and other early coast tribes, who, in concentrating in the Oriskany valley, after the close of the revolutionary war, dropped their respective languages, learned the English, and assumed the name of Brothertons. Both these migrated tribes were in an advanced state of semi-civilization, and were good farmers and herdsmen at the era of their removal.

I am, sir,
With respect,
Your obd't servant,
HENRY R. SCHOOLCRAFT,
Marshal under the 15th section of the census act.

Hon. NATHANIEL S. BENTON,
Secretary of State.

SUPPLEMENTARY REPORT

Of Henry R. Schoolcraft to the Secretary of State.

ANTIQUITIES—HISTORY—ETHNOLOGY.

New-York, January 7th, 1846.

Sir :—I have now the honor to submit a supplementary report, embracing minutes and remarks on the aboriginal history, antiquities and general ethnology of western New-York, made in accordance with an expression permitting the collection of such materials in your general instructions of the 25th of June last.

To these details I have prefixed some general considerations on the early period of the Iroquois history, the affinities of the several tribes, and the era and principles of their confederation ; the antiquarian remains and general archaeology of the western counties ; the ancient state of Indian art ; some traits of their traditions and religion ; and a few connected topics which, it is hoped, will tend to render the report more acceptable and valuable.

I regret, indeed, that time has not permitted me to enter more fully on some of the topics introduced, and that of others, I have been obliged to cut them short or omit them altogether, including the subject of their languages, geographical terminology, and personal names, the latter of which is a very curious inquiry in itself. I confess it would have fallen in with my inclinations, as well as my conceptions of the true nature and extent of the inquiries confided to me, to have extended them to other parts of the State, and given a more complete view of our ethnology, had it been practicable to do so before the meeting of the Legislature.

I cannot, however, close this note without expressing the hope that the Legislature will authorize you to take further measures for completing the work. There are a large number of the class of antique, circular and elliptical works scattered over the western and south-western part of the State, of an age anterior to the discovery, which it would be important to examine and describe. These chiefly lie west of Cayuga, and upon the sources of the Susquehanna. Interspersed amid this system of common ring-forts of the west there are some of a still earlier period, which exhibit squares and parallelograms, yet without any defensive work in the nature of bastions.

The area of early French occupancy, or attempt at colonization, within the State, extends east and west, between the waters of the Cayuga and Oneida lakes, as general boundaries, having the county of Onondaga as its chief and central point. This area will comprehend the most striking part of the numerous remains of implements of art and other antiquities of European origin, which have heretofore excited attention. How far these evidences extend north is not known. But any examination of either the aboriginal or foreign remains would be incomplete which did not extend also along the line of the St. Lawrence and the waters of Lake Champlain.

The valley of the Hudson, and the southern part of the State generally, although it has not been explored with this view, is known to have some antiquarian features worthy examination. And were there none others than the artificial shell mounds and beds on the sea coast, and the fossil bones of the valley, so remarkable in themselves, these would alone be entitled to the highest interest in studying the ancient history of the races of man in this area.

Geological action subsequent to the period of the habitation of the globe, has not been examined with this view, but is believed to be important in denoting eras of former occupancy; it is known that various parts of the State have yielded, at considerable depths below the surface, many curious evidences of artificial remains, along with relics of the animal and vegetable kingdoms.

There is an apparent extension of the system of works which characterize the fort and mound period of the Ohio valley, reaching from the Alleghany waters in Chautauque and Cattaraugus, along the southern shore of Lake Erie, indefinitely eastward, which it would be interesting to trace.

One of the most reliable proofs of eras and races of men is found in the remains of art.

There are some striking coincidences in this respect between the antiquities of New-York and the Mississippi valley, which denote precisely the same state of arts and the same eras of occupancy. Such are the Minace Alleghanic which occurs alike in the Grave Creek mound and the simple places of sepulture in Onondaga, the Nabikoaguna Antique, which has been found at Upper Sandusky and at Onondaga ; and the Medaëka Missouric, from the valley of the Sciota, in Ohio, and the Kasonda, in New-York.

Accurate descriptions of the whole class of our antiquarian remains could not, if thoroughly executed, but throw much light on, and introduce precision in, periods of remote history in this State, and indeed the continent, which are now either involved in obscurity, or constitute themes of mere conjecture.

I. HISTORICAL AND ETHNOLOGICAL MINUTES.

MADE ON TAKING THE CENSUS OF THE IROQUOIS OF NEW-YORK, IN CONFORMITY WITH AN ACT OF THE LEGISLATURE, IN 1845.

[a.] A Sketch of the Iroquois Groupe of Aboriginal Tribes.

On the discovery of North America, the Iroquois tribes, were found seated chiefly in the wide and fertile territory of western and northern New-York, reaching west to the sources of the Ohio;* north, to the banks of Lake Champlain and the St. Lawrence; and east, to the site of Albany. They had as much nationality of character, then, as any of the populous tribes, who, in the 4th century wandered over central and western Europe. They were, in a high degree, warlike, handling the bow and arrow with the skill and dexterity of the ancient Thracians and Parthians. They were confederated in peace and war, and had begun to lay the foundations of a power, against which, the surrounding nations, in the Mississippi valley, and along the St. Lawrence, the Hudson, and the Delaware, could not stand. The French, when they effectually entered the St. Lawrence in 1608,† courted their alliance on the north, and the Dutch did the same in 1609, on the Hudson. Virginia had been apprised of their power, at an early day, and the other English colonies, as they arrived, were soon made acquainted with the existence of this native confederacy in the north.

---

* They always denominated the Alleghany river by the name of Ohio. This I found o be the term constantly used for that river in 1845. They give the vowel i, in this word, he sound of i, in machine.

† They actually discovered this river, in 1535.

By putting fire-arms into their hands, they doubled the aboriginal power, and became themselves, for more than a century, dependant on their caprice or friendship.

The word Iroquois, as we are told by Charlevoix, who is a competent and reliable witness on this point, is founded on an exclamation, or response, made by the sachems and warriors, on the delivery to them, of an address. This response, as heard among the Senecas, it appeared to me, might be written *eoh*; perhaps, the Mohawks, and other harsher dialects of this family, threw in an r, between the vowels. It is recorded in the term Iroquois, on French principles of annotation, with the substantive inflection in *ois*, which is characteristic of French lexicography. It is a term which has been long, and extensively used, both for the language and the history of this people; and is preferable, on enlarged considerations, to any other. The term Five Nations, used by Colden, and in popular use during the earlier period of the colony, ceased to be appropriate after the Tuscarora revolt in North Carolina, and the reunion of this tribe with the parent stock, subsequent to 1712. From that period they were called the Six Nations,* and continued to acquire inceased reputation as a confederacy, under this name, until the termination of the American Revolution in 1783, and the flight of the Mohawks and Cayugas to Canada, when this partial separation and breaking up of the confederacy, rendered it no longer applicable.

The term NEW-YORK INDIANS, applied to them in modern days, by the eminence in their position, is liable to be confounded, by the common reader, with the names of several tribes of the generic Algonquin family, who formerly occupied the southern part of the State, down to the Atlantic. Some of these tribes lived in the west, and owned and occupied lands, among the Iroquois, until within a few years. And, at any rate, it is too vague and imprecise a term to be employed in philology or history.

By the people themselves, however, neither the first nor the last of the foregoing terms appear ever to have been adopted, nor are they now used. They have no word to signify "New-York" in a sense more specfiic, than as the territory possessed by themselves—a claim

* In 1723, they adopted the NECARIAGES, as a Seventh Nation, as will be noticed under the appropriate head.

which they were certainly justified in making, at the era of the discovery, when they are admitted, on all hands, to have carried their conquests to the sea.

The term *Ongwe Honwe*, or a people surpassing all others, which Colden was informed they applied proudly to themselves, may be strictly true, if limited, as they did, to mean a people surpassing all other red men. This they believed, and this was the sense in which they boastfully applied it. But it was a term older than the discovery, and had no reference to European races. The word *Honwe*, as will appear by the vocabulary hereto appended, means man. By the prefixed term *Ongwe*, it is qualified according to various interpretations, to mean real, as contradistinguished from sham men, or cowards; it may also mean strong, wise, or expert men, and, by ellipsis, men excelling others in manliness. But it was in no other sense distincttive of them. It was the common term for the red race of this continent, which they would appear, by the phrase, to acknowledge as a unity, and is, the word as I found it, used at this day, as the equivalent for our term "Indian."

Each tribe had, at some period of their progress, a distinctive appellation, as Onondaga, Oneida, &c. of which some traditionary matter will be stated, further on. When they came to confederate, and form a general council, they took the name of KONOSHIONI, (or as the French authors write it, *Acquinoshioni*), meaning literally, People of the Long House, and figuratively a UNITED PEOPLE, a term by which they still denominate themselves, when speaking in a national sense. This distinction, it is well to bear in mind, and not confound. This Long House, to employ their own figure, extended east and west from the present site of Albany to the foot of the great lakes, a distance, by modern admeasurement, of 325 miles, which is now traversed by railroad. An air palace, we may grant them, having beams and rafters, higher and longer than any pile of regal magnificence, yet reared by human hands.

Thus much may be said, with certainty, of the name of this celebrated family of red men, by which they are identified and distinguished from other stocks of the hunter tribes of North America. Where they originated, relatively to their position on this continent, the progress of ethnology does not, at this incipient period of that science, enable us to determine, nor is it proposed, save with the merest brevity, now to inquire. Veiling their own origin, if anciently known, in allegory, or designing by fancy to supply the utter want of early history, to the intent, perhaps, that they might put forth an undisputed title to the country they occupied, the relations of their old sages affirm that they originated in the territorial area of western New-York. Their tradition on this point, as put on record by the pen of one of their own people, (see extracts from Cusic's historical and traditionary tract, hereto appended,) fixes the locality of their actual origin at an eminence near the falls of the Oswego river. To cut short the narration, they assert that their ancestors were called forth, from the bowels of a mountain, by TARENYAWAGON, the Holder of the Heavens. It represents them as one people, who moved first towards the east, as far as the sea, and then fell back, partly on their own tracks, towards the west and southwest. So far, and so far only, the tale appears credible enough, and as there is no chronology established by it, although dates are freely introduced, and consequently nothing to contradict it, their track of migration and countermigration from the Oswego, may be deemed as probable.

The diversities of language, and the separation into tribes, are represented to have taken place, according to known principles of ethnological inference.

Ondiyaka, an Onondaga sage, and the ruling chief of the confederacy, who died on an official visit to the Oneidas in 1839, at the age of ninety, confirmed these general traditions of the Tuscarora scribe. He informed Le Fort, who was with him in that journey and at his death, that the Onondagas were created by NEO,* in the country where they lived ; that he made this island or continent, " Hawoneo," for the red race, and meant it for them alone. He did not allude to or acknowledge any migration from other lands. This, Le Fort, himself an Onondaga, a chief, and an educated man, told me during the several interviews I had with him, the present year, at the Onondaga Castle.

* The term " Neo," God, is generally used reverently, with a syllable prefixed in the different Iroquois dialects, as Yawa-Neo, in the Tuscarora, Howai-Neo in the Seneca, Hawai-Neo, Onondaga, Lawai-Neo, Mohawk, &c.

Ondiyaka proceeded to say, as they walked over the ancient ruins in the valley of the Kasonda,* that this was the spot where the Onondagas formerly lived, before they fixed themselves in the Onondaga valley, and before they had entered into confederation. In those days they were at enmity with each other; they raised the old forts to defend themselves. They wandered about a great deal. They frequently changed their places of residence. They lived in perpetual fear. They kept fighting, and moving their villages often. This reduced their numbers, and rendered their condition one of alarms and trials. Sometimes they abandoned a village, and all their gardens and clearings, because they had encountered much sickness, and believed the place to be doomed. They were always ready to hope for better luck in a new spot. At length they confederated, and then their fortifications were no longer necessary, and fell into decay. This, he believed, was the origin of these old ruins, which were not of foreign construction.† Before the confederacy, they had been not only at war among themselves, but had been driven by other enemies.‡ After it, they carried their wars out of their own country, and began to bring home prisoners. Their plan was to select for adoption from the prisoners, and captives, and fragments of tribes whom they conquered. These captives were equally divided among each of the tribes, were adopted and incorporated with them, and served to make good their losses. They used the term, WE-HAIT-WAT-SHA, in relation to these captives. This term means a body cut into parts and scattered around. In this manner, they figuratively scattered their prisoners, and sunk and destroyed their nationality, and built up their own.

At what period they confederated, we have no exact means of deciding. It appears to have been comparatively recent, judging from traditionary testimony.§ While their advancement in the economy of living, in arms, in diplomacy and in civil polity, would lead conjecture to a more remote date. Their own legends, like those of

---

* Butternut Creek, which runs through parts of the towns of Pompey, Lafayette and De Witt, Onondaga county.

† This remark must be considered as applied only to the class of simple ring forts, so frequent in western New-York. These forts are proved by antiquarian remains, forest growth, &c. to be the most ancient of any works, in Onondaga county, in the shape of forts.

‡ Colden represents them as driven by the Algonquins, on the discovery of Canada.

§ Vide Pyrlaus.

some other leading stocks of the continent, carry them back to a period of wars with giants and demons and monsters of the sea, the land, and the air, and are fraught with strange and grotesque fancies of wizards and enchanters. But history, guiding the pen of the French Jesuit, describes them first as pouring in their canoes through the myriad streams that interlace in western New-York, and debouching, now on the gulf of the St. Lawrence, now on the Chesapeake—glancing again over the waves of Michigan, and now again plying their paddles in the waters of the turbid Mississippi. Wherever they went, they carried proofs of their energy, courage, and enterprise.

At one period we hear the sound of their war cry, along the straits of the St. Mary's and at the foot of Lake Superior. At another under the walls of Quebec, where they finally defeated the Hurons under the eyes of the French. They put out the fires of the Gahkwas and Eries. They eradicated the Susquehannocks. They placed the Lenapees, the Nanticokes, and the Munsees under the yoke of subjection. They put the Metoacks and the Manhattans under tribute. They spread the terror of their arms over all New-England.

They traversed the whole length of the Appalachian chain, and descended like the enraged Yagisho and Megalonyx, on the Cherokees and the Catawbas. Smith encountered their warriors, in the settlement of Virginia, and La Salle on the discovery of the Illinois. Nations trembled when they heard the name of the KONOSHIONI.

They possessed a fine physical structure—they lived in a climate which imparted energy to their motions. They used a sonorous and commanding language, which had its dual number, and its neuter, masculine, and feminine genders. They were excellent natural orators, and expert diplomatists. They began early to cherish a national pride, which grew with their conquests. They had, like the Algonquins, in the organization of the several clans, or families, which composed each tribe, a curious *heraldic* tie, founded on original relationship, which exercised a strong influence, but which has never been satisfactorily explained. They were governed by hereditary chieftaincies, like others of the aboriginal stocks, but contrary to the usage of these other stocks, the claims of their chiefs, were subjected to the decision of a national council. The aristocratic and democratic principles, were thus both brought into requisition, in candidates for office. But in all that constituted national action, they were a pure Republic. So far was this carried, that it is believed the veto of any one chief, to a public measure, was sufficient to arrest its adoption by the Council.

In the development of their nationality, they have produced several men of energy and ability, who were equal, in natural force of character, to some of the most shining warriors and orators of antiquity. Few war captains have exceeded Hendrick, Brant or Skenandoah. The eloquence and force of Garangula, Logan and Red Jacket, in their public speeches, have commanded universal admiration. Mr. Jefferson considered the appeal of Logan to the white race, after the extirpation of his family, as without a parallel; and it has been imitated in vain, by distinguished poets and orators.

Such were the aboriginal people who occupied western New-York, and their memory will forever live in the significant names which they have bestowed upon Niagara and Ontario, and a thousand lesser waters, which beautify and adorn the land. Viewed as one of the Indo-American stocks, they possessed some very striking traits.

Few barbarous nations have ever existed on the globe, who have shown more native energy, and distinctiveness of character. Still fewer who have evinced so firm a devotion to the spirit of independence. Yet all their native manliness and energy of character and action, would have failed, or become inoperative, had they not abandoned the fatal Indian principle of tribal supremacy, or independent chieftainships, and made common cause in a national confederacy. The moment this was done, and each of the component clans or tribes, had surrendered the power of sovereignty to a general council of the whole, the foundation for their rise was laid, and they soon became the most powerful political body among the native tribes of North America, this side of the palace of Montezuma.

In visiting the descendants of such a people, after a lapse of more than two centuries and a quarter from the discovery, it was the impulse of the commonest interest, to make some inquiries into their former history, and antiquities. These have been pursued under favorable circumstances, for the most part, at all points of my journey, and have been resumed, when broken off, whenever practical. The only method pursued, was to obtain all the facts possible, from red or white men, of reliable testimony. There was no time and no intention, to digest them, into a connected history. They were collected in the pauses which intervened, in the obtaining of the statistics of the census, and they are contributed herewith, in the simple garb and freshness of the original minutes. Those who related the traditions, did not suppose themselves to be delivering the important lore of their history. They were related, along the road, or seated around the evening circle, as the current belief of the people. Sometimes the fields or hills, disclosing the localities of old forts, were the scene of the narrations; sometimes the Indian burial ground; sometimes more formal interviews. He who gleans popular traditions among this race, must have his ear ever open, his memory under notice "to retain," and his pen or pencil ever ready.

Historical and biographical notices, names of places, and sketches of antiquarian remains, were thus entered on or dropped, as time or occasion prompted. To make minutes of what occurred, was all that time permitted me; but it was a rule, to make them promptly and on the spot. This much seemed necessary in despatching this portion of my report, with the miscellaneous details accompanying it; and having accomplished this object, my present task is terminated.

[*b*.] Ethnological Suggestions.

Where we have nothing else to rely upon, we may receive the rudest traditions of an Indian nation, although they be regarded as mere historical phenomena, or materials to be considered. Whether such materials are to be credited or disbelieved wholly, or in part, is quite another thing. Our Indians, like some of the ancient nations of Asia, whom they resemble in many points of character, were prone to refer their origin to myths and legends, under which they doubtless, sometimes meant to represent truths, or at least, to express opinions. The Indian tribes, very much like their ancient prototypes of the old world, seemed to have felt a necessity for inventing some story of their origin, where it is sometimes probable there was little or nothing of actual tradition to build it upon. They were manifestly under a kind of self-reproach, to reflect that they had indeed no history ; nothing to connect their descent from prior races ; and if they have not proved themselves men of much judgment in their attempts to supply the deficiency in their fabrications and allegories, they must often come in, it must be confessed, for no little share of imagination.

There appears, throughout the whole race, to be the vestiges of a tradition of the creation and the deluge, two great and striking points in the history of man, which, however he wandered, he would be most likely to remember. They uniformly attribute their origin to a superior and divine power. They do not suppose that they came into existence without the act of this pre-existing almighty power, who is called Neo, or Owaneo. This is the third great and leading point in their traditions. And these three primary vestiges of the original history of the race are to be found among the rudest tribes, between the straits of Terra del Fuego and the Arctic Ocean, notwithstanding the amount of grotesque and puerile matter which serves as the vehicle of the traditions.

Between the creation and the deluge and the present era of the world, there is nearly an entire blank. Ages have dropped out of their memory, with all their stirring incidents of wars and migrations, and the first reliable truth we hear is, that at such a time they lived on the banks of the Mississippi, the Ohio, the Lakes, or the St. Lawrence, &c. Nothing but this kind of *proximate* origin could indeed be expected to be retained. They acknowledge relationship to no prior race of man. We see that they are sui generis with, and much resemble some of the eastern nations in color and features. Physiologists have never been able to detect a bone or muscle, more or less, than the Caucassian race possess. Philologists listen to their speech and admit that in one tribe or another they possess all the powers of articulate utterance known to that race. We know by this kind of evidence, physical and moral, that they are a branch of the original Adamic stock, without reference to the pages of revelation, where we learn the same truth, and are told in so many words, that "God out of one flesh, formed all men." And we must perforce infer, that the Indian race is of foreign origin, and must have crossed an ocean to reach the continent.

Ask not the red sage to tell you how? or when? or where? He knows it not, and if he should pretend to the knowledge, it would be the surest possible evidence, philosophically considered, that his responses were fabulous. Three hundred and fifty-three years only has America been known to Europe, and yet should we strike our history out of existence, what should we know of the leading facts of the discovery and the discoverer from Indian tradition? Still the inquisitive spirit of research leads us to ask, where were this race eighteen hundred and forty-five years ago? or at the invasion of Britain by Julius Cæsar? or at the outpouring of the Gothic hordes under Alaric or Brennus? Scandinavian research tells us they were here in the 10th century. The Mexican picture writings inform us that some of them reached the valley of Mexico in the 11th century. Welsh history claims to have sent one of her princes among them in the 12th century. The mounds of the Mississippi valley do not appear to have had an origin much earlier. The whole range of even historical conjecture is absolutely limited within eight or nine hundred years. Nothing older, of their presence here certainly, is known, than about the time of the crowning of Charlemagne, A. D. 800, unless we take the Grecian tradition of Atalantis.

That we have nothing in the way of tradition older than the dates referred to, is no positive proof that the tribes were not upon the continent long prior. There are some considerations, in the very nature of the case, which argue a remote continental antiquity for these tribes. It is hardly to be supposed that large numbers of the primitive adventurers landed at any one time or place ; nor is it more probable that the epochs of these early adventurers were very numerous. The absolute conformity of physical features renders this improbable. The early migrations must have been necessarily confined to portions of the old world peopled by the RED RACE—by a race, not only of red skins, black hair and eyes, and high cheek bones, who would reproduce these fixed characteristics, *ad infinitum*, but whose whole mental as well as physiological development assimilates it, as a distinct unity of the species. While physiology, however, asserts this unity, in the course of the dispersion and multiplication of tribes, their languages, granting all that can be asked for on the score of original diversity, became divided into an infinite number of dialects and tongues. Between these dialects, however, where they are even the most diverse, there is a singular coincidence in many of the leading principles of concord and regimen, and polysynthetic arrangement. Such diversities in sound, amounting, as they do in many cases, for instance, in the stocks of the Algonquin and Iroquois, to an almost total difference, must have required many ages for their production. And this fact alone affords a proof of the continental antiquity of the American race.

[c.] Indian Cosmogony.

ORIGIN OF THE CONTINENT, OF THE ANIMAL CREATION, AND OF THE INDIAN RACE: THE INTRODUCTION OF THE TWO PRINCIPLES OF GOOD AND EVIL INTO THE GOVERNMENT OF THE WORLD.

Iroquois tradition opens with the notion that there were originally two worlds, or regions of space, namely, an upper and lower world. The upper was inhabited by beings similar to the human race; the lower by monsters, moving in the waters. When the human species were transferred below, and the lower sphere was about to be rendered fit for their residence, the act of their transference or reproduction is concentrated in the idea of a female, who began to descend into the lower world, which is depicted as a region of darkness, waters and monsters. She was received on the back of a tortoise, where she gave birth to male twins, and expired. The shell of this tortoise expanded into the continent, which, in their phraseology, is called an "island;" and is named by the Onondagas, AONAO. One of the infants was called INIGORIO, or the Good Mind; the other, INIGOHATEA, or the Bad Mind. These two antagonistical principles, which are such perfect counterparts of the Ormusd and Ahriman of the Zoroaster, were at perpetual variance, it being the law of one to counteract whatever the other did. They were not, however, men, but gods, or existences, through whom the "Great Spirit," or "Holder of the Heavens," carried out his purposes. The first labor of Inigorio was to create the sun out of the head of his dead mother, and the moon and the stars out of other parts of the body. The light these gave, drove the monsters into deep water, to hide themselves. He then prepared the surface of the continent, and fitted it for human habitation, by diversifying it with creeks, rivers, lakes and plains, and by filling these with the various species of the animal and vegetable kingdoms. He then formed a man and woman out of earth, gave them life, and called them "Ea-gwe-ho-we," or, as it is more generally known to Indian archæologists, Ong-we-Hon-we; that is to say, a real people. [D.]

Meanwhile the Bad Mind created mountains, waterfalls, and steeps and morasses, reptiles, serpents, apes, and other objects supposed to be injurious to, or in mockery of mankind. He made attempts also to conceal the land animals in the ground, so as to deprive man of the means of subsistence. This continued opposition to the wishes of the Good Mind, who was perpetually busied in restoring the effects of the displacements and wicked devices of the other, at length led to a personal combat, of which the time and instruments of battle were agreed on. They fought for two days, the one using deer's horns, and the other flag roots, as arms.* Inigorio, who had chosen horns, finally prevailed; his antagonist sunk down to a region of darkness, and became the Evil Spirit, or Kluneolux,† of the world of despair. Inigorio, having obtained this triumph, retired from the earth.

This piece of ingenuity, or philosophy of the Indian mind, much of which is pure allegory, under which truths are hid, stands in the remote vista of Iroquois tradition, and it seemed necessary to notice it, in preparing to take up their more sober traditions. It is picked out of a mass of incongruous details, published by a native, [see App. D.] which only serve, peradventure, to denote its genuineness, for divested of absurdity, in the original, we should not ascribe much antiquity to it, or be prone to attribute it to an ignorant, superstitious, pagan people, living in all their earlier times without arts, letters or civilization. Futile as it is, it will be found veritable philosophy, compared with most of the earlier theories of the renowned nations of antiquity. Take, as an instance, the account Sanconeathus gives of the theology of the Phœnicians.‡

* By reference to the Algonquin story of the combat between Manabozho and his father, the West Wind, as given in Algic Researches, vol 1, p. 134, it will be seen that the weapons chosen by the parties were the same as those employed by Inigorio and Inigohatea, namely, deer's horns and flag roots.

† Oneida.

‡ Gowan's Ancient Fragments, 1 vol. 8vo., N. Y., 1835.

[*d*.] Gleams of their General Ancient History.

ITEMS : Indians claim to be the offspring of an independent act of creation. The Iroquois name themselves in proud allusion to their supposed supremacy. Tribes on the St. Lawrence and the lakes live in disputes. War with a race of giants called Ronongweca: the fiend Shotrowea,--contests with the great Kwiss Kwiss, or Mastodon,--the Big Elk,—and the Horned Serpent. A meteor falls in the camp. Northern tribes confederate ; send an unfortunate embassage to a great chief south,—war with him,—war with each other, and the country thereby depopulated and left to its original desolation.

When we come to draw the minds of the sages and chroniclers of the Iroquois cantons, to the facts of their early history and origin, they treat us with legendary fables, and myths of gods and men, and changes and freaks in elementary matter, which indicate that such ideas, were common to their progenitors, whatever part of the world they occupied. We have adverted to their notions on this head, in the preceding remarks on their cosmogony, tinctured, as it strongly is, with the old Persian philosophy.

They deny, as do all the tribes, a foreign origin. They assert, that America, or AONAO, was the place of their origin. They begin by laying down the theory, that they were the peculiar care of the Supernal Power who created all things, and who, as a proof of his care and benevolence of a race whom he had marked by a distinct color, created the continent for their especial use, and placed them upon it. None of the tribes pretend to establish dates, nor have they any astronomical data, to fix them. But they all give to the story of their origin, or creation, a locality, which is generally fixed to some prominent geographical feature near to their present respective place of abode, or at least, a spot well known. This spot, among the Iroquois cantons, is located in the northern hemisphere.

The term, Ongwe Honwe, is used by these tribes, very much in the manner in which the ancient Teutons called themselves, Allamanna, or Ghermanna, from which we have the modern terms, Allemand and German. If they did not litterally call themselves "all-men," as did these proud tribes, they implied as much, in a term which is interpreted to mean, real men, or a people surpassing all others. It is the common term for the red race, as contradistinguished from all other races, and the true equivalent of the phrase, "Indian."

By their earliest traditions, we are told that a body of the Ongwe Honwe, encamped on the banks of the St. Lawrence, where they were invaded by a nation few in number, but of giant stature, called Ronongweca.* After a war, brought on by personal encounters and incidents, and carried on with perfidy and cruelty, they were delivered at length, by the skill and courage of Yatontea,* who, after retreating before them, raised a large body of men and defeated them, after which they were supposed to be extinct. They next suffered from the malice, perfidy, and lust of an extraodinary person called Shotrowea,* who was finally driven across the St. Lawrence, and came to a town south of the shores of lake Ontario, where, however, he only disguised his intentions, to repeat his cruel and perfidious deeds. This person, who assassinated many persons, and violated six virgins, they point to as a fiend in human shape.

At this time the Big Quisquis† invaded the country, who pushed down the houses of the people, and created great consternation and disturbance. After making ineffectual resistance, they fled, but were at length relieved by a brave chief, who raised a body of men to battle him, but the animal himself retired. In this age of monsters, their country was invaded by another monster called the "Big Elk," who was furious against men,‡ and destroyed the lives of many persons, but he was at length killed after a severe contest.

A great horned serpent next appeared on Lake Ontario, who, by means of his poisonous breath, produced diseases, and caused the death of many, but he was at last compelled to retire by thunderbolts. This fourth calamity was not forgotten, when a fifth happened. A blazing star fell into a fort situated on the banks of the St. Lawrence, and destroyed the people. Such a phenomenon caused great panic and dread, and they regarded it as ominous of their entire destruction. Prior to this, a confederation had taken place among these northern tribes, situated north of and along the banks of the great lakes, and they had a ruling chief over all. This ruler repaired to the south to visit a ruler of great fame and authority, who resided at a great town in

* I abreviate these words from the originals, for the sole purpose of making them readable to the ordinary reader.

† Kwis Kwis is the name of a hog in modern Iroquois.

‡ Carnivorous—but this is not a characteristic of the Elk.

A LODGE OF GOLD. But it only proved to be an embassy of folly, for this great ruler, exercising an imperial sway, availing himself of the information thus derived, of a great country full of resources, built many forts throughout the country, and almost penetrated to the banks of Lake Erie. The people who had confederated on the North resisted. A long war of a hundred years standing ensued, but the northern people were better skilled in the use of the bow and arrow, and were more expert woodsmen and warriors. They at length prevailed, and taking all these towns and forts, left them a heap of ruins.

But the prediction of the blazing star was now verified. The tribes who were held together by feeble bands, fell into disputes, and wars among themselves, which were pursued through a long period, until they utterly destroyed each other, and so reduced their numbers, that the land was again overrun by wild beasts. [D.]

II. ORIGIN AND HISTORY OF THE IROQUOIS, AS A DISTINCT PEOPLE.

The first period of Indian history having thus terminated in discords, wars, and the mutual destruction of each other, tradition does not denote how long the depopulation of the country continued. It begins a second period by recollections of the Konoshioni, or Iroquois. They do not indicate what relation they bear to the ancient, broken down confederacy glanced at, in the preceding paper; but leave us to suppose that they may have been fragmentary descendants of it. That such a conclusion should not be formed, however, and in order to prove themselves an original people in the land, they frame a new myth, to begin their national existence. They boldly assert, that they were, through some means, confined in a mountain, from whose subterraneous bowels they were extricated by Taryenyawagon, the Holder of the Heavens. They point to a place at or near the falls of the Oswego river, where this deliverance happened, and they look to this divine messenger, who could assume various shapes, as the friend and patron of their nation.*

As soon as they were released, he gave them instructions respecting the mode of hunting, matrimony, worship, and other points. He warned them against the Evil Spirit, and gave them corn, beans, squashes, potatoes and tobacco, and dogs to hunt their game. He bid them go towards the east, and personally guided them, until they entered a valley called Tenonanatchi, or the Mohawk. They followed this stream to its entrance into the Sanatatea, or, as called by the Mohawks, Kohatatea, which they pursued to the sea.

* Where the Indians dwelt for a long time, it is customary for them to affirm, in their metaphorical language, that they originated, or were created. When they date from such a spot, we find they frame a story, saying that they came out of a hill, &c. at that spot. In 1791, an extensive work, consisting of ditches, &c. was found about 40 miles south of Oswego, which is not remote from the probable place of origin their traditions refer to; and it may be worthy of examination with this particular view. Some account of this old fort appeared in the N. Y. Mag. 1792.

From this point they retraced their steps towards the west, originating as they went, in their order and position, the Mohawks, the Oneidas, the Onondagas, the Cayugas, and the Senecas. They do not omit the Tuscaroras, whom they acknowledged, after a long period of wandering and a considerable change of language, and admitted as the Sixth tribe of the confederacy.

The Tuscaroras affirm, that, after reaching the lake waters, they turned southwest, to the Mississippi river, where a part of them crossed on a grape vine, but it broke, leaving the remainder east. Those who went west, have been lost and forgotten from their memory. The remainder, or eastern Tuscaroras, continued their wanderings, hunting, and wars, until they had crossed the Alleghanies and reached the sea again, at the mouth of the Cautoh, or Neus river, in North Carolina.

Each tribe was independent of the others. They increased in numbers, valor and skill, and in all sorts of knowledge necessary in the forest. But they began to fight and quarrel among themselves, and thus wasted and destroyed each other. They lived a life of perpetual fear and built forts to defend themselves, or to protect their women and children. Besides this, the country was wide and covered with large forests and lakes, and it gave shelter to many fierce wild animals and monsters, who beset their paths and kept them in dread. The evil spirit also plagued them with monstrous visitations. They were often induced to change their villages, sometimes from the fear of such enemies, and sometimes from sickness or bad luck. In this manner, and owing to their perpetual hostility, their population was often reduced. How long they wandered and warred, they do not know. At length it was proposed by some wise man that they should no longer fight against each other, but unite their strength against their enemies, the Alleghans, the Adiriondacks, the Eries, and other ancient and once powerful tribes, who figure in the foreground of their early history, and who, if accounts be true, once greatly excelled them both in war and arts, the skill of making implements, canoes and utensils, &c.

To this league, which was formed on the banks of Onondaga lake, they in time, gave the name of the Long House, using the term symbolically, to denote that they were tied and braced together by blood and lineage, as well as political bonds. This house, agreeably to the allusion so often made by their speakers, during our colonial history, reached from the banks of the Hudson to the Lakes. At its eastern door stood the Mohawks, at the west the Senecas, who guarded it with vigilance.

[*a*.] The Mohawks.

The Mohawks are supposed to be the eldest brother, in the symbolical chain of the Six Nations. Their own tradition assigns them this rank, and it appears to be consonant to other traditions.

When Tarenyawagon, their liberator from their subterranean confinement, bid them travel east, he gave them his personal conduct and care until they had entered the Mohawk valley. Some of their western brethren call this stream Tenonanatche, or a river flowing through a mountain. In due time, they went on into the valley of the Hudson, and thence, if we credit their annals, to the sea. The seat of their power and growth was, however, in the genial valley where they had at first located. Here they lived when the country was discovered, and here they continued to live and flourish until the events of the American revolution, and the determined cruelty which they exercised, under the authority and influence of the British crown, drove them out of it, and lost them the inheritance.

It does not appear, from any thing history or tradition tells us, or from any monumental remains in the valley or its immediate vicinity, that it had before been occupied by other nations. They do not speak of having driven out or conquered any other tribe. There are no old forts or earthen walls, or other traces of military or defensive occupancy, of which we have heard. Their ramparts were rather their own brawny arms, stout bodies and brave hearts. From the earliest notices of them, they were renowned for wielding the war club and arrow with great dexterity. They raised corn on the rich intervales, and pursued the deer, bear and elk in the subjacent forests. Their dominion extended from the head waters of the Susquehanna and Delaware to Lake Champlain. They had pursued their forays into the territorial area of New-England, as far, at least, as the central portions of the Connecticut, and had made their power felt, as temporary invaders, among the small independent tribes who lived about the region of the present city and harbor of New-York. Wherever they went, they carried terror. Their very name, as we learn from Colden, was a synonyme for cruelty and dread.* No tribe, perhaps, on the continent, produced better warriors, or have ever more fully realized, as a nation, the highest measure of heroism and military glory to which hunter nations can reach.

In passing over the country which they once occupied, there is little to stimulate historical interest, beyond the general idea of their power and military renown. Their history is connected with the rise and influence of one of our most distinguished anti-revolutionary citizens, Sir William Johnson. The influence he obtained over them was never exceeded, if equalled by that of any other man of European lineage. He moulded them to his purposes in peace and war. They followed him in his most perilous expeditions, and sustained him manfully, as we know, in the two great contests to whose successful issue he owed his laurels, namely, Lake George and Niagara. So completely identified were they in feeling and policy with this politic and brave man, that after his death, which happened at the crisis of '76, they transferred their attachment to his family, and staking their all on the issue, abandoned their beloved valley and the bones of their fathers, and fled to the less hospitable latitudes of Canada, from which they have never permanently returned.

Some twenty or more persons of this tribe are mingled as residents of the villages of their brethren, the Senecas, Tuscaroras, and Oneidas. A much greater number exist with intermixture of other kindred tribes, in the St. Regis canton of St. Lawrence county ; but the greater number of the parent tribe reside on lands appropriated for

---

* The word Mohawk itself, is not a term of Mohawk origin, but one imposed upon them, as is believed, by the Mohegan race, who inhabited the borders of the sea. Among this race the Dutch and English landed, and they would naturally adopt the term most in vogue for so celebrated a tribe. The Dutch, indeed, modified it to Maaquas—a modification which helps us to decypher its probable origin, in Mauqua (by kindred tribes, Mukwa, &c.) a bear. By others, it may be traced to mok, wa, a wolf, and awki, a country.

their use by the British government, at Brantford, on the Grand river of Canada West. To this place at the close of the war, they followed their distinguished leader, Thayendanegea, the Jephtha of his tribe, who, against the custom of birth and descent, and every other obstacle, after the failure of the line of wise and brave chiefs to lead them to battle, was made their Tekarahogea and leader, and displayed a degree of energy and firmness of purpose, which few of the aboriginal race in America have ever equalled.

What light the examination of the old places of burial of this tribe in the valley would throw on their ancient history or arts, by entombed articles, cannot be told without examinations which have not been made. Probably the old places of Indian interment about Canajoharie, Dionderoga, and Schenectady, would reveal something on this head, conforming at least, in age and style of art, with the stone pipes, tomahawks and amulets of the Onondaga and Genesee countries. The valley of the Schoharie and that of the Tawasentha, or Norman's kill, near Albany, might also be expected to reward this species of research. [Vide B.] A human head, rudely carved in stone, apparently aboriginal, was sent to the New-York Historical Society early in 1845, which was represented to have been found in excavating a bank at Schenectady. If this piece of sculpture, which denoted more labor than art, be regarded as of Mohawk origin, it would evince no higher degree of art, in this respect, than was evinced by similar outlines cut in the rock, but not detached, by some of the New-England tribes.*

---

* Rude carvings of this kind are represented to exist on the banks of the Connecticut, at Bellows' Falls, &c.

[b.] Origin and History of the Oneidas.

This canton of the Iroquois nation, deduces its origin in a remote age, from the Onondagas, with the language of which, the Oneida has the closest affinity. According to a tradition which was related to me, and which is believed to be entitled to respect, they are descended from two persons, who, in their obscure ages, and before a confederation had been thought of, went out from the people at Onondaga, and first dwelt at the head of the Oneida river. After increasing in numbers, they removed to the outlet of the Oneida creek, which flows into Oneida lake. Here they fortified themselves, and farther increased in numbers and power. Remains of this fortification are said still to exist. Their next removal was up the Oneida creek valley, to the storied locality of the Oneida stone, from which, by a figure of speech, they represent themselves to have sprung. This stone is in the town of Stockbridge, Madison county. It lies on a very commanding eminence, from which the entire valley, as far as the Oneida lake, can be seen in a clear atmosphere. The day of my visit being hazy at a distance, the lake could not be seen, although the view down the valley, was both magnificent and picturesque. This eminence was formerly covered with a butternut grove. Old, and partly decayed trees of this species, still remain in a few places. The ancient town extended in a transverse valley, south of this ridge of land, covered as it was, with nut wood trees, and was completely sheltered by it, from the north winds. A copious and clear spring of water issued at the spot selected for their wigwams. Here in seclusion from their enemies, the tribe expanded and grew in numbers. When it was necessary to light their pipes, and assemble to discuss their national affairs, they had only to ascend the hill, through its richly wooded grove, to its extreme summit, at the site of the Oneida stone. This stone, represented on the succeeding page, became the national altar.

Standing at its side, at a probable elevation of 400 or 500 feet above the Stanwix summit, they could survey the whole valley of the Oneida ; and a beacon fire lighted here, was the signal for assembling their warriors, from all the surrounding lateral plains and vallies. Time and usage rendered the object sacred, and as they expanded into nationality and power, while located around it, their sages asserted with metaphorical truth, that they sprang from this rock. Stone in this language is Onia. They called themselves, Oniota-aug, people of, or who sprung from the stone. There is some variety in the pronunciation. The Mohawks call them Onéota. The French wrote it Aneyoute, the English and Dutch, Oneida, which latter has prevailed. Neither retained the plural inflection in *aug*, which carries the idea of people.

With a knowledge of these traditions, I approached the spot with deep interest. It occupies the extreme summit, as shown in the print. The first feeling, on approaching it, was one of disappointment at its size, but this feeling soon subsided in the interest of its antiquity and national associations. It is a large, but not enormous boulder of syenite,* of the erratic block groupe, and, consequently, geologically foreign to the location. There are no rocks of this species in situ, I believe, nearer to it, in a northerly or easterly direction, than the Kayaderosseras or the Adirondach mountains.† The summit upon which, partly embedded, it reposes, is now a cleared field, in grass. A few primitive and secondary boulders, all of lesser size, are strown about the ridge, and several of weight and magnitude rest upon its flanks, and in the vallies at its base. One of the largest of these is the White Stone at the spring, which has been spoken of, I think, in some early notices of the Oneidas, as the

* A specimen of the rock before me, brought thence, consists of flesh colored feldspar, quartz and hornblende.

† If the passage of the Mohawk through the Astorenga or Astogan hills, at Little Falls, discloses syenite, I am not aware of the fact.

true Oneida Stone; but this opinion is erroneous, by the concurrent testimony of red and white men, cognizant of the facts, whom I consulted. This white stone, figured below, has been removed, by the proprietor of the land,* from its ancient position near the spring, to constitute part of a stone fence; it is a carbonate of lime.

TSHEJOANA, one of the Oneidas, who served as my guide in visiting this interesting location, took me to see still another stone, of note, lying a mile or more distant, in a southerly direction, on a farm of Gen. Knox. This stone, of which a figure is annexed,

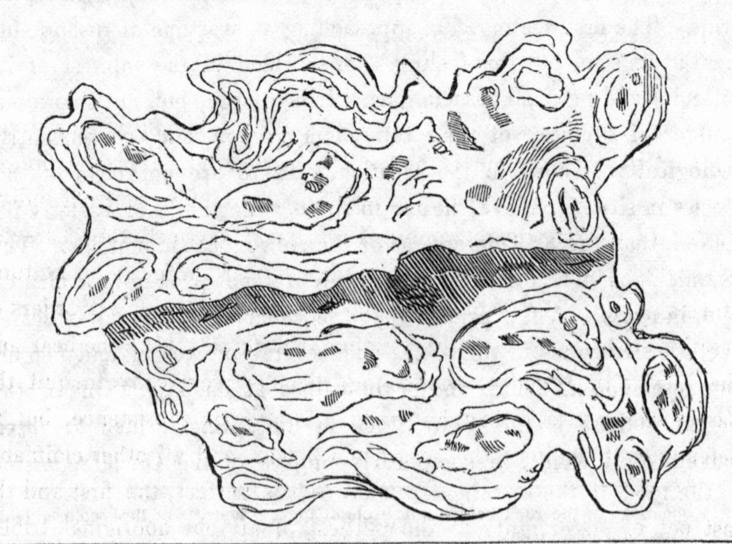

* Mr. Job Francis.

I found to be a large boulder of dark, compact limestone, with organic remains.

It was observable that the encrinites contained in this mass, were red. My Indian guide would have this color to be the result of the ancient Indian war paint. But the most striking characteristic of this rock, aside from its massy and flattened size and channelled centre, consists in the evidences it affords of the action of water, in rounding and polishing it. In several places, my guide would have this wearing effect to have been produced by the rubbing and sharpening of the Indian war axes; for he averred that it was customary for war parties who went out south against the Cherokees, to come and sharpen their axes upon this stone, and paint themselves for war. Whatever there was in this custom, I think he was probably mistaken in his locality; yet it is a question in which others may differ. At any rate, geology had been quite beforehand with the Oneida legendary and philosopher, in producing and accounting for these two phenomena, namely, the red color and smoothed and channelled surfaces. Geology having been mentioned, I may add the following incident. I told Skanawadi, one of my guides, while standing at the Oneida stone, lying on its proud ancient elevation, that there was no stone like this, in place, till we went north to the Adirondachs or Tehawas, or great lakes, and that this block of syenite had been brought here by the ocean, when it covered the whole land, and left on its recession. He replied, after a moment's reflection, that "he believed this."

At the time the Oneidas came to fix their location at this stone, the Konoshioni or Iroquois had not confederated. This people, in the early eras of their history, like the Algonquins, sent out individuals and bands, who became powerful, and assumed the character of separate and independent tribes, making war and peace ad libitum. If this mode of multiplication be compared to the lower orders of creation, it had some striking analogies with it. Like the bear and the hawk, the moment the young member was ready to quit the parent lair or nest, it had not only to forage for subsistence, but to defend itself against other bears and hawks, and all other claimants to the food of the forest. To make war is, in fact, the first and the last act of sovereignty of the pettiest of all our aboriginal tribes.

War is with them the road, and the only road to fame, and the readiest way to secure a supply of spontaneous food. They fight to increase or defend the boundaries of their hunting grounds. Thus, doubtless, arose the first difficulties between the Oneidas and the other branches of the Iroquois. As soon as they were important enough to be noticed, and bold enough to defend themselves, they had to raise barriers around their villages, and when these were carried, as they probably were, or were threatened to be, at two points, on the Oneida waters, they fled to the hill country, at the site of the Oneida stone. How long they abode here, and made it the seat of their council fire, we can only conjecture. They cannot and do not pretend to tell. Wisdom, at length, taught the Iroquois sages, that they had enemies enough, without fighting with each other, and the idea of a confederation was suggested. Tradition has preserved the name of Thaunowaga as the original suggestor: but it has preserved nothing more of his biography. The delegate from the Oneidas was Otatschechta. That he came from, and lived *at*, the locality of the stone, and was renowned for his deeds and wisdom, is probable. This comprises the brief biography of two celebrated aboriginal sages and statesmen. Three periods of transference, of their council fire, have been named, all of which were probably prior to the confederation. Their fourth remove was down the valley to the present site of Oneida Castle—a place which then, as now, they called KUNAWALOA, meaning a man's head on a pole. At this place they lived and held their council fire, when the Dutch, in 1609, discovered and ascended the Kohatatea, or, Hudson river. Such are the accounts of their sachems and wise men. It is a general confirmation of them, that the other members call them Younger Brother.

By another and older Indian tradition, an earlier date is assigned to the Oneida canton, which is regarded as one of the original subdivisions of the generic stock. It represents this stock as moving from the west to the east, and at another period, returning towards the point of sun-setting, leaving the several separate tribes, or cantons, in their order as they passed. In this migration, the Oneidas are named as the second in geographical position and order of chronology.

They located themselves, says the Tuscarora annalist,* at a stream called Kaw nah taw te ruh, or Pineries, a tributary, of the Susquehanna, which originates according to this authority, in Allen's lake, ten miles south of Oneida Castle. They were called Ne haw retahgo,† or Big-Tree, a name, it may be remarked, which does not occur as the patronymic for this tribe in other authors, nor has it been retained by them. The distance and course denoted, coincide very nearly with that of the Oneida stone. It is not known, however, that any tributary of the Susquehanna exists in that vicinity.

The two traditions may indeed be reconciled to truth, by supposing the latter the more ancient one, and that the Onondaga families before mentioned, constituted a subsequent accession to, and union with a band who had seated themselves at a prior era, at the spot denoted ; or this band may have remained there, on the general passage of the people eastward, and thus been the nucleus of the tribe, on the general return of the people west. In any view, however, they were called and are still called by the Iroquois, "Younger Brother," which must be considered conclusive, that their nationality is of a period subsequent to that of the Mohawks, Onondagas, Cayugas, and Senecas. This fact too, is adverse to the theory, which has too much the aspect of a mere theory, that the re-migration of the Iroquois westward from the Atlantic, proceeded like a marching army, leaving tribes here and there as they went, in a regular chronological order, each of which took a name, and "altered," as his phrase is, the language. The writer seems all along, to have had the Jewish Tribes in his mind. The truth is, ethnologically speaking, no tribe or nation, alters by an authoritative decision, or pre-thought, its language or idoims. Such alterations flow from time and circumstances. Least of all, do wandering savage tribes gravely determine to "alter" their dialects. Accident, usage, or caprice, little by little, and at long intervals, is the parent of new dialects and languages.

A few deductions may be added. By data before introduced, it will have been seen that it is probable the present confederation, whatever had preceded it, did not take place till about 1539, or seventy years before the arrival of Hudson. It may be considered

* Cusick. † In Tuscarora.

as probable, that the Oneidas did not remove from the Oneida stone, into the valley and plains of Oneida Castle, until after the event of the final confederation between the Five Tribes, gave them security against internal enemies. The date of this transfer of the council fire, is rather remote, but not very ancient. A new forest has grown upon the old cornfields which were once cultivated at their ancient settlement at the Oneida stone. The appearance of corn hills in rows, is still clearly perceptible in some parts of this forest. To an inquiry how such a preservation of the outlines of corn hills could be possible, my informant, who was an Oneida, answered, that in ancient times, the corn hills were made so large, that three clusters of stalks or sub-hills were raised on each circle or hill. There being no ploughs or other general means of turning up the earth, the same hill was used year after year, and thus its outlines became large and well defined. In a black walnut tree, standing on the site of one of these ancient corn-fields, which was partly cut, and partly broken off, I counted on the cut part, one hundred cortical layers, and measuring the broken part, estimated it to have 140 more. Allowing a year for each ring, the commencement of the growth was in 1555, or 16 years after the supposed date of the confederacy, and 290 years from the present date.

The remaining history of the Oneidas can only be glanced at, but has some points of peculiar interest. They are the only tribe of the ancient Konoshioni who adhered to us, at least the better part of them, in our life and death struggle of the revolutionary war, saving some portion of the Tuscaroras; whose aid, however, is justly due to the Oneida influence. It was by the Oneidas that the Tuscaroras were brought off from the south. The Oneidas had long distinguished themselves in their war excursions against the southern Indians. Their traditions are replete with accounts of these war parties against the Oyada, or Cherokees. They had found allies at the south in the Tuscaroras, who were themselves engaged in desperate wars, at various periods, against the Catabas, and Cherokees, and others. Besides this, Iroquois tradition claims the Tuscaroras as one of their original cantons, or rather as a band of the original Eagwe Heowe, who had, in early times gone south.* And when a crisis happened in their affairs, they nobly went to their relief, and seated

* Vide Cusick's pamphlet.

them on their western confines, between themselves and the Onondagas, where they remained during the revolution. The Oneidas bore their full share in the long and bloody wars waged by Iroquois for more than two centuries, against the French in the Canadas, and against the distant Algonquins, Hurons and Illinese. And he who scans the ancient records of treaties and councils, will find that their sachems were represented in the conferences assembled on this continent, by the kings and potentates of Europe, who planted colonies at various times, between the respective Gulphs of Mexico and the St. Lawrence. After the flight of the Mohawks, in 1776, they were in the van of the Konoshioni, and to use their symbolic phraseology, stood in the eastern door of the Long House. When the mixed Saxon population of New-York and New-England began, after the war of 1776, to move westward, the Oneidas first felt the pressure upon their territory. By siding with the colonists, they had secured their entire ancient domain, from which they ceded to the State, from time to time, such portions as they did not want for cultivation, taking in lieu money annuities. Nor did they fail to profit, in a measure, by the example of industry set before them in agriculture and the arts. For a while, it is true, they reeled before the march of intemperance, and sunk in numbers, but many of them learned the art of holding the plough. From the earliest times they were noted, along with their more western brethren, for the cultivation of Indian corn, and the planting of orchards. They also became tolerable herdsmen, and raised in considerable numbers, neat cattle, horses and hogs.

To preserve their nationality, their sachems, about the year 1820, sent delegates west to look out a location for their permanent residence. They purchased a suitable territory from the Monomonees of Wisconsin, a wandering and non-idustrious race, seated about Green Bay, and expended a part of their annuities in the payment. This turned out a wise measure. They soon began to remove, and have at this time a very flourishing settlement on Duck river, in that territory. At that location they have established schools, temperance societies and a church. They bear a good reputation for morals and industry, and are advancing in civilization and the arts.

By an official return of the date of 1844, they numbered 722 persons at that settlement. Two hundred and ten are still seated within the boundaries of New-York, mostly in Oneida county. They are a mild people, of a good stature, and easy manners, and speak a soft dialect of the Iroquois, abounding in the liquid *l*, which, together with a mild enunciation, imparts a pleasing character to their speech.

[*c*.] Onondagas.

Onondaga was, from the remotest times, the seat of the Iroquois government. Granting credence to the account of their own origin, on the high grounds or falls of the Oswego, they had not proceeded far up the course of the widely gathered waters of this stream, when a portion of them planted their wigwams in this fertile region. Whatever was the cause of their migrating from their primary council fire, nothing was more natural than that, by pursuing this stream upward, they should separate into independent tribes, and by further tracing out its far spread forks, gradually expand themselves, as they were found by the discoverers and first settlers, over the entire area of western New-York. On reaching the grand junction of Three River Point, a part went up the Seneca river, who subsequently dividing, formed the Senecas and Cayugas. The bands who took the eastern fork, or Oneida river, pushed forward over the Deowainsta, or Rome summit, into the first large stream, flowing east, and became the Mohawks. The central or Onondaga fork was chosen by the portion who, from the hill country they first located in, took this name ; and from them, the Oneidas, pursuing in fact the track of the Mohawks, were an off-shoot. That such was the general route, and causes of their separation, appears as evident as strong probabilities, in coincidence with their own traditions and modern discovery, can make it. That the whole of the original number who started from the south banks of Lake Ontario, did not keep together till they reached the valley of the Hudson and the sea, and then go back to the west,—for so their general tradition has it, is also both reasonable and probable to suppose. Large bodies of hunters cannot keep long together. They must separate to procure food, and would separate from other causes. The first effect of their separation and spread into various rich vallies, abounding in game, nuts and fish, was a rapid increase in population. The next, to become overbearing, quarrel about territory, and fight. They were compelled to build forts to defend their stations, or secure their women and children, at night, and by this system, kept down their population to about its first point of increase. It is altogether probable that they did not more than maintain, for ages, a stationary population, which occasionally went down by disease and other calamities, and again revived, as we know that natural causes, in the laws of vitality, will revive a people quickly, after the scourge of pestilence.

The idea of a confederation was, it is believed, an old one with this people, for the very oldest traditions speak of something of this kind, among the lake and St. Lawrence tribes of older days. When the present league was formed, on the banks of the Onondaga lake, this central tribe had manifestly greatly increased in strength, and distinguished itself in arms, and feats of hunting and daring against giants and monsters, for in such rencontres their traditions abound.

Most distinguished, however, above all others, east or west, was a leader of great courage, wisdom and address, called Atotarho; and when they proposed to form a league, this person, who had inspired dread, and kept himself retired, was anxiously sought. He was found, by the Mohawk embassy, who were charged with the matter, sitting as he is represented in the annexed cut, composedly in a

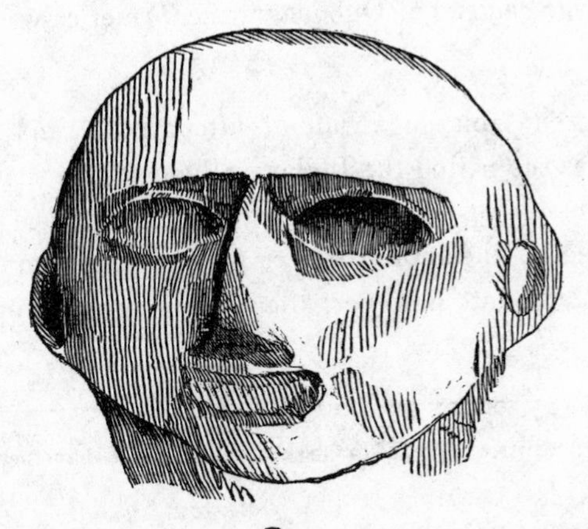

swamp, smoking his pipe, and rendered completely invulnerable, by living serpents. These animals extended their hissing heads from all parts of his head and body. Every thing about him, and the place of his residence, was such as to inspire the utmost fear and respect. His dishes and spoons were made of the skulls of enemies, whom he had slain in battle. Him, when they had duly approached with presents and burned tobacco in friendship, in their pipes, by way of frankincense, they placed at the head of their league, as its presiding officer. They collected a large quantity of wampum, and invested him with a broad belt of this sacred article. I found the original drawing of this personage, from which the above is reduced, in the summer of 1845, in the house of a Seneca on the Cattaragus reservation. The owner of this curious pictorial relic, on being asked, proceeded to a chest and carefully took it from its envelope, and allowed me to make a copy. It represents Atotarho, at the moment of his discovery, by the Mohawk delegation.

The right thus awarded to the Onondagas, to furnish a presiding officer for the league, has ever been retained, and is still possessed by that canton. To the Mohawks, at the same time, was awarded the Tekarahogea, or chief war captain—an office, however, of the general recognition of which, there is a disagreement amongst interpretors.

A singular tradition may be here added. It is said that the XIIIth Atotarho reigned at Onondaga when America was discovered. [D.]

Giving to each Atotarho* a rule of fifteen years, and taking Hudson's voyage as the period the Indians allude to, we should have A. D. 1414, as the era of the present confederacy, in place of 1539, before mentioned on the authority of a general tradition recorded by Pyrlaus. We cannot, however, place much reliance upon Cusick's chronology.

---

* Incidental circumstances have led to the substitution of the above head for the original figure.

[*d.*] Cayugas.

The history of this canton does not stand out prominently among the Iroquois while it will be found that as one of the inclusive tribes who carried their name and fame so high among the aborigines, they have performed their due part, and produced warriors, sages and speakers of eminence. Were every thing else, indeed, blotted out of their history, the fact of their having produced a Logan* would be sufficient to rescue their memory from oblivion. In their early search after a place to hunt, fish and plant corn, as an independent tribe, they, on the assumption of their own traditions, passed up the Seneca river, into the sylvan and beautiful lake which bears their name. In visiting this lake the present year, in search of their ancient sites, it was not without a melancholy interest, that I surveyed, within the boundaries of Aurora, the remains of one of those apple orchards, which were ruthlessly cut down by a detachment of the army of Gen. Sullivan, in his severe but necessary expedition in 1778. Many vestiges of their ancient residence still remain in Cayuga county, nor has local memory, in its intelligent and hospitable inhabitants, dropped from its scroll the names of several of its distinguished chiefs, and their places of abode. They point to a spot at Springport, now trenched on by the road, where lie the remains of Karistagea, better known by his English appellative of Steeltrap, one of their noted chiefs and wise men, who extended the hospitalities of his lodge to the first settlers on the "Military Tract." The nation itself, although they had fought strenuously under the Red Cross of St. George in the Revolutionary war, appeared to be composed of mild and peaceable men, of friendly dispositions towards the settlers. They brought venison, fish and wild fruits for sale to the doors of families, whose elder branches yet dwell upon the shores of the Cayuga.

Yet their history is a melancholy one, and their decline, on the settlement of Western New-York, was probably one of the most

* Logan was the son of Skellelimus, a Cayuga, and went early to the Ohio valley, if he were not born there.

striking instances of the rapid depopulation of a tribe in modern days. Their first cession of land to the State was in 1789. This was confirmed at the general treaty of Fort Stanwix in 1790, and such had been the pressure of emigration into that quarter, that in 1795, at a treaty held at Cayuga bridge, they ceded their reserve of one hundred miles square in the valley of the Seneca outlet and the basin of Cayuga lake, reserving but four miles square. In these treaties they deemed themselves wise to change into large money annuities,* a territory which was no longer useful for hunting, and which they did not cultivate.

Experience has shown, however, throughout America, that Indian tribes, who live on annuities, and not by agricultural labor, are in the most dangerous condition of rapid decline. To render the danger eminent, it needs but the close proximity of a European population, who present the means of indulging selfish gratifications. Among these means, so seductive to the Indian mind, ardent spirits have ever been the most baneful. It proved so at least with the Cayugas, for within sixteen years after the treaty of Fort Stanwix, they had all emigrated west. Some of them had rejoined their brethren, who followed Brant and the Mohawks to Canada. Some had migrated to Sandusky, in Ohio, and others found a refuge among the Senecas, near Buffalo. With the Senecas they have ever been on most intimate terms. Whilst they lived on the Cayuga lake, and the latter on the Seneca, they were separated by a midland range of forest, little more than 16 miles broad. They intermingled freely in their hunting parties, and even in their villages. The inhabitants still point to a large tree near Canoga, on the banks of Cayuga lake, where the celebrated orator Red Jacket was born.

In investigating the Indian population of New-York, under the provisions of the census act, I found 114 Cayugas residing in twenty families, on the Cattaragus reservation. These families cultivate 316 acres of land, and during the year 1845, they raised 1,970 bushels of corn, 1,622 of oats, 210 of wheat, 955 of potatoes, and 277 of buckwheat, besides esculents and small articles. They were found to possess 43 milch cows, 39 horses, 40 sheep, and 109 hogs. Besides

* A perpetual annuity of $2,300 was secured by one of these treaties.

the Cayugas residing on the Cattaragus, there were found, dispersed among the other cantons, 83 persons; making the whole number within the boundaries of New-York, 197. The style of their dwellings is, generally, that of squared timber, plainly but comfortably furnished, with glass windows, and plain common furniture. Sixteen of the number are members of Protestant churches. The males dress exclusively in the European fashion, and their condition and prospects are, like those of the Senecas, among whom they dwell, in a high degree encouraging to the friends of humanity. Of the number out of the bounds of the State, there have been no accurate means of judging. The vocabulary of their language (vide appendix O) will denote its close affinities with other tribes of this family.

From a remark made to me, by a daughter of Brant, (the late Mrs. Kerr,) at her house near Wellington square, Canada, in 1843, I am inclined to think, that in the early wars waged by the Iroquois against the Virginia Indians, the Cayugas defeated and made prisoners the remnant of the Tuteloes, whom they brought and settled among them, in the Cayuga country.

[*e.*] History and origin of the Senecas.

One of the first traits which strikes an observer on entering the territory of this tribe, is the fact that they are called by a name which is not known in their vocabulary, and which they only recognize from having long been thus designated by others. Identical as it is in its present orthography, with the name of the Roman moralist, it is yet wholly improbable that it had any such origin; it must be regarded as an accidental coincidence of sound in some other Indian tongue. That this tongue is the Mohawk, a people who stood first in position east on the Iroquois borders, is probable, but not certain. The earlier authors spelt it with a *k*, with the *a* final, which probably had the usual broad sound. It occurs on a map of 1614, which was brought over from Holland recently, by the historical agent of the State, and has been laid, by that gentleman, before the New-York Historical Society, with the proofs of its genuineness, thus bringing the use of the word within five years of the voyage of Hudson.

The term by which they call themselves is NUNDOWAGA, or the People of the Hill. A name which leads us at once to consider the accounts of their own origin. Various relations of this story have been given, differing in some of their details, but all coinciding in the main events, namely : that they originated and lived on a well known hill, at the head of Canandaigua lake, where they were put in eminent peril of utter destruction by a monstrous serpent, which circled itself about the fort and lay with its mouth open at the gate. The following is given from a native source, and has some novel details to recommend it.

While the tribe had its seat and council fire on this hill, a woman and her son were living near it, when the boy, one day caught a small two-headed serpent, called Kaistowanea, in the bushes. He brought it home as a pet to amuse himself, and put it in a box, where he fed it on bird's flesh and other dainties. After some time it had become so large that it rested on the beams of the lodge, and the hunters were obliged to feed it with deer ; but it soon went out and made its abode on a neighboring hill, where it maintained itself. It often went out and sported in the lake, and in time became so large and mischievous that the tribe were put in dread of it. They consulted on the subject one evening, and determined to fly next morning; but with the light of the next morning the monster had encircled the hill and lay with its double jaws extended before the gate. Some attempted to pass out, but were driven back ; others tried to climb over its body, but were unable. Hunger at last drove them to desperation, and they made a rush to pass, but only rushed into the monster's double jaws. All were devoured but a warrior and his sister, who waited in vain expectancy of relief. At length the warrior had a dream, in which he was showed that if he would fledge his arrows with the hair of his sister, the charm would prevail over their enemy. He was warned not to heed the frightful heads and hissing tongues, but to shoot at the heart. Accordingly, the next morning he armed himself with his keenest weapons, charmed as directed, and boldly shot at the serpent's heart. The instantaneous recoiling of the monster proved that the wound was mortal. He began in great agony to roll down the hill, breaking down trees and uttering horrid noises, until he rolled into the lake. Here he slaked his thirst, and tried by water to mitigate his agony, dashing about in fury. At length he vomited up all the people whom he had eaten, and immediately expired and sunk to the bottom.*

The fort was immediately deserted, and all who had escaped went with their deliverer to, and fixed their council fire on, the west shores of Seneca lake, where Geneva now stands.

The general course of the migration and conquests of the Senecas has, however, been towards the west. Taking their own general and ancient traditions of the parent stock, to wit, their origin in the valley of the Oswego, they may be supposed to have followed the Seneca branch of those outspread waters to the banks of the Seneca and Canandaigua lakes, and thence into the rich valley of the Genesee. At an early day they were limited to the region east of this capital stream, which, crossing the country in a transverse direction, formed a natural boundary. There lived west of it, in ancient times, a tribe who are known as Alleghans, Andastes and Eries, or, as the Senecas call them, Kah-Kwas. They had their council fires at or near Buffalo, extending west and also east. The people called by the French the Neuter Nation, had placed themselves, so far as we can learn, on the waters of Oak-Orchard creek, which draws its tributaries in part from the fertile districts of Genesee, Niagara and Orleans counties. From the accounts of the Tuscaroras, [D.] this people were governed in early times by a queen, who ruled over twelve forts in that quarter. North of them, embracing the Niagara ridge and the country below it, dwelt a branch of the Algonquin nation, who are called by the same authority, TWANKANNAH. Other names occur, which are believed to be either synonymes for these, or minor divisions of the three principal tribes named, of which some further notice will be taken in a subsequent paper on the antiquarian remains of the country.

That these Trans-Genessean people were populous and warlike, not only maintaining their grounds against the Senecas, but often de-

---

* If this be viewed as an allegory, it may admit of this interpretation. Internal feuds created by somebody brought up in their own lodges, originated hatred and hot blood. In a long and bloody war, the nation was nearly exterminated ; at length the affections of a woman prevailed. Harmony was restored, and a new era of prosperity began, by removing the council fire to another place.

feating them and driving them back, is proved not only by the traditions of the Senecas themselves, but by the striking evidences of their military strength and skill, denoted by the remains of forts and intrenchments and cemeteries, yet existing throughout the extensive area, included between the Genesee and the Niagara, extending up the southern shores of Lake Erie to Chautauque and the other principal known Indian routes to the waters of the Alleghany and Ohio. There is, at least, one authority* for believing that the Eries themselves were remotely descended from the Senecas, and we have living tradition to prove [VIII,] that, at the time of their final defeat and so called extermination, some of them fled west, whilst the remainder of them, scattered, cut up and depressed, were incorporated in the Seneca canton.

To the Twankannas, the Neuter Nation, and other tribes and bands, not being Eries, who lived in this portion of the State, the Iroquois applied the general term of Adirondacks,† a bold, warlike, northern race, who spread over many degrees of latitude and longitude in former days, covering, by generic affiliation with other tribes, all New-England and the Atlantic coast, to North Carolina, and who are still, in their numerous and subdivided descendants, in the upper lakes and the west, the most numerous of any of the aboriginal stocks yet existing east of the Mississippi and Missouri. So long as the Iroquois remained divided, the Eries and their Algonquin allies kept their ground ; and there is no reason to believe that they began to decline until a considerable period after the era of the Onondaga league. That league was at first but little more than an agreement to stand by each other, and to send delegates and forward news to a central council ; but it put an end to intestine wars, and its popular capacities soon developed themselves, and made it formidable to their neighbors. Thus much by way of prelude to their wars, to be noticed hereafter.

The Senecas were from the earliest times the most powerful of the Iroquois, nearly doubling, in its best estate, the Mohawks. Their population in past days has been variously estimated, and often exaggerated. Perhaps Dalton, who puts it at 400 warriors, or 2,000 souls, during the American war, verges to the opposite extreme, and

---

* Cusick. † Called Algonquins by the French.

actually underrates it. Be this as it may, I found the entire Seneca population, within the State, to be 2,383, residing on four reservations in the counties of Niagara and Genesee, Erie, Chautauque, Cattaraugus and Alleghany. They were found to be divided into 538 families, who cultivated, in the aggregate, 8,416 acres of land. The produce of this land, as near as it could be obtained, as some declined stating it, was 21,341 bushels of corn, 3,745 of wheat, 20,039 of oats, and 12,469 of potatoes, besides buckwheat, turneps, peas, and smaller articles. They possess 1,537 neat cattle, 510 milch cows, 626 horses, 335 sheep, and 2,269 hogs. Other details of their advance in agriculture were equally flattering. They cut large quantities of meadow land, possess an adequate supply of farming utensils, carts, wagons, including many tasty buggies and sleighs. Very little of their means of subsistence, even in the most unfavored positions, is derived from the chase. Upwards of 4,000 fruit trees were counted. The style of their buildings, fences and household furniture, as well as the dress of the males, is not essentially different, and little, often nothing at all, inferior to that of their white neighbors. Temperance and temperance societies exist in a good state in each canton. Fifteen of their youth have received a collegiate or academic education. A number of these have studied professions. About 350 of the children attend private or missionary schools, and so far as I could obtain returns, some 250 adults are enrolled as members of Protestant churches. Of this number, there are several catechists and intelligent educated translators and interpreters of the language. On the four reservations, there are fifteen native mechanics and three physicians.

Thus it appears that the energies once devoted by their ancestors to war and hunting, are in good earnest now directed to husbandry and the arts ; and there is every encouragement to hope, and reason to believe, that by a continuance in the best measures, they will be wholly reclaimed and added to the number of useful, intelligent and moral citizens. In viewing the condition of such a people, hardy, well formed and active, and pressing forward, as they are, in the great experiment of civilization, humanity consoles itself with the hope, that the energy and firmness of purpose which once carried them, in pursuit of warlike glory, far and wide, will develope itself, as it has already signally commenced to do, in the labors of the field and the workshop. Their rude picture-writing upon the bark of trees, has given place to the school. Their prophets' lodges have been converted into churches; their midnight orgies, at the Indian dancing house, into societies to promote temperance. It is but applying present experience to future results, to predict that these results may become general. The eloquence thrown out by a Red Jacket, in opposition to the further curtailment of their territory,, may shine out, in some of his descendants, to enlighten his people in agriculture, morals and political economy. Nor ought we to doubt that the desk and the forum are yet to resound with Seneca eloquence.

[*f.*] Tuscaroras.

The traditions of this canton affirm, that they are descendants of the original family of Iroquois, who began their existence, or their nationality, at least at or near the falls of the Oswego. After the migration of the parent tribe towards the sea, and their return west and separation into tribes, this band went on west till they reached Lake Erie. From hence they travelled southwest till they reached the Mississippi. Part of them crossed the river, and they were thus divided. Those who went over, became, in time, the enemies of such as remained on its eastern banks, and were finally lost and forgotten from their memory.

Terenyawagon, the Holder of the Heavens, who was the patron of the home bands, did not fail, in this crisis, to direct their way also. After giving them practical instructions in war and hunting, he guided their footsteps in their journies, south and east, until they had crossed the Alleghanies, and reached the shores of the sea, on the coasts which are now called the Carolinas. They were directed to fix their residence on the banks of the Cau-tan-o, that is, a Pine in the water, now called Neuse river, in North Carolina. By this time their language was altered, but not so much but that they could understand each other. Here Terenyawagon left them to hunt, increase and prosper, whilst he returned to direct the remaining Five Nations to form their confederacy. Thus far the Tuscarora annalist. History picks up the Tuscaroras precisely where tradition and fable leave them. On the settlement of Virginia and the Carolinas, they were found to be the first nation of any stability of purpose, after passing the Powhatannic tribes, in proceeding south. The intervening coast tribes were petty chieftaindoms, few in numbers and disunited in action or policy. They were essentially ichthiopagi. They soon fell before the two-fold influence of idleness and rum, and have left little or no history, or traits worth preserving. Such is the history of the Chowanokes,* the Maratocks, and the Mangoacks, who, in one hundred and twenty years from the date of Raleigh's patent, had dwindled from 6,000 to forty-six bowmen.†

The Tuscaroras, who lived in the game country, on the skirts of the mountains, showed themselves at the mouths of Cantano or Neuse, Contentny, and Taw rivers. They were, at the time, numerous and warlike, and as inimical to the inhabitants of the Carolinas, as they were numerous. They were at war with the Catabas, the Cowetas and the Cherokees. Numbers, bravery and success, and abundance of animal food, made them haughty, and they evinced the disposition of their northern brethren, by trying to subjugate and break down their neighbors. What they had done with red men, very effectually, it must be confessed at least with the Catabas, they thought they might do with the Hugenots of France, the cavaliers of England, and the protestants of the baronetcy of Graffenried in Germany. It is not improbable, indeed, that, at a prior era, the Tuscaroras were the very people who had exterminated the colony left on Roanoke island, under the first attempts of Sir Walter Raleigh to colonize Virginia. But, if such were the fact—a mere conjecture at best—they mistook their present neighbors and their own position in attempting to repeat the act.

This scheme was, however, deeply laid, although it appeared to be a matter hastily executed. They had long felt a growing jealousy of the encroaching settlements, and gave vent to it, the first occasion that offered, by seizing Lawson the surveyor-general of the Province, on a trip up the Neuse, and after a kind of trial before a council, putting him to death. The Baron Graffenried, who was with him,

* Mr. Jefferson thinks (vide Notes, p. 152, London ed. of 1787,) that this tribe was connected with the Tutelos, Nottaways and Meherrins of Virginia.

† Williamson.

and was also condemned, but saved, on an appeal on the ground of his being a man of rank and not an Englishman; but they kept him a prisoner, while they proceeded to execute their ill-advised and nefarious plot, which was nothing less than the massacre of the entire colony in one day. The day fixed for this tragedy was the 22d of September, 1711. Williamson* thinks it was an impulsive movement arising from the killing of Lawson, who being a public officer, they felt themselves committed in a war, and resolved to proceed with the bloody work. For this purpose they divided themselves into small bands of six or seven, and entering the settlements at various points, theys truck down with the tomahawk on one day one hundred and thirty persons. To conceal their intentions, they had left their arms, and relied on theirhatchets alone. In this plot, they were assisted by the sea-coast bands of Corees, Mattamuskeets and Bear-river Indians, some three or four tribes, denoting a league and maturity in the attempt. But the plan did not succeed to their wishes, for besides that the colony consisted then of nearly two thousand men, much spread, it must needs have happened that many at the time of attack, would be absent from their homes. The colonists rallied, and prepared to carry the war home to their subtle assailants. They asked the aid of South Carolina, which came gallantly to their rescue. The Legislature of of that Province having granted four thousand pounds, placed Col. Barnwell at the head of a small detachment of armed men, supported by a large body of Cherokees, Creeks and Catabas, the deadly enemies of the Tuscaroras. He killed, in various actions, thirty Tuscaroras, and fifty of the sea-coast auxiliaries, and took two hundred women and children of the latter prisoners, and returned. The war thus commenced was continued, with various results for some few years. The aid of Virginia, as well as South Carolina was invoked the next year. The Tuscaroras also made vigorous exertions. They were well provided with arms and ammunition, and despatched runners to the Senecas for aid. Their auxiliaries, the Mattamuskets, Corees and others killed or made prisoners the next winter, forty inhabitants of the Island of Roanoke or Croatan. The Tuscaroras prepared to maintain their power by entrenching themselves behind a picketed work on the river Taw. This work, called fort NAHARUKE, stood on a plain beside a creek, and consisted of a rampart of earth, covering the whole ground occupied, defended with palisades. To

* Hist. North Carolina.

protect themselves from artillery, they had dug within this wall, square pits of earth, six feet deep, covered with poles, and connected by a wall of earth. They were well provided with corn and ammunition, and had the means of standing a siege, had they made a wise provision for water. To obtain this necessary article, they relied on an artificial ditch leading to the stream.

To this aboriginal fort Col. Moore of South-Carolina, drove them from the lower country with 40 musketeers and 800 Indians, in the early part of the winter of 1713, after having been detained on his march by a deep snow. He immediately saw the mistake of the water trench, and placed cannon to rake it. He then fortified the only passage or point of land, where the Indians would be likely to escape, and began regular approaches to the work, which he entered on the 26th of March, 1713, taking 800 Tuscaroras prisoners. It is not said how many were killed. He had lost of his army, during the seige, 22 white, and 36 red men killed, and 29 of the former, and 50 of the latter wounded. The Cherokees and their allies claimed the prisoners, who were taken to the south, and sold as slaves, a part, as we are left to infer, being offered by the southern Indians, to appease the spirit of retaliation for prior losses by them.

This brought the tribe to terms, and they entered into preliminaries of peace, by which they agreed to deliver up twenty men, who were the contrivers of the plot, and who took Lawson and Graffenried ; to restore all prisoners, horses and cattle, arms and other property ; to treat and pursue the Mattamuskeets and their other allies, as enemies ; and finally, to give two hostages for the peaceable conduct of each of their towns.

During the following summer, the chief called "King Blount," brought in thirty scalps from his miserably treated allies ; "but the greater part of the nation," says the historian before quoted, "unable to contend, and unwilling to submit, removed to the northward, and joined the Seneka, and other confederate tribes on the frontiers of New-York.* Those who remained, were to have settled between the Neuse and Taw rivers ; but an Indian war having broken out in the southern colonies in 1715, only three months after the peace, with the Corees and their other former allies, the Tuscaroras, now the

* Williamson.

remains of a broken down tribe, feeble in numbers and power, obtained permission to settle on the *north* side of the Roanoke river, on a reservation, where some of them were living in 1803.

The whole number of Indians living in North Carolina in 1708, estimating their fighting men, were 1,608, of whom, the Tuscaroras constituted 1,200, which would give them, on the ordinary principle of estimating their population, 6,000 souls. Two thirds of the whole number of their fighting men were captured at the taking of fort NAHARUKE in 1713. How many were killed on other occasions is not certainly known ; but it is probable that in this short war of but three years duration, and owing to the desertion of families, death by sickness, want, and other casualties consequent upon the surrender of Naharuke, they sunk to almost immediate insignificance. Those who fled to their kindred in western New-York, were never counted. They were estimated, perhaps high, at 200 warriors, in 1776. They were located at first, immediately west of, and in juxtaposition to the Oneidas, along with whom, they are mentioned as being secured in their rights, by the treaty of Fort Stanwix, in 1784. But in fact, they had no independent claim to territory, living merely as guests, although the confederacy had admitted them as an integral member, after their disastrous flight from North Carolina, calling themselves no longer the FIVE, but the SIX NATIONS. The Senecas gave them lands on the Niagara Ridge, after the American revolution ; these were subsequently secured to them in a reservation made by the State, in the present bounds of Niagara county. Here they have continued to dwell, having added to their possessions, by an early purchase from the Holland Land Company, made with the avails of the sale of their reservation north of the Roanoke, in North Carolina.

But if the Tuscaroras have erred in policy, and sunk in numbers, with a rapidity and in a ratio unequalled by any other members of the confederacy, if we except the Onondagas and Cayugas, they may be said to have grown wise by experience. Low as their present numbers are, they hold an exalted rank among their brethren for industry, temperance, and their general advance in arts, agriculture and morals.

I found, on making the enumeration, 283 persons living in 53 families, of whom 151 were males and 167 females. These families cultivated the past year 2,080 acres of land, on which they raised 4,897 bushels of wheat, 3,515 of corn, 4,085 of oats, 1,166 of potatoes, besides limited quantities of peas, beans, buckwheat and turnips. They possess 336 neat cattle, 98 milch cows, making 7,537 pounds of butter, 153 horses, 215 sheep, and 596 hogs.

When it is considered that this enumeration gives an average of six neat cattle, three horses, (nearly) two milch cows, (nearly) 10 hogs, and 92 bushels of wheat, 966 of corn to each family, their capacity to sustain themselves, and their advance as agriculturists will be perceived. Fifty-nine ploughs were found amongst fifty-three families. They cut 195 acres of meadow to sustain their cattle. They have over 1,500 fruit trees, and dwell in excellent frame or square-timber houses, well finished, and for the most part well furnished. I noticed one edifice of stone, in the process of building, seated on rising grounds, amidst shade trees, which denotes both wealth and taste. Other results of civilization are to be already observed. Among these there are no slight indications of classes of society, arranging themselves, as rich and poor, intelligent and ignorant, industrious and idle, moral and immoral.

Of the entire population, 63 are church members, and 231 members of temperance societies, which is a far higher proportion than is found in any other of the cantons.

[g.] Necariages.

The Tuscaroras were probably admitted into the confederacy about 1714. Nine years afterwards the Iroquois received the Nicariages. Under this name the long expatriated Quatoghies, or Hurons, then living at Teiodonderoghie or Michilimackinac, were taken into the confederacy as the Seventh Tribe, or canton. This act was consummutated in the reign of George II., at a public council held at Albany on the 30th May, 1723, on their own desire. A delegation of 80 men, who had their families with them, were present. Of this curious transaction but little is known. For although done in faith, it was not perceived that a tribe so far separated from the main body, although now reconciled, and officially incorporated, could not effectually coalesce and act as one. And accordingly, it does not appear, by the subsequent history of the confederacy, that they ever came to recognize, permanently, the Necariages as a Seventh Nation. The foundation for this act of admission had been laid at a prior period by the daring and adroit policy of Adario, who had so skilfully contrived to shift the atrocity of his own act, in the capture of the Iroquois delegates on the St. Lawrence, on the Governor-General of Canada.

It has been mentioned, in a preceding page of this report, that the Iroquois recommended their political league as a model to the colonies, long before the American revolution was thought of. And it is remarkable that its typical character, in relation to our present union, should have been also sustained, in the feature of the admission, if not "annexation," of new tribes, who became equal participants of all the original rights and privileges of the confederacy.

[*h.*] St. Regis Colony, or Band.

This community is an off-shoot of the Iroquois stock, but not a member of the confederacy. It originated in the efforts commenced about the middle of the 17th century, by the Roman Catholic church of France, to draw the Iroquois into communion with that church. It was, however, but a part of the public policy, which originated in the reign of Louis XV., to colonize the Iroquois country, and wrest it from the power of the British crown. When this effort failed,—replete as it was with wars, intrigues and embassies, battles and massacres, which make it the heroic age of our history, the persons who had become enlisted in the ritual observances of this church, were induced to withdraw from the body of the tribes, and settle on the banks of the St. Lawrence, in the area of the present county of St. Lawrence. It was, in effect, a missionary colony. Its members were mostly Mohawks, from Caughnawaga, with some Oneidas, and perhaps a few of the Onondagas, amongst whom there had been Catholic missions and forts established, at early dates.

The exertions made to organize this new canton were, politically considered, at direct variance with the colonial policy of New-York, and were therefore opposed by the persons entrusted by the crown with Indian affairs, and also by the councils of the confederacy.

Those persons who composed it assimilated in faith, and almost as a necessary consequence, they soon did so in politics.* They went off in small parties, secretly, and after they had become embodied and located, they were regarded, in effect, as foreign Indians, and were never recognized or admitted to a seat in the confederacy. The feeling caused by this separation, among the tribes themselves, amounted to bitterness, and it is a feeling which, I had occasion to observe on one occasion, is not forgotton by the existing cantons even at this day.

The St. Regis colony increased rapidly, but had some extra stimulants to promote its growth, its success being equally dear to the political and ecclesiastical policy of France. It became a thorn to the frontier towns and settlements of New-England, during the whole of the old French war, so called, and of the American revolution. Some of the forays of this band into the Connecticut valley were productive of thrilling and heart rending events, as those must have realized who have had their youthful sympathies excited by narrations of the touching captivities of the Hows and the Williams, of that valley.

When the 54° parallel came to be drawn, under the provision of the treaty of Ghent, it cut the St. Regis settlement unequally in two, leaving the church and the larger portion of the Indian population within the bounds of Canada. Those who reside within the limits of New-York, numbered, the past summer, three hundred and sixty souls.

---

* Some exceptions to this existed. The noted chief called Col. Louis, who rendered the American cause such essential service, during the siege of Fort Stanwix, in 1777, was of the St. Regis tribe, agreeably to information given to me, at Oneida Castle, the present year, by Abraham Dennie.

III. EPOCH AND PRINCIPLES OF THE IROQUOIS LEAGUE.

[*a.*]

Something on this head appears desirable, if it be only to mitigate, in some degree, our historical ignorance, and want of accurate or precise information, touching it. The question of the principles of their social and political association, is one of equal interest and obscurity, and would justify a more extended inquiry than is here given.

[*b.*] Era of the Confederation.

Chronology finds its most difficult tasks in establishing dates among our aboriginal tribes. Pyrlaus, a missionary at the ancient site of Dionderoga or Fort Hunter, writing between 1742 and 1748, states, as the result of the best conjectures he could form, from information derived from the Mohawks, that the alliance took place "one age, or the length of a man's life, before the white people came into the country."* He gives the following as the names of the sachems of the Five Nations, who met and formed the alliance :

TOGANAWITA, *for the Mohawks.*
OTATSCHECHTA, *for the Oneidas.*
TATOTARHO, *for the Onondagas.*
TOGAHAYON, *for the Cayugas.*
GANIATARIO, } *for the Senecas.*
SATAGARUYES, }

The name of THANNAWAGE is given as the first proposer of such an alliance. He was an aged Mohawk sachem. It was decided that

* Trans. Hist. and Lit. Com. Am. Philo. Soc. vol. 1, p. 36.

these names should forever be kept in remembrance by naming a person in each nation, through succeeding generations, after them.

Taking 1609, the era of the Dutch discovery, and estimating "a man's life" by the patriarchal and scriptural rule, we should not at the utmost have a more remote date than 1539,* as the origin of the confederacy. This would place the event 18 years after the taking of Mexico by Cortes, and 47 years after the first voyage of Columbus. Cartier, who ascended the St. Lawrence to Hochelaga, the present site of Montreal, in 1535, demonstrates clearly, by his vocabulary of words, that a people who spoke a branch of the Iroquois language, was then at the place. This people is usually supposed to have been the Wyandots, or Hurons. But he makes no remark on a confederacy. He only denotes the attachment of the people to an old and paralytic sachem, or head chief, who wore a frontlet of dyed porcupine's skin.†

Curious to obtain some clue to this era, or test of the preceding data, I made it a topic of inquiry. The Onondagas, the Tuscaroras, and the several bands, unite in a general tradition of the event of a confederacy, at the head of which they place Atotarho, (the same doubtless whose name is spelt Tatotarho above,) but amongst neither of these tribes is the era fixed. The dates employed by Cusick, the Tuscarora legendary, giving an extravagant antiquity to the confederation, are more entitled to the sympathy of the poet than the attention of the historian, although other traditions stated by him debarring the dates, may be regarded as the actual traditions of his tribe. Were the dates moderate, which he generally employs to confer antiquity on his nation, they might inspire respect. But like the Chinese astronomers, he loses no little as a native archæologist, by aspiring after too much.

Atotarho, who by these traditions was an Onondaga, is the great embodiment of Iroquois courage, wisdom and heroism, and in their narrations he is invested with allegoric traits, which exalt him to a kind of superhuman character. Unequalled in war and arts, his fame had spread abroad and exalted the Onondaga nation to the high-

---

* For other data on this topic, see the subsequent paper, entitled "Onondagas," in which an earlier date is assigned. See also the article "Oral Traditions."

† Oneota, p.

est pitch. He was placed at the head of the confederacy, and his name, like that of King Arthur of the Round Table, or those of the Paladins of Charlemagne, was used after his death as an exemplar of glory and honor ; while like that of Cæsar, it became perpetuated as the official title of the presiding chief. What is said by Pyrlaus re-respecting the mode of the transmission of the names of the first delegates to the council forming the confederacy, appears to be probable. It is true, so far as is known, but it seems that not only the name of the ruling chief, but the title of each minor officer in the council, as he who presents the message ; he who stands by the chief or Atotarho, &c. is preserved to this day by its being the name of an individual who exercises a similar office.

The best light I could personally obtain from tradition of the date of the event, viz. the era of the confederacy, came through a tradition handed down from Ezekiel Webster, an American, who at an early day settled among the Onondagas, learned their language, married the daughter of a chief, and became himself a man of great influence among them. Mr. Tyler of Seneca-Falls, son of one of the first settlers in the present county of Onondaga, informed me in a casual interview at Aurora, on the 13th of August, that his father had received this account from Webster's own lips, namely, that the confederation, as related by the Onondagas, took place about the length of one man's life before the white men appeared. A remarkable confirmation of the statement of Pyrlaus.* It must be admitted, however, that we cannot, without rejecting many positive traditions of the Iroquois themselves [D.] refuse to concede a much earlier period to the first attempts of these interesting tribes to form a general political association. For eighty years before the American Revolution they, in friendly recommendation, held up their confederacy as a political model to the English colonies. (See Colden.) Their own first attempts to form themselves into one nation may have borne the same relation to them and their subsequent condition as our early confederation of States bears to the present Union ; and this, instead of lasting a few years, as did ours, may have continued even for centuries, among so rude a people, before it could ripen into the bonds of empire.

---

* A Seneca tradition which is hereafter noticed, places the event of the confederation four years before the appearance of Hudson in his ship, in the bay of New-York.

Two elementary powers existed at an early day in the Iroquois cantons, namely, the civil and war chieftainships. There is abundant evidence, both in their own traditions, and in existing antiquarian remains, to show that they were at variance, in the early periods of their history, and fought against each other, and built fortifications to defend themselves. Partial leagues would naturally fail. League after league probably took place. When they came to see the folly of such a course, and proposed to confederate on enlarged principles, and direct their arms exclusively against others, the question doubtless arose, how they should be represented in the general council. It is clear, from the preceding remarks on the era of the confederation, whatever age we assign to the era itself, that the Rakowanas,* or leading chiefs of each of the five cantons, did not assemble. Power was assigned to, and concentrated on one individual, who stood as the federal representative of his canton in its sovereign capacity. It was only to the Senecas that two representatives, of this senatorial dignity, were assigned; a conclusive evidence that they were, at this era, estimated at double the numerical strength of the highest of the other four cantons. By these six men, who appear rather in the capacity of ambassadors, forming the principles of a treaty, or league, the modern confederacy, as known to us, was organized. Tradition says that this treaty of alliance was held at Onondaga, where the central council fire of the confederacy, organized under it, was also originally fixed, and has permanently remained. Of the nature and powers of this general council, or congress of sachems, acting for the whole cantons, some views are expressed in the following paper.

[*c.*] Principles of the Iroquois Government.

No one has attended to the operations of the Iroquois government and polity, as they are developed in their councils and meetings for general consultation and action, without perceiving a degree of intricacy in its workings, which it is difficult to grasp. Or rather, the obscurity may be said to grow out of the little time and the imperfect opportunities which casual observes have to devote to the object.

* Mohawk.

For, maturely considered, there is no inherent difficulty in the way. It seems clear that they came together as independent tribes, who, at an early age, had all proceeded from the same parental stock, but who, after an indefinite period of fightings and wars, became convinced of the short-sightedness of such a course, and fell on the plan of a confederation which should produce general action, and yet leave the several members free, both in their internal polity, and in the exercise of most of their co-tribal powers. It was clearly a confederation for common purposes of defence and offence, and not a perfect union. Each tribe, or more properly speaking, canton, was still governed by its own chiefs, civil and military. They came together in general councils, by sachems, exercising the power of delegates.

These delegates or sages came in their hereditary or elective character, as the case might be, or as the customs and laws of the tribe in its popular character had decided. But their voices were, in all cases, either prompted by prior expressions of the warriors and wise men, or were to be ratified by these known powers. However invested with authority they but spoke the popular will. The relative power of the cantons is denoted, and appears as a question that was already settled, at the first formal general council for the purpose of confederating. For we there see precisely the same tribal representation, which has obtained ever after and still prevails; that is to say, the Mohawks, the Oneidas, the Onondagas, and the Cayugas, had each one chief, and the Senecas two, making six supreme dignitaries or state counsellors. That their powers were merely advisory and interlocutory, and that they aimed to come to harmonious results, by the mere interchange of opinion, without any formal or solemn vote, is evident, from all that we know, or can gather from their still existing institutions. There appeared to have been no penalties—no forfeiture of rights—no binding or coercive power, to be visited on tribes or chiefs beyond that of OPINION. Popular disapproval was the Iroquois penalty here and elsewhere. It is equally clear, however, that a single negative voice or opinion, was of the highest efficacy. A unanimous decision, not a decision, on the majority principle, was required. The latter was a refinement, and an advance in polity, which they had not certainly reached, although they seem inclined now to follow it; and herein we may perceive the great power and efficacy of their old decisions. These decisions were, in their effects, clothed with all the power of the most full popular will. For what each of the senatorial chiefs or delegates, and all the cantons, pronounced proper, there was no one, in a patriarchal community, to lisp a word against.

So little power was abstracted from each tribe, and conceded to the federative council as a fixed government, that it seems not without scrutiny, that we can perceive there is *any*. This is, however, certain. One of the six primary sachems, was selected to preside over the general councils. His power was, however, exclusively of a civil character, and extended but little beyond that of a moderator, but he was a moderator for life, or during the time he retained the right and full use of his faculties, or until just cause of dissatisfaction should bring the question of a successor before the council. This head officer, had also authority to light the council fire,—that is to say, he could send messengers, and was if so desired, bound to send messengers to assemble the general council. The act, and the symbol of the act were both in his hands. He summoned the chiefs, and actually lit the sacred fire, at whose blaze their pipes were lighted. Thus limited, and having no other administrative power, but to appoint his own Har-yar-do-ah, aid or pipe-bearer, and messengers, he enjoyed his executive dignity ; but had little more power when the sessions were closed, than belonged to every leading chief of the component tribes. He was himself bound to respect the messages of the tribal chiefs, and receive the runners who were sent to him from the frontiers with news, and he thus performed merely and exactly the will of each tribe, thus expressed. He was never in advance of the popular will. The whole hereditary machinery was made subservient to this. And he was limited to the performance of these slender, and popular duties. He might, it is true, if a man of eloquence. talents or bravery, be also the ruling civil chief of his tribe, and furthermore, its war captain in the field. And such is known to have actually been the character and standing of Atotarho, the first presiding chief in their federative councils. He was a man of energy and high renown. And such was the estimation in which he was held in his life time, and the popular veneration for his character after death, that as above denoted, his name became the distinctive title for the office. Thus much is preserved by tradition, and the office and title of the Atotarho as presiding sachem, is not yet extinct, although the tribes have no longer wars to prosecute, or foreign embassadors to reply to.

But how, it may be asked, is a government so purely popular, and so simple and essentially advisory in its character, to be reconciled with the laws of hereditary desent, fixed by the establishment of heraldic devices, and bringing its proportion of weak and incompetent minds into office, and with the actual power it exercised, and the fame it acquired ? To answer this question, and to shew how the aristocratic and democratic principles were made to harmonize, in the Iroquois government, it will be necessary to go back, and examine the law of desent among the tribes, together with the curious and intricate principles of the TOTEMIC BOND.

Nothing is more fully under the cognizance of observers of the manners and customs of this people, than the fact of the entire mass of a canton or tribe's being separated into distinct clans, each of which is distinguished by the name and device of some quadruped, bird, or other object in the animal kingdom. This device is called, among the Algonquins, (where the same separation into families or clans, exists,) TOTEM, and we shall employ the term here, as being already well known to writers. But while the Algonquins have made no other use of it, but to trace consanguinity, or at least, remote affinities of families, and while they have also separated into wild independencies and tribes, who have assumed new tribal names, and wandered and crossed each other's track and boundaries in a thousand ways, the Iroquois have turned it to account by assuming it as the very basis of their political and tribal bond. How far fixity of territorial possession and proximity of location may have favored or led to the establishment of this new bond, need not be inquired into here, but, while we express no opinion favorable to the remote antiquity of their residence in the north, it must be evident that this tie would have lost all its binding force if the Alleghanies, the Great Lakes, or any other very wide geographical areas, had been interposed between them, and thus interrupted frequent and full intercourse and united action. A government wholly verbal, must be conceded to have required this proximity and nearness of access. The Senecas may be selected as an example of the influence of the Totemic bond. This canton is still the most numerous of the existing Iroquois tribes. By the recent census, the results of which accompany these papers, they number over two thousand four hundred souls. This population is, theoretically, separated into eight clans or original families, who are distinguished respectively by the totems of the wolf, the bear, the turtle, the deer, the beaver, the falcon, the crane and the plover. Theory at this time, founded doubtless an actual consanguinity in their inceptive age, makes these clans brothers. It is contrary to their usages that near kindred should intermarry, and the ancient rule interdicts all intermarriage between persons of the same clan. They must marry into a clan whose totem is different trom their own. A wolf or turtle male cannot marry a wolf or turtle female. There is an interdict of consanguinity. By this custom the purity of blood is preserved, while the tie of relationship between the clans themselves is strengthened or enlarged.

But by far the most singular principle connected with totems, the sign manual of alliance, is the limitation of descent exclusively to the line of the female. Owing to this prohibition, a chieftain's son cannot succeed him in office, but in case of his death, the right of descent being in the chief's mother, he would be secceeded not by one of his male children, but by his brother ;* or failing in this, by the son of his sister, or by some direct, however remote, descendant of the maternal line. Thus he might be succeeded by his own grandson, by a daughter, but not by a son. It is in this way that the line of chieftainships is continually deflected or refreshed, and family dynasties broken up.

While the law of descent is fully recognized, the free will of the female to choose a husband, from any of the other seven clans, excluding only her own, is made to govern and determine the distribution of political power, and to fix the political character of the tribe. Another peculiarity may be here stated. The son of a chief's daughter is necessarily destined to inherit the honors of the chieftainship ; yet the validity of the claim must, on his reaching the proper age, be submitted to and recognized by a council of the whole canton. If approved, a day is appointed for the recognition, and he is formally installed into office. Incapacity is always, however, without

---

* Thus Hendrick, who fell at the battle of Lake George, in 1755, was succeeded, in the Mohawk canton, by his brother Abraham, and not by his son.

exception, recognized as a valid objection to the approval of the council.

Had this law of descent prevailed among the Jews, whose customs have been so often appealed to, in connection with our red race, neither David nor Solomon would ever have sat on the throne. It would be easy, did the purposes of this paper require it, to show by other references the futility of the proofs, derived from the supposed coincidence of customs, which have been brought forward with so much learning, and so little of the true spirit of research, to prove the descent of the American aborigines from that ancient and peculiar people. But if theorists have failed on this ground, what shall we say of that course of reasoning which lays much stress on the most slender evidences of nativity, in the instance of the great Mohawk sachem, to prove the superior chances of recurring talent in the line of hereditary descent, and the legitimacy of his actual claims to the chieftainship, on the score of paternal right?* Vide Appendix C., notes at Oneida Castle.

What was true of the totemic organization of the Senecas, was equally so of the Mohawks, and of each of the other cantons. Each canton consisted, like the Senecas, of the clans of the wolf, bear, turtle, beaver, deer, falcon, plover and crane. But each of these clans were increments of re-organizations of one of the eight original clans. They were brothers, and appealed to their respective totems as a proof of original consanguinity. They were entitled to the same rites of hospitality, in the lodges of their affiliated totems abroad, that they were entitled to at home. The affiliated mark on the lodge was a sufficient welcome of entrance and temporary abode. It results, therefore, that there were but eight original family clans, estimating at the maximum number existing in six cantonal departments, or tribes, and that the entire six tribes were bound together politically by these eight family ties. As a matter of course, each clan

* This remark is not made to depreciate the literary merits of the esteemed and lamented author of the Life of Brant, but as being simply due to the cause of truth. Few men have better earned the respect and remembrance of the public than William L. Stone, whose whole life was an example of what energy and talents can achieve. It was not, indeed, to be expected that the incessant duties of the diurnal press should permit historical scrutiny into a matter, very obscure in itself, and of which the details are only to be gleaned after laborious search at remote points.

was not equally numerous in each tribe. This would depend on accidental circumstances and natural laws; but it is an argument in favor of the antiquity of the people, or the confederacy, that each of the tribes had organized in each of the respective clans. For we cannot suppose that at first there was a systematic, far less, an equal division of the clans, or that their original separation into separate tribes, or cantons, was the result of a considerate formal public act. This would be to reverse the ordinary progress of tribes and nations who, in early ages, separate from circumstances and causes wholly casual, such as the ambition or feuds of chiefs, the desire of finding better places to live, easier means of subsistence, &c.

In the condition of a people, living in a governmeut so purely patriarchal, following game for a subsistence, and making wars to enlarge or defend their hunting grounds, the oldest and most respected man of his clan or totem, would necessarily be its sachem or political head. We must assume that to be a fixed and settled principle of their simple constitution and verbal laws, which appears, from all we know, to have been so. Letters, they had none, and their traditions on this head are to be gleaned from scattered and broken sources which do not always coincide.

If each clan had its leading sachem or chief, there were eight principal chiefs in each canton. Consequently, when the confederacy consisted of five cantons, there were forty Rakowanas,* or head chiefs. These were the recognized leaders and magistrates in the villages; but in effect, in a community thus constituted, each Rakowana or ruling chief of a clan, has a number of aids, Mishinawas† and minor officials, who were also regarded as semi-sachems, or chiefs. This number is always indefinite and fluctuating, but may be supposed to be, in relation to the ruling Rakowana, as at least five to one.

This would give to each canton forty inferior chiefs, and to the five cantons, two hundred, denoting a distribution of power and civil organization, which acting in union must have been very efficacious; and the more so, when we consider that all their political movements were entirely of a popular cast, and carried with them the voice of every man in the canton.

* Mohawk. † Algonquin.

This appears to have been the standing civil organization; but it was entirely independent of the military system. War chiefs appear ever to have derived their authority from courage and capacity in war, and to have risen up as they were required in each canton. The Tekarahogea, or war captain, founded his rights and powers in the Indian camp, on former triumphs and present capacity; but the office does not appear to have been a general one recognized by their constitution. All males were bound to render military service by custom and opinion, but by nothing else. Disgrace and cowardice were the penalties, but they were penalties more binding than oaths or bonds among civilized communities, and always kept their ranks full. All war parties were, of course, volunteers. It seems that all able-bodied males over fourteen were esteemed capable of taking the war path; the early development of martial power being considered of all traits the most honorable. No title was more honored than that of Roskeahragehte,* or Warrior.

There was no baggage to encumber the march of an Iroquois army. The decision of Alexander and the policy of Bonaparte were alike unnecessary here. Each Iroquois warrior supplied and carried his own arms and provisions. He joined the war dance, the analogous term for enlistment, for the particular expedition in hand. If it failed, or another force was required, other captains called for other volunteers, and sung their war songs to inflame the ardor of the young. Taunts and irony of the deepest character were, on these occasions, flung at the character of the enemy. The war chief lifted his tomahawk as if actually engaged in combat, and in imagination he stamped his enemy under foot, while he symbolically tore off his scalp, and uttered his sharp Sasakwon,† or war whoop.

If it be inquired why this people, with so comparatively small a population, carried their wars to such an extent, and acquired, probably in no great time, so wide a sway and power over the other tribes of the continent, the reply will appear, in a great measure, in this efficient war organization. It may be said that other tribes had the same principles. But these eastern and western tribes had feeble or divided counsels. Each tribe was a sovereignty by itself, and their powers were tasked by home wars, without attempts at remote

---

* Mohawk. † Algonquin.

conquest. There is nothing to denote that the number of war chiefs was ever settled or fixed. Time and chance determined this, as we observe it in the Algonquin and other American stocks. Fixity, in the number of the civil chiefs, was indeed rather a theory than an actuality, and the number must have been perpetually fluctuating, according to obvious circumstances.

But while the theory of the Iroquois government thus distributed its powers between two classes of chiefs, one of which ruled in the council, and the other in the field, there was a third power of controlling influence in both, which respected, it is true, this ancient theory, but which annulled, confirmed, originated, or set aside all other power. I allude to the popular will as exercised by the warriors. Whatever was proposed had to come under the voice of the armed men, who had the free right, at all times, to assemble in council, and put their approval or veto on every measure. Practically considered, a purer democracy, perhaps, never existed. The chiefs themselves had no power in advance of public sentiment, or else it was their policy, as we see it at this day, to express no such power, but rather to keep in abeyance of, or be the mere agents of the popular will. In all negociations such absolute power is disclaimed by them. Acting on principles of the highest diplomacy, they invariably defer general answers, until a reference can be had to the warriors or men. They risk nothing by taking grounds in doubtful positions in advance, and the consequence is that the results of most Indian councils are unanimous.

There was yet a reserved power in the Iroquois councils which deserves to be mentioned. I allude to the power of the matrons. This was an acknowledged power of a conservative character, which might, at all times, be brought into requisition, whenever policy required it. And it exists to-day as incontestibly as it did centuries ago. They were entrusted with the power to propose a cessation of arms. They were literally peace-makers. A proposition from the matrons to drop the war club could be made without compromitting the character of the tribe for bravery; and accordingly, we find, in the ancient organization, that there was a male functionary, an acknowledged speaker, who was called the representative or messenger of the matrons. These matrons sat in council, but it must needs have been seldom that a female possessed the kind of eloque[illegible] able to public assemblies; and beyond this there was a sentim[illegible] respect due to the female class, which led the tribes, at their gen[illegible] organization, to create this office.

Councils, so organized—so perpetually and truly swayed by popular will, gave the greatest scope for eloquence. Eloquence, in the aborigines, takes the place entirely of books and letters. It is the only means of acting on the multitude, and we find that it was, from the earliest times, strenuously and successfully cultivated by the Iroquois. By far the best and most abundant specimens of native eloquence we possess are from this stock. And their history is replete in proofs that they employed it, not only in their internal affairs and negociations, but in teaching to appreciate their rights and the principles of their government.

[*d.*] Ancient Worship.

SACRED FIRE.—THE SUN A SYMBOL OF DIVINE INTELLIGENCE.

It was a striking peculiarity of the ancient religious system of the Iroquois that, once a year, the priesthood supplied the people with sacred fire. For this purpose, a set time was announced for the ruling priest's visit. The entire village was apprized of this visit, and the master of each lodge was expected to be prepared for this annual rite. Preliminary to the visit, his lodge fire was carefully put out and ashes scattered about it, as a symbolic sign of desolation and want. Deprived of this element, they were also deprived of its symbolic influence, the sustaining aid and countenance of the supreme power, whose image they recognized in the sun.

It was to relieve this want, and excite hope and animation in breasts which had throbbed with dread, that the priest visited the lodge. Exhibiting the insignia of the sacerdotal office, he proceeded to invoke the Master of Life in their behalf, and ended his mission by striking fire from the flint, or from percussion, and lighting anew the domestic fire. The lodge was then swept and garnished anew, and a feast succeeded.

This sacred service annually performed, had the effect to fix and increase the reverence of the people for the priestly office. It acted as a renewal of their ecclesiastical fealty ; and the consequence was, that the institution of the priesthood among these cantons was deeply and firmly seated. Whether this rite had any connection with the period of the solstices, or with the commencement of the lunar year, is not known, but is highly probable. That men living in the open air, who are regardful of the celestial phenomena, should not have noted the equinoxes, is not probable. They must have necessarily known the equinoxes by the observation of capes and mountains, which cast their shadows from points and describe angles so very diverse at the periods of the sun's greatest recession, or return. Yet we know not that the time of such extreme withdrawal and return marked and completed the circle of the year. Their year was, in all the Algonquin tribes, a lunar year. It consisted of thirteen moons, each of which is distinctly named. Thirteen moons of 28 days each, counting from visible phase to phase, make a year of 364 days, which is the greatest astronomical accuracy reached by the North American tribes.

That the close of the lunar series should have been the period of putting out the fire, and the beginning of the next, the time of relumination, from new fire, is so consonant to analogy in the tropical tribes, as to be probable.

The rite itself offers a striking coincidence, with that solemn performance at the close of each year, by the Azteek priests, in the valley of Mexico, and may not unreasonably be supposed to denote a common origin for the belief. The northern tribes had, however, dropped from the ritual, if it ever was in it, that of their remote ancestors, the horrid rite so revolting in the Azteek annals, of *human sacrifice*. For although prisoners were burned at the stake, this was not an act of the priesthood. It was a purely popular effervescence of revenge for losses of friends in war, or some other acts done by the enemy. Such sacrifices appeased the popular cry—all classes, young and old, rejoiced in them. They were looked on alone as an evidence of their nation's power ; and by it the warriors also shewed their regard for the relations of the bereaved. The widow of the warrior dried her tears. The children rejoiced—they hardly knew why—it was the triumph of the nation. And they were thus educated to regard the public burning of prisoners as a proper and glorious deed. Women, indeed, rejoiced in it apparently more than men. It seemed a solace for the loss of their progeny. And all authors agree in attributing to the older females the most extravagant and repulsive acts of participation and rejoicing in these warlike rites.

[e.] Witchcraft.

The belief in witchcraft prevailed extensively among the North American tribes. It is known that even in modern times, it was one of the principal means used by the Shawnee prophet to rid himself of his opponents, and that the venerable Shawnee chief Tarhe and others were sacrificed to this diabolical spirit.

Among the Iroquois the belief was universal, and its effects upon their prosperity and population, if tradition is to be credited, were at times appalling. The theory of the popular belief, as it existed in the several cantons, was this. The witches and wizzards constituted a secret association, which met at night to consult on mischief, and each was bound to inviolable secrecy. They say this fraternity first arose among the Nanticokes. A witch or wizzard had power to turn into a fox or wolf, and run very swift, emitting flashes of light. They could also transform themselves into a turkey or big owl, and fly very fast. If detected, or hotly pursued, they could change into a stone or rotten log. They sought carefully to procure the poison of snakes or poisonous roots, to effect their purposes. They could blow hairs or worms into a person. [D.]

While in Onondaga, James Gould, one of the original settlers on the Military Tract, told me that he had been intimate with Webster, the naturalized Onondaga, who told him many things respecting the ancient laws and customs of this people. Amongst them there was a curious reminiscence on the subject of witchcraft. Webster had heard this from an aged Onondaga, whom he conversed with during a visit which he once made to Canada. This Onondaga said that he had formerly lived near the old church on the Kasonda creek, near Jamesville, where there was in old times a populous Indian village. One evening, he said, whilst he lived there, he stepped out of his lodge, and immediately sank in the earth, and found himself in a large room, surrounded by three hundred witches and wizzards. Next morning he went to the council and told the chiefs of this extraordinary occurrence. They asked him whether he could not identify the persons. He said he could. They then accompanied him on a visit to all the lodges, where he pointed out *this* and *that* one, who were marked for execution. Before this inquiry was ended, a very large number of persons of both sexes were killed. He said ——* hundred.

Another tradition says that about fifty persons were burned to death at the Onondaga castle for witches. [D.]

The delusion prevailed among all the cantons. The last persons executed for witchcraft among the Oneidas, suffered about forty years ago. They were two females. The executioner was the notorious Hon Yost of revolutionary memory. He entered the lodge, according to a prior decree of the Council, and struck them down with a tomahawk. One was found in the lodge; the other suffered near the lodge door. [B.]

[*f*.] Wife's Right to Property.

Marriage, among the Iroquois, appears to be a verbal contract between the parties, which does not affect the rights of property. Goods, personal effects, or valuables of any kind, personal or real, which were the wife's before, remain so after marriage. Should any of these be used by the husband, he is bound to restore the property or its worth, in the event of separation. It is not uncommon at present to find a husband indebted to a wife for moneys loaned of her,

* Having doubts, I omit to fill this blank.

derived from payments or property, which she owned, and still owns, in her own right; and it is a cause of union in some cases where, without this obligation, a separation would probably ensue.

Marriage is therefore a personal agreement, requiring neither civil nor ecclesiastical sanction, but not a union of the rights of property. Descent being counted by the female, may be either an original cause or effect of this unique law.

IV. ARCHÆOLOGY.

In considering the subject of American antiquities it may facilitate the object, to erect separate eras of occupancy, to which the facts may be referred. Such a division of the great and almost unknown period, which preceded the arrival of Europeans, will at least serve as convenient points to concentrate, arrange and compare the facts and evidences brought forward; and may enable the observer, the better to proceed in any future attempts to generalize.

There appear to have been three eras in the aboriginal occupancy of the continent, or more strictly speaking, three conditions of occupancy, which may be conveniently grouped as eras, although the precise limits of them, may be matters of some uncertainty. To make this uncertainty less than it now is, and to erect these eras on probable foundations, the proofs drawn from monuments, mounds, fortifications, ditches, earth-works, barrows, implements of art, and whatever other kind of evidence antiquity affords, may, it is thought, be gathered together in something like this shape, namely:

1. Vestiges and proofs of the original era of the aboriginal migration from other parts of the globe. These, so far as arts or evidences of a material character are denoted, must necessarily be exceedingly limited, if any, of undoubted authenticity, shall indeed now be found. The departments of physiology, and philology, which have heretofore constituted the principal topics of research, are still an attractive, and by no means a closed field.

2. Proofs and vestiges of their continental migrations, wars, affinities and general ethnological characteristics, prior to the discovery of the continent. Such are the grouping of languages; the similarity, or dissimilarity of arts, modes of defence, and means of subsistence.

Proofs and vestiges of occupancy, change, and progress, subsequent to the Columbian period.

With regard to the first era, it is almost wholly the subject of general and profound scientific and philosophical investigations, which require a union of great advantages for successful study. The second and third eras, fall within the compass of ordinary observation. Both kinds of proof may exist at the very same localities. They do not necessarily imply diverse or remote geographical positions. We know that some of the leading tribes, the Cherokees, (till within a few years,) and the Iroquois, for instance, have continued to live in the very same positions in which they were found by the first explorers.

As their chiefs and warriors died, they carried to their places of burial, (such was the result of ancient and general custom,) those kinds of ornaments, arms and utensils, which were the distinguishing tokens of art, of the several eras in which they lived.

The coming of European races among them introduced fabrics of metal, earths, enamels, glass, and other materials more or less durable, and capable of resisting decomposition. These would necessarily take the place of the aboriginal articles of stone and shell, before employed.

If, then, places of sepulture were permanent, the inquirer at the present day would find the various fabrics of the second and the third era, in the same cemeteries and burial grounds, and sometimes in the same barrows and mounds.

Modes of defence would also alter by the introduction of the second period. The simple ring-fort, with palisades, crowning a hill, which would serve as a place of excellent defence, against bows and arrows and clubs, would prove utterly useless, as the Tuscaroras found at Naharuke in 1712, after the introduction of artillery. A trench to obtain water, from a spring or creek, leading from one of the works of the older period, might have been so covered as to afford full protection from the simple aboriginal missiles. Besides this, the combination of several tribes, as the Iroquois, the Algonquins, the Eries, Alleghans and others, might render these simple forts, defended with ditches, mounds, and otherwise, no longer necessary, in the interior of their territory, after the time of such general combinations or confederacies. And in this case, these works would be deserted and become ruins, long before the period of the discovery.

It is affirmed by their traditions, that, in the older periods of their occupancy of this continent, they were even obliged, or their fears suggested the measure, to build coverts and forts to protect themselves and families from the inroads of monsters, giants and gigantic animals. We are not at liberty to disregard this, be the recitals symbolic or true. Such places would afford convenient shelters for their women and children, at the particular times of such inroads, while the warriors collected to make battle against the common enemy. Whether this enemy carried a huge paw or a spear we need not determine. The one was quite as much an object of aboriginal terror as the other. Whatever be the character of the antiquarian object to be examined, it will be well to bear in mind these ancient and changing conditions of the aboriginal population. If no absolute historical light be elicited thereby, we shall be the more likely to get rid of some of the confessed darkness enveloping the subject, and thus narrow the unsatisfying and historically hateful boundaries of mystery.

In applying these principles to the antiquarian remains of the area of western New-York, which has been a theme of frequent allusion and description, at least since the life time of De Witt Clinton, it is merely proposed to offer a few contributions to the store of our antiquities, in the hope that other and abler hands may proceed in the investigation.

[*a.*] Vestiges of an Ancient Fort or Place of Defence in Lenox, Madison county.

Some years have elapsed since I visited this work,* and the plough and spade may have further obliterated the lines, then more or less

---

* 1812.

fully apparent. But in the meantime no notice of it has been published. The following outlines denote its extent and character.

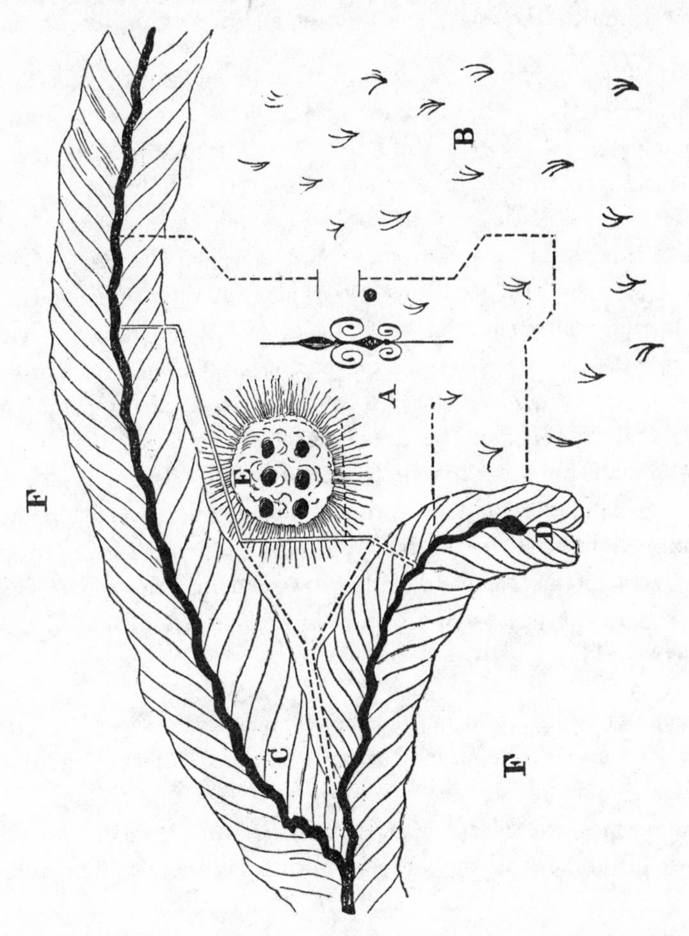

A. indicates the lines of a picketted work. B. is an extensive plain, covered with wild grass and some shrubbery, which had once been in cultivation. The northern edge of this plain is traversed by a stream, which has worn its bed down in the unconsolidated strata, so as to create quite a deep gorge, C. This stream is joined from the west, by a small run, having its origin in a spring, D. Its channel, at the point of junction, is as deep below the level of the plain as the other.* The point of junction itself forms a natural horn-

* Some few miles below this stream is the site of an iron cupola or blast furnace, where the red or lenticular oxyd is reduced.

work, which covered access to the water. The angle of the plain, thus marked, constituted the point defended. The excavations E. may have once been square. They are now indentations, disclosing carbonaceous matter, as if from the decay of wood. No wood, or coal, however, existed. Their use in this position is not apparent, connected with the designated lines of palisades, unless it be supposed that they were of an older period than the latter, and designate pits, such as the aborigines used in defence. This idea is favored by the ground being a little raised at this point, and so formed that it would have admitted the ancient circular Indian palisade. If such were the case, however, it seems evident that the spot had been selected by the French, at an early period, when, as is known, they attempted to obtain a footing in the country of the Oneidas. The distance is less than ten miles northwest of Oneida Castle. It probably covered a mission. The site, which my informant, living near, called the OLD FRENCH FIELD, may be supposed to have been cultivated by servants or traders connected with it.

The oak and maple trees, which once covered it, as denoted by the existing forest, F. F., are such, in size and number, as to have required expert axmen to fell.

With the exception of two points, in the Oneida Creek valley, where there are still vestiges of French occupation, supported by tradition, this work is the most easterly of those known, which remain to testify the adventurous spirit, zeal and perseverance which marked the attempt of the French crown to plant the flag and the cross in western New-York.

The bold nature of this scheme to colonize the country, and bring the Iroquois to acknowledge their dependence upon France, and the importance of the experiment and the issue, cannot be well conceived without reference to the history of those times. Pending the famous expedition of the Chevalier de Vandreiul, 1696, into the Iroquois country, it is known that the Jesuit Milet was stationed among the the Oneidas, over whom he had so much influence, that soon after the termination of this vain display of power, thirty Oneidas deserted to the French, and desired that Milet might be appointed their pastor.*

* Colden's Five Nations, p. 193.

[*b.*] Ancient site of the Onondagas in the valley of the Kasonda, or Butternut creek of Jamesville.

The fact that the ruins of asquare fort, with extensive sub-lines in the nature of an enclosure, had existed on the elevated grounds on the right banks of this stream, a mile or two from Jamesville, at the period of its first settlement, led me to visit it. There was the more interest imparted to this well attested tradition of the present inhabitants, by the accounts of the Onondagas, that this valley, in its extent above and below Jamesville, was one of their earliest points of settlement, prior to the era of their establishing their council fire at Onondaga Hollow. The subjoined sketch, although not plotted from actual measurement, will convey an idea of the relative position and former importance of the principal features, geographical and artificial, denoted.

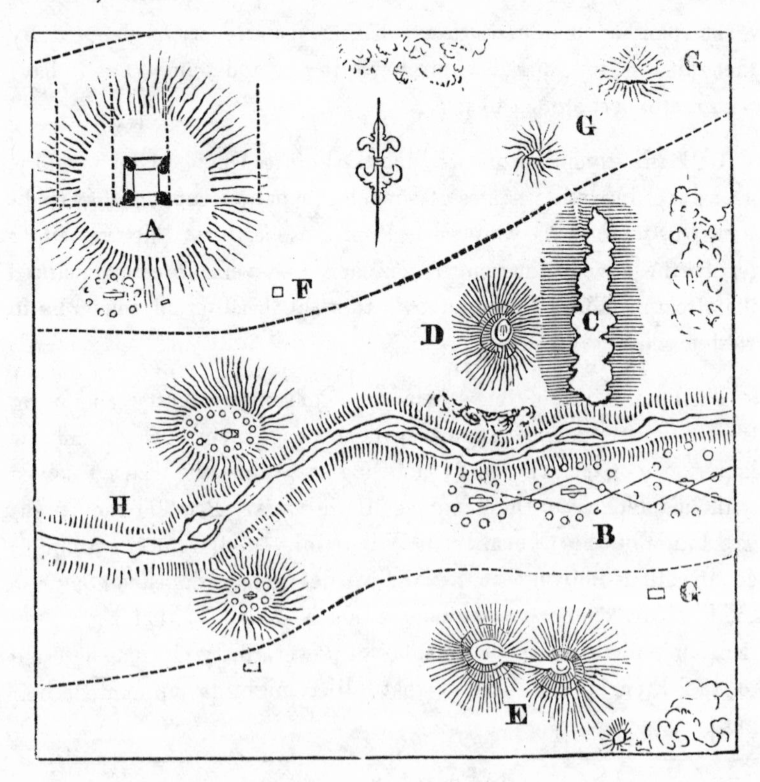

A. indicates the site of the fort, which, at the time of my visit, was covered with a luxuriant field of wheat, without a feature to denote that it had ever been held under any other jurisdiction but that of the plough. The farm which embraces it, is owned and occupied by Isaac Keeler, who remarks that, at the time he came to settle here, the site of the old fort was an extensive opening in the forest, bearing grass, with some clumps of wild plumb trees, and a few forest trees. On this opening, the first regiment of militia that ever paraded in Onondaga county, met. It was commanded by Major De Witt, after whom the township is now named.

About the year 1810, he felled an oak, near the site of the fort, measuring two feet six inches in diameter. In recutting it for fire wood, after it had been drawn to his door, a leaden bullet was found, covered by one hundred and forty-three cortical layers. From its position, embedded as it was in the compact wood, it was still some distance to the heart of the tree. He thinks this tree may have been a sapling when the bullet was fired. Whether this conjecture be true or not, one hundred and forty-three years appear to have elapsed since the bullet assumed its position. This would give A. D. 1667 as the era.

In 1666, the Governor of Canada concluded a treaty with the Onondaga Iroquois, as is seen from the "Paris Documents" obtained by Mr. Broadhead. Colden's history of the Five Nations, which has been the principal source of information heretofore, after a brief summary of traditionary matter,* in the first chapter, opens with the transactions in 1665. This matter is more fully and satisfactorily stated by Charlevoix in his history of New France, from whom it is presumable, Colden drew his information of the former power and pre-eminence of the Adirondacks.

During this year De Traci came out as viceroy of New-France, and the same year Monsieur Coursel, who is notorious for his perfidy in executing the Iroquois sachem, Agariata, arrived with the commission of Governor-General of Canada. But there is little to be found bearing directly on the subject before us.

* The States General of Holland surrendered New-York to the English crown in 1664.

It would appear from the journal of the Jesuit, Father Le Moyne, as given in the missionary "Relacions," that the country of the Onondagas was not discovered and explored until the year 1653. Facts disclosed by him in the same letter denote, however, prior negociations with the French authorities, and we are probably to understand only that as yet, no missionaries from his or any other order, had visited, or been established amongst this tribe. In this view, and from the incidental light which he throws on some other topics, such as the new breaking out of the war with the Eries, the discovery of the salt springs, and the existence of the buffalo in the country, this letter is important to the early Iroquois history, and a translation of it is hereto appended. It is certain that no mission or fort had then been introduced. A footing may, however, have been gained by the French within the next fourteen years, that is, at the time of the apparent date of the existence of the old fort on the right banks of the Kasonda.*

Where history fails, we may appeal to tradition and to the proofs drawn from antiquarian remains. Isaac Keeler, who is above mentioned, exhibited to me one-half of the brass circle of a dial plate, three inches (less two-tenths) in diameter, which had been ploughed up by him on the site of the fort, or from that general area. This circle had engraved, in good Roman characters, the numbers II, III, IV, V, VI, VII, VIII. He likewise exhibited the box of a small brass pocket compass, with a screw lid one inch and two-tenths in diameter. From this instrument the needle had been removed and its place supplied by vermillion, the highly prized war pigment of the Indians. When plowed up and found at the bottom of a furrow, it wrs encrusted with oxide, but restored by washing and friction to its original color and even surface. On being opened, it was found to contain the pigment, of which I examined a portion. It appeared to me to have been, not the Chinese vermillion of the trade, but the duller red article, which is, I believe, a peroxide of lead prepared by the Dutch.

---

* Fire-arms began to be first introduced among the Iroquois in 1609, the very year that Hudson explored the river now bearing his name. In this year, Champlain, heading the Algonquins, with some regular troops, in lake Corlear, (since called Champlain,) defeated the Mohawks by the use of fire-arms.

Among the articles which he had preserved were the following :

1. A crucifix of brass of two inches in length, ornamented by a human figure, and having a metallic loop for suspending it.

2. An octagonal medal, four-tenths of an inch, of the same material, bearing a figure with the name "St. Agatha," and the Latin word "ora"—a part of the Gregorian chant.

3. A similar medal, five-tenths of an inch in length, with a figure, inscribed "St. Lucia," and the same fragment of a chant.

4. A rude medal of lead, an inch and four-tenths long, ovate, with the figure of the Savior, as is supposed, being that of a person suspended by the outstretched hands, however, and the figure of a serpent, as if this form of temptation had been presented during his advent. On the reverse, is a sitting figure, which bears most resemblance to a common and characteristic position of one of the native priests or prophets. Should this conjecture be correct, this figure may have been intended, adopting the Indian method, to teach the office of the Savior by a symbol. He is thus shown, however, to be merely the priest and prophet of men—an idea which does not coincide with Catholic theology, and which, if not enlarged and corrected by verbal teaching, would convey no conception of his divine character and atonement, and thus leave the Onondaga neophyte as essentially in the dark as before. To figure the Savior as the great Jesukeed of men, as is done in this medal, is indeed the most extraordinary and audacious act of which the history of missions among rude nations affords any parallel. The novelty of this feature in this apparently home-wrought model, gives it a claim to be hereafter figured.

5. An iron horse-shoe, four and a half inches long nearly, and five inches, lacking two-tenths, broad, with three elongated nail holes in each side, and a clumsy steel cork, partially worn. The peculiar fabric of this shoe, its clumsiness and spread, and the little mechanical skill which it evinces in the hammering and general make, denote it to be very clearly the workmanship of a Canadian blacksmith, such as a rude Canadian blacksmith is still to be witnessed, in the lake country, and to have been, at the same time, intended for the unfarriered hoofs of the Canadian horse.

6. A pair of iron strap hinges, common and coarse. These my informant had turned to account, by employing them to hang the lit-

tle gate which led, through a small flower plat, to his dwelling house. See figure F.

These articles have been selected for notice from many of more common occurrence, such as beads of coarse paste, enamel and glass, of various sizes and colors, which are evidently of European make. My informant further stated that a blacksmith's anvil, vice, horn, and almost every other article of a smith's shop, had been from time to time found on the site or in the vicinity, but there was nothing of this kind in his possession. On the south declivity of the hill, near the present road leading east to Pompey hill, there is a spring still sheltered with shrubbery, which he supposes furnished the fort with water.

This fort constitutes but a part of the very marked evidences of former occupancy by man in a civilized state, and in a forgotten age, which occur in this portion of Onondaga, chiefly in the present towns of Pompey, Lafayette, Dewitt, Camillus and Manlius. For such of these evidences as did not pass under my personal notice, reference is made to letter C in the documentary appendix. Other observed localities and facts derived from other witnesses, illustrating the character of this fort, and of the ancient Indian settlements in the Kasonda valley, are marked H in the annexed sketch.

In this plat B denotes the site of an ancient Onondaga town or village, immediately on the banks of the stream, where water could be readily obtained for all purposes. C is the locality of the cemetery used at the period, on the ascending grounds on the north banks of the stream. It constitutes a well marked transverse ridge. Immediately west of it rises a natural mound, marked D, of large size, nearly conical in its shape, and terminating in a flat surface or plain, of an ovate border, some twelve by seventeen paces. James Gould, the propietor of the land, who, from his residence, guided me to the spot, remarks that this conical hill, was formerly covered with a hard wood forest, similar in its species to those of the surrounding country, with the exception of a spot, some four or five paces diameter on its apex. This spot was, however, completely veiled from sight by the overtopping trees until the arcanum was entered. From the peculiar character of this eminence, and its relative position to the village and burial ground, it may be supposed to have been the site of the seer's lodge, from which he uttered his sacred responses.

Speaking of the old fort of Kasonda, this informant remarked, that when he came into the country, its outlines could still be traced, that it was a square fort, with bastions, and had streets within it. It had been set round with cedar pickets, which had been burned to the ground. Stumps of these ancient palisades were struck by the plough. It is on this testimony, which at the same time, denotes a violent destruction of the work, that the geometrical figure of it, represented in A, is drawn. He had, I think, been in the revolutionary army, and drawn his bounty lands, as many of the original settlers on the military tract had done. He knew therefore, the import of the military terms he employed.

In a collection of aboriginal antiquarian articles at his house, he permitted me to make drawings of any taken from the fort grounds, or disinterred from ancient Indian graves, which appeared to me to merit it. Of these, but a few are pertinent to the present inquiry. These are as follows :

Number 1, represents an antique collar or medal, [Nabikoágun,] wrought out of sea shell. It is crossed with two parallel, and two horizontal lines, ornamented with dots, and dividing the surface into four equal parts. An orifice exists for introducing a string to suspend it about the neck. This species of article, is found in Indian graves of the period preceding the discovery of the continent, or not extending more than one or two generations into the new period. It was probably an elegant ornament when bright and new, and exhibiting the natural color and nacer of the shell. Inhumation has so far served to decompose the surface, as to coat it with a limy or chalky exterior, which effervesces in mineral acids. By scraping deep into it, the shelly structure is detected. This kind of ornament, varying much in size, was probably soon replaced by the metallic gorget and medal introduced by the trade, and has long been unknown both to Indians and traders. I found it first in Indian cemeteries of the west, without, however, for some time suspecting its real nature, supposing it some variety of altered pottery, or enamel paste ; but have since traced it over the entire area of the ancient occupation of western New-York, and, so far as examined, of Canada.

No. 2. A stone ring, one inch and two-tenths in diamater, made of a dark species of somewhat hard steatite or slaty rock. Its character istic trait is found in its adaptation to the middle finger, (of a male) and its having eleven distinct radiating lines.

No. 3. A globular bead or amulet, [Minace,] of sea shell one inch and a half in diameter, solid and massy, having an orifice for suspending it. It is slightly ovate. Its structure from shell, is distinctly marked. Like the flat medal-shaped Nabikoágun (No. 1.) of the same material, it has a limy coating from the effects of partial decomposition. In the remaining features of the sketch, referred to, letters G. G., denote ancient remains of a European character in the contiguous part of the town of Pompey, which are more particularly described in the documentary appendix.

E. represents the Twin Mounds, two natural formations of fine gravel and other diluvial strata, situated on the south side of the creek, on the farm of Jeremiah Gould. These mounds are conspicuous features in the landscape, from their regularity, and position on elevated grounds, as well as from their connection with the ancient Indian history of the valley. These pyramidal heaps of earth are connected, by a neck of earth, in the manner represented. They exhibit the appearance of having been cleared of the forest, almost entirely, at an ancient date. The surface exhibits numerous pits or holes, which excite the idea of their having served as a noted locality for the Indian Assenjigun, or pit for hiding or putting *en cache*, corn or other articles, to preserve it from enemies, or as a place of deposit during temporary absences from the village. There can, I think, be little question that this was the true use and relation these geological eminences bore to the ancient town on the Kasonda, marked B. Such, too, is the general impression derived from local tradition. Some years ago, a skeleton was exhumed from one of these *caches*.

[c.] Antiquities of Pompey and adjacent parts of Onondaga county.

No part of western New-York has furnished a larger number of antiquarian remains, or been more often referred to, than the geographical area which constituted the original town of Pompey. There is, consequently, the less need of devoting elaborate attention to the details of this particular locality. It was first visited and described by De Witt Clinton, in 1810–11,* and the plough has since rendered it a task less easy than it then was, to examine the lines of its ancient works and its archæological remains. It is quite evident, from the objects of art disclosed at and about these antique sites of security and defence, that civilized man dwelt here in remote times, and there must be assigned to this part of the State a period of European occupancy prior to the commonly received historical era of discovery and settlement, or, at least, if falling within it, as there is now reason to believe, yet almost wholly unknown, or forgotten in its annals. Sismondi has well remarked, that only the most important events come down to posterity, and that fame, for a long flight, prepares to forget every thing which she possibly can. That no accounts should remain of obscure events, in a remote part of the country, at an early date, is not surprising. As it is, we must infer both the dates and the people, from such antiquarian remains of works of art and historical comparisons as can be obtained.

There appear to have been two or three nations, who supplied very early visitors or residents to ancient Onondaga, namely, the Dutch, French and Spanish, the latter as merely temporary visitors or explorers. Both the Dutch and the French carried on an early trade here with the Iroquois. It is most probable, that there are no remains of European art, or have ever been any disclosed, in this part of the country, one only excepted,† which are not due to the early attempts of the Dutch and French, to establish the fur trade among these populous and powerful tribes. To some extent, missionary

---

* Trans. of Philo. and Lit. Society of New-York.

† Antique stone with an inscription, Albany Academy.

operations were connected with the efforts of both nations. But whatever was the stress laid on this subject, by Protestants or Catholics, neither object could be secured without the exhibition of firearms and certain military defences, such as stockades and picketted works, with gates, afforded. No trader could, in the 16th and 17th centuries, securely trust his stock of goods, domestic animals,, (if he had any,) or his own life, in the midst of fierce and powerful tribes, who acknowledged no superior, and who were, besides, subject to the temporary excitement created by the limited use of alcohol. For we can assign absolutely no date to the early European intercourse with these tribes, in which there was no article of this kind, more or less, employed. Probably we should not have been left, as we are, to mere conjectures, on this subject, at least between the important dates of 1609 and 1664, had not the directors of the State paper office in Holland decided, in 1820, to sell the books and records of the Dutch West India company, as waste paper.*

In examining the archæology of this part of New-York, we are, therefore, to look for decisive proofs of the early existence of this trade in the hands of the two powers named. The Dutch were an eminently commercial people, at the epoch in question, and pursued the fur trade to remote parts of the interior, at an early date. They had scarcely any other object at the time but to make this trade profitable. Settlements and cultivation was a business in the hands of patroons, and was chiefly confined to the rich vallies and intervales of the southern parts of the State. They were, at the same time, too sagacious to let any thing interrupt their good understanding with the natives ; and on this account, probably, had less need of military defences of a formidable kind than the French, who were a foreign power. It was, besides, the policy of New-France,—a policy most perseveringly pursued,—to wrest this trade, and the power of the Indians, from the hands of the Dutch and their successors, the English. They sought not only to obtain the trade, but they intrigued for the territory. They also made the most strenuous endeavors to enlist the minds of the Indians, by the ritual observances of the Romish church, and to propagate among the Iroquois its peculiar doctrines. They united in this early effort the sword, the cross, and the purse.

* Vide Mr. Brodhead's report.

Were all the libraries of Europe and America burned and totally destroyed, there would remain incontestible evidences of each of the above named efforts, in the metallic implements, guns, sword-blades, hatchets, locks, bells, horse-shoes, hammers, paste and glass beads, medals, crucifixes and other remains, which are so frequently turned up by the plough in the fertile wheat and cornfields of Onondaga.

Looking beyond this era, but still found in the same geographical area, are the antiquities peculiar to the Ante-Columbian period, and the age of intestine Indian wars. These are found in various parts of the State, in the ancient ring forts, angular trenches, moats, barrows, or lesser mounds, which constituted the ancient simple Indian system of castramentation.

This era is not less strongly marked by the stone hatchets, pestles, fleshing instruments, arrow-heads and javelins of chert and hornstone; amulets of stone, bone and sea-shells, wrought and unwrought; needles of bone, coarse pottery, pipes, and various other evidences of antique Indian art. The practice of interring their favorite utensils, ornaments and amulets with the dead, renders their ancient grave-yards, barrows and mounds the principal repositories of these arts. They are, in effect, so many museums of antiquity.

The field for this species of observation is so large and attractive to the antiquarian, that far more time than was at my command, would be required to cultivate it. Early in the present year, Mr. Joshua V. V. Clark visited some of the principal scenes mentioned. Subsequently, at my suggestion and solicitation, he re-visited the same localities and extended his inquiries to others of an interesting character, in the county of Onondaga, descriptions of which are presented under letter [C] of the documentary appendix.

[*d.*] Ancient fortification of Osco,* at Auburn, Cayuga County.

The eminence called "Fort Hill," in the southwestern skirts of the village of Auburn, has attracted notice from the earliest times. Its height is such as to render it a very commanding spot, and crowned, as it was, with a pentagessimal work, earthen ramparts and palisades of entire efficacy against Indian missiles, it must have been an impregnable stronghold during the periods of their early intestine wars. The following diagram, drawn by James H. Bostwick, surveyor, and obligingly furnished by S. A. Goodwin, Esq. exhibits its dimensions :

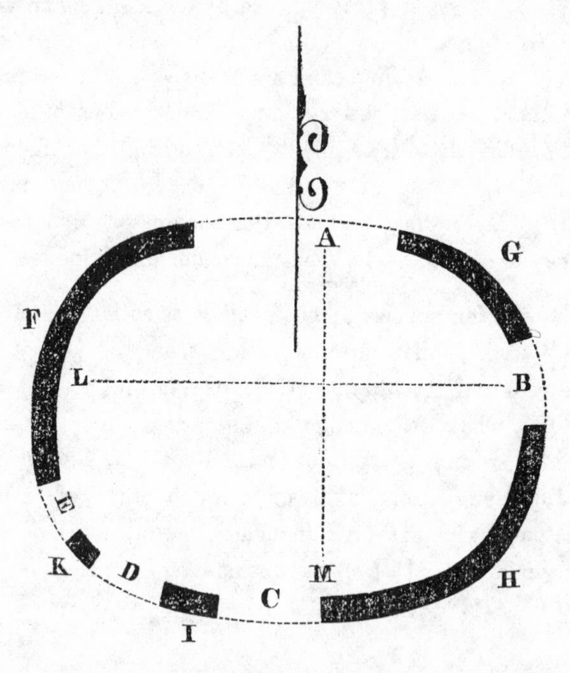

* This ancient name for the site of Auburn, was communicated to me by the intelligent Onondaga Taht-kaht-ons, or Abraham Le Fort. It is descriptive of the ford or crossing place, which anciently existed above the falls, near the site of the present turnpike bridge. This was crossed by stepping stones, &c. The barks, which made a part of a rude Indian bridge, were, at the time the name was bestowed, nearly overflowed; the crossing was very dangerous, as it was just above the brink of the falls, and it was an act of daring to pass over. The name bestowed at this time became perpetual, although there may have been but little danger in crossing afterwards.

The site of this work is the highest land in the vicinity, and a visit to it affords one of the best and most varied views of the valley of the Owasco, and the thriving and beautiful inland town of Auburn, with its public buildings, prison,* and other noted public edifices. The ellipsis enclosed by the embankments, with their intervening spaces, has a circumference of 1200 feet. Its minor dimensions are as follows, namely :

From A. to	M., 310	feet.
" B. to	L., 416	"
Opening at	A., 166	"
"	B., 66	"
"	C., 78	"
"	D., 60	"
"	E., 50	"
Wall at	F., 275	"
"	G., 145	"
"	H., 278	"
"	I., 52	"
"	K., 30	"

Viewed as a military work, the numerous breaks or openings in the wall, marked from A. to C., constitute rather its characteristic trait. They are of various and irregular widths, and it seems most difficult to decide why they are so numerous. If designed for egress or regress, they are destitute of the principle of security, unless they were defended by other works of destructible material, which have wholly disappeared. The widest opening [of 166 feet,] opens directly north, the next in point of width [78 feet,] directly south ; but in order to give these or any of the other spaces the character of entry or sally ports, and, indeed, to render the entire wall defensible, it must have had palisadoes.

Immediately below the openings at E. D. C., and a part of the embankment F., there are a series of deep ravines, separated by acute ridges, which must have made this part of the work difficult of approach. In front of the great (north) opening, the ground descends

* One of the most striking evidences of that tendency of the surface limestone stratification of western New-York to assume a fissured character, marked by the cardinal points, is seen in the banks of the Owasco, a short distance below the State prison.

gradually about seventy feet, when there is a perfect acclivity. The hill has its natural extension towards the east, for several hundred yards, in the course of which, a transverse depression in the surface separates the eastern terminus of the ridge from its crown at the site of the fort.

It is not known that excavations have been made for antiquarian remains, so that there is no accessory light to be derived from this source. The entire work conforms to the genius and character of the red races who occupied the Ohio valley, and who appear to have waged battle for the possession of this valuable part of the country, prior to the era of the discovery of America, and ere the Iroquois tribes had confederated and made themselves masters of the soil. That the art of defence by field works was cultivated by the ancient American tribes, is denoted by their traditions, as well as by the present state of our antiquarian knowledge. This art did not aspire to the construction of bastions, at the intersection of two right angled lines, by means of which a length of wall might have been enfiladed with arrows. Even where the works were a square or parallelogram, of which there are one or two instances among the oldest class of forts, such an obvious advantage in defence does not appear to have occurred. Fire, and the coal chisel, or digger, were the ready means of felling trees and of dividing the trunks into suitable lengths for palisades. To heap a pile of earth *within and without* such lines, was the mode adopted by the Tuscaroras at the siege of Naharuke, in 1712, and it is probable that this *then* powerful and warlike nation had inherited much of the skill in fort building possessed by their northern predecessors.

The chief point, in addition to its numerous breaks in the wall, before noticed, in which this work differs from the generality of antique native forts of the oldest period in this State, is its very well preserved elliptical form. A circle is the usual form of the antique forts of Indian origin in western New-York; and these works are generally placed on the apex of a hill, covered by ravines as a natural moat, or they occupy an eminence which commanded other advantages. For the original communication and survey, above referred to, see letter E., documentary appendix.

[*e*.] Vestiges of an Ancient Elliptical Work at Canandaigua.

The Senecas deduce their descent from a noted eminence, bearing the title of "Fort Hill" at the head of the sylvan expanse of Canandaigua lake. The term of Fort Hill, is however, not confined to that spot, but is, as in the work under consideration, one of common occurrence, in sundry parts of the ancient and extended area of the Six Nations. The subjoined sketch, denotes the vestiges of an ancient strong-hold of the Senecas, of an elliptical form, on elevated lands about a mile northerly from the village.

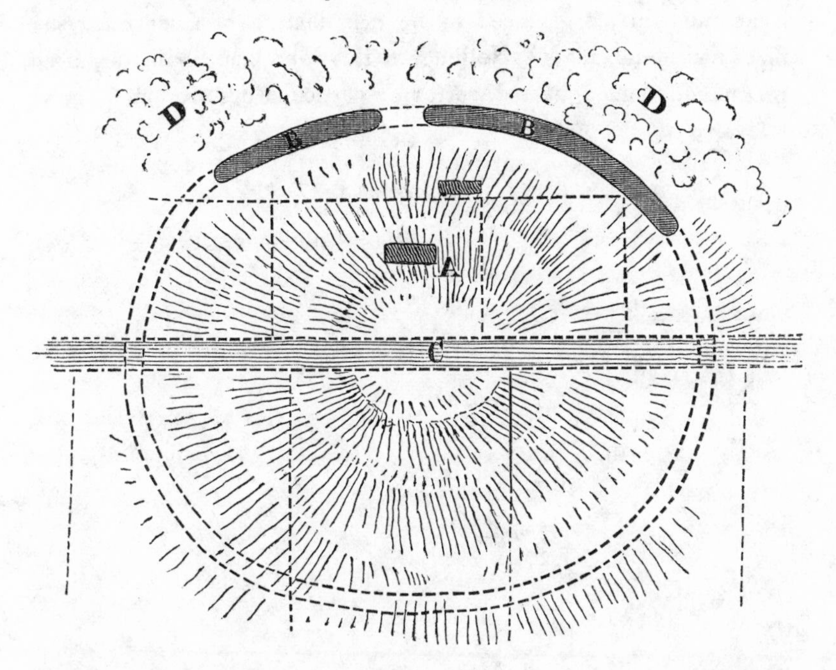

This work has been nearly obliterated by the plough. The only portions of the ancient wall yet remaining, are indicated by the letters B. B. At A, a dwelling house has been erected, flanked by gardens. C, is a turnpike or rectangular town road, passing over the apex of the elevation. The dotted angular lines denote fields in cultivation, and the dotted ellipses, through these grounds, are laid down from tradition, rather than from any well defined vestiges in these fields of the original wall yet visible. D, D, represents a native forest. Judging from the curves of the portions of wall entire at B, B, in connection with the era pointed out by the occupant, this work may have had a circumference of one thousand feet. It occupied a commanding site. The sections of the wall remaining, denote the labor of many hands, and if this rampart was crowned with palisades, and secured in the usual manner with gates, it must not only have furnished a garrison to a large body of warriors, but have been a work of much strength.

In excavating the grounds for the road, in the approach to the village, human bones were found, in considerable quantities, on the descent of the hill, together with some of the usual vestiges of ancient Indian art, as evinced in the manufacture of stone and clay pipes and implements. Nothing of this kind had, however, been preserved, which appeared worthy of particular description.

[*c*.] Ancient entrenchments on Fort Hill, near Le Roy, Genesee county.

The following diagram of this work has been drawn from a pen-sketch, forwarded by the Rev. Mr. Dewey, of Rochester.

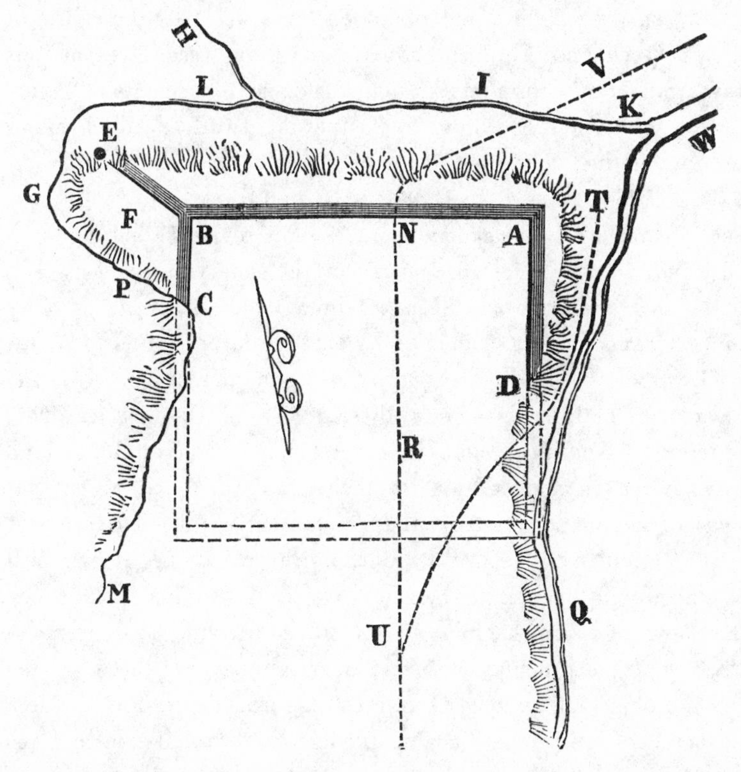

The work occurs on an elevated point of land formed by the junction of a small stream, called Fordham's brook, with Allen's creek, a tributary of the Genesee river. Its position is about three miles north of the village of Le Roy, and some ten or twelve northeast of Batavia. The best view of the hill, as one of the natural features of the country, is obtained a short distance north of it, on the road from Bergen to Le Roy.

To attain a proper conception of its susceptibilities and capacity, as the site of a work of defence, it is essential to conceive the country, for some distance, to have had the level of the extreme plain, forming the highest part of the fort. The geological column of this plain, after passing down through the unconsolidated strata, appears to be composed of various strata of corniferous limestone, Onondaga or hydraulic limestone, and perhaps Medina sandstone. Geological causes, originating, so far as we can immediately perceive, in the two streams named, have cut down this series of stratifications, on the north, east and west, unequally, to the depth of some eighty or ninety feet, isolating the original plain, on three sides, by the vallies of Allan's creek and Fordham brook. Availing themselves of this heavy amount of natural excavation, the ancient occupants of it further strenghtened its position, by casting up a wall and ditch along the brow of the two vallies, at the points of their junction, from A. to B., 60 rods; from A. to D., 30 rods; and from B. to C. 15 rods. This is as much of the embankment as now remains; but tradition adds, that, on the earliest occupancy of the county, there were evidences that the work had been continued south from the extreme points, C. and D., and connected by an enclosure, parallel to A. B., which would have given it a regular quadrangular shape. The encroachments of the respective vallies, at C. and D., now terminate the trench. And if we concede that geological changes of this kind must have required some time for their production, by the present power of action possessed by the streams named, it is an argument for the antiquity of the work. But, however antique, it was still the effort of a rude, and at best half civilized people, at an epoch when bows and arrows, clubs, spears and stones, and the stone *cassetete*,* were the principal weapons of defence. For these are the the chief objects of antiquarian interest dug from the ground. There are also disclosed by the place or its vicinity, the amuletum archæus and other amulets of sea shell, bone and fossile stone, which were so

* I find the French word cassetete more exactly descriptive of the probable and exclusive uses of the antique stone tomahawk, than any other which has been met with. The shape of this warlike instrument resembled strongly the ancient crossbill. It presents the figure of a crescent, tapering gradually to the ends, which are rounded, and proceed to a sharp point. In the concave centre of the crescent is an orifice for a helve. It is an instrument denoting skill, and the possession of some mechanical tool for carving it harder than the dark silecious slate, from which it is generally made. One of these instruments, sent to me by Mr. Follet, of Batavia, and which, from an inscription, was found "in that vicinity by Jerome A. Clark, Esq. on the 16th May, 1844," is worthy the chisel of a sculptor.

much prized by the ancient red races of this continent, by whom they were manufactured, and exclusively used before the era of the discovery. That the spot continued, however, whether a ruin or not, to be visited or occupied, after this era, is proved by some remains of art, which were found here and described by Mr. Follet, in a letter, which constitutes a valuable part of the materials employed in this description. [See appendix.] But the most remarkable and distinctive trait connected with its archæology is the discovery of human bones denoting an uncommon stature and development, which are mentioned in the same communication. A humerus or shoulder bone, which is preserved, denotes a stature one-third larger than the present race, and there is also a lower jaw bone, preserved by a physician at Batavia, from the vicinity, which indicates the same gigantic measure of increase.

To supply the fort with water, a trench was continued about fifteen rods, from B at the northeast angle to E, in order to reach a spring below the declivity. In the isolated portion of the hill, marked F. haiks of moderate sized round stones have been found, which were probably one of the ancient means of defence. This spot, from the remains found, appears also to have been an ancient place of burial. Among the articles exhumed, were several curious pipes of stone and earthenware. One of these was formed out of granular limestone; another was of baked clay in the form of a man's head and face, the nose, eyes and other features being depicted in a style resembling some of the figures in Mr. Stephens' plates of the ruins of Central America. The top of the head is surrounded by a fillet; on the occipital part are also two fillets. The neck has a similar ornament, and there is another on the breast. The orifices of the ears are denoted, and the whole evinces no little degree of art. This is the most curious relic found.

Another pipe of reddish baked clay is ornamented with dots; two rows of which extend round it, and another in festoons, like a chain looped up.

Other parts of the topography are denoted by the plot. Q, W, is Allen's creek. H, I, K, Fordham's brook. L, P, M, a branch of Fordham's brook. R, N, V, denote the road, which passes through the centre of the work. A former road led from U down the ravine to T.

There was formerly a bridge at N, to cross the ditch. This trench was estimated by early observers at from eight to ten feet deep, and as many wide. The earth in making it, had been thrown either way, but much of it inwards. Forest trees were standing, both in the trench and on its sides. In size and age they appeared to be equal to the general growth of the forest. Prostrate upon the ground, there were found numerous trunks of the heart-wood of black cherry trees of large size. These were evidently the remains of a more antique forest, which had preceded the existing growth of beech and maple. They were in such a state of soundness as to be employed for timber by the first settlers.

There were no traditions among the Indians of the country respecting the use and design of this work. It was to them, as to the first settlers, an object of mystery. About half a mile below the hill, Allen's creek has a fall of some eighty feet. It is a perpendicular fall of much beauty. At this place the hydraulic limestone is seen to be the underlying rock. This rock had also been struck in excavating the north line of the trench, on "Fort Hill," and some portions of it had been thrown out with the earth.

Such are the interesting facts communicated to me, by the gentlemen whose names have been mentioned. The notice of the present altered state of the site, and the following just reflections naturally springing from the subject, may be stated in the exact words of Dr. Dewey:

"The forest has been removed. Not a tree remains on the quadrangle, and only a few on the edge of the ravine on the west. By cultivating the land, the trench is nearly filled in some places, though the line of it is clearly seen. On the north side the trench is considerable, and where the road crosses it, is three or four feet deep at the sides of the road. It will take only a few years more to obliterate it entirely, as not even a stump remains to mark out its line.

"From this view it may be seen or inferred,

"1. That a real trench bounded three sides of the quadrangle. On the south side there was not found any trace of trench, palisadoes, blocks, &c.

"2. It was formed long before the whites came into the country. The large trees on the ground and in the trench, carry us back to an early era.

"3. The workers must have had some convenient tools for excavation.

"4. The direction of the sides may have had some reference to the four cardinal points, though the situation of the ravines naturally marked out the lines.

"5. It cannot have been designed merely to catch wild animals to be driven into it from the south. The oblique line down to the spring is opposed to this supposition, as well as the insufficiency of such a trench to confine the animals of the forest.

"6. The same reasons render it improbable that the quadrangle was designed to confine and protect domestic animals.

"7. It was probably a sort of fortified place. There might have been a defence on the south side by a *stockade*, or some similar means, which might have entirely disappeared.

"By what people was this work done ?

"The articles found in the burying-ground at F, offer no certain reply. The axes, chissels, &c. found on the Indian grounds in this part of the State, were evidently made of the greenstone or trap, of New-England, like those found on the Connecticut river in Massachusetts. The pipe of limestone might be from that part of the country. The pipes seem to belong to different eras.

"1. The limestone pipe indicates the work of the savage or aborigines.

"2. The third indicates the age of French influence over the Indians. An intelligent French gentleman says such clay pipes are frequent among the town population in parts of France.

"3. The second and most curious, seems to indicate an earlier age and people.

"The beads found at Fort Hill are long and coarse, made of baked clay, and may have had the same origin as the third pipe.

"Fort Hill cannot have been formed by the French as one of their posts to aid in the destruction of the English colonies. In 1689, or 156 years ago, the French in Canada made serious attempts to destroy the English colony of New-York. If the French had made Fort Hill a post as early as 1660, or 185 years ago, and then deserted it, the trees could not have grown to the size of the forest generally in 1810, or in 150 years afterwards. The white settlements had extended 'only twelve miles west of Avon' in 1798, and some years after 1800, Fort Hill was covered with a dense forest. A chesnut tree cut down in 1842, at Rochester, showed 254 concentric circles of wood, and must have been more than 200 years old in 1800. So opposed is the notion that this was a deserted French post.

"Must we not refer Fort Hill to that race, which peopled this country before the Indians, who raised so many monuments greatly exceeding the power of the Indians, and who lived at a remote era ?"

[g.] Antique rock citadel of Kienuka, in Lewiston, Niagara county.

In the preceding sketches, evidences have been presented of the readiness and good judgment of the aboriginal fort builders of western New-York,* in availing themselves of steeps, gulfs, defiles, and other marked localities, in establishing works for security or defence. This trait is, however, in no case more strikingly exemplified than in the curious antique work before us, which is called, by the Tuscaroras, KIENUKA. The term Kienuka is said to mean the stronghold or fort, from which there is a sublime view. It is situated about

* It is not without something bordering on anachronism, that this portion of the continent is called New-York, in reference to transactions not only before the bestowal of the title, in 1664, but long before the European race set foot on the continent. Still more inappropriate, however, was the term of New-Netherland, i. e. New-Lowland, which it bore from 1609 to 1664, many parts of the State being characterized by lofty mountains, and all having an elevation of many hundreds of feet above the sea. In speaking of these ancient periods, a title drawn from the native vocabulary would better accord with the period under discussion, if not with the laws of euphony. But the native tribes were poor generalizers, and omitted to give generic names to the land. The term of Haonao for the continent, or "island," as they call it, occurs, but this would have no more pertinence applied to New-York, than to any other portion of it. The geographieal feature most characteristic of the State, is NIAGARA, and next in prominence, ONTARIO, and either would have furnished a better cognomen for the State, had they been thought of in season. But it is too late now to make the change, and even for the remote era alluded to, the name under which the country has grown great, is to be preferred. It is already the talismanic word for every honorable and social reminiscence.

three and a half or four miles eastward of the outlet of the Niagara gorge at Lewiston, on a natural escarpment of the ridge.

This ridge, which rises in one massy, up-towering pile, almost perpendicularly, on the brink of the river, developes itself, as we follow its course eastward for a mile or two, in a second plateau, which holds nearly a medium position in relation to the altitude of the ridge. This plateau attains to a width of a thousand yards or more, extending an unexplored distance, in the curving manner of the ridge, towards Lockport. Geologically considered, its upper stratum is the silurean limestone, which in the order of superposition, immediately overlies the red shaly sandstone at the falls. Its edges are jagged and broken, and heavy portions of it have been broken off, and slid down the precipice of red shaly under grit, and thus assumed the character of debris. Over its top, there has been a thin deposit of pebble drift, of purely diluvial character, forming, in general, not a very rich soil, and supporting a growth of oaks, maples, butternut, and other species common to the country. From the ascent of the great ridge, following the road from Lewiston to Tuscarora village, a middle road leads over this broad escarpment, following, apparently, an ancient Indian trail, and winding about with sylvan irregularity. Most of the trees appear to be of second growth ; they do not, at any rate, bear the impress of antiquity, which marks the heavy forests of the country. Occasionally there are small openings, where wigwams once stood. These increase as we pass on, till they assume the character of continuous open fields, at the site of the old burying ground, orchard and play ground of the neighboring Tuscaroras. The soil in these openings appears hard, compact and worn out ,and bears short grass. The burial ground is filled almost entirely with sumach, giving it a bushy appearance, which serves to hide its ancient graves and small tumuli. Among these are two considerable barrows, or small elliptic mounds, the one larger than the other, formed of earth and angular stones. The largest is not probably higher than five feet, but may have a diameter of twenty feet, in the longest direction.

Directly east of this antique cemetery, commences the old orchard and area for ball playing, on which, at the time of my visit, the stakes or goals were standing, and thus denoted that the ancient games are kept up on these deserted fields, by the youthful popula tion of the adjacent Tuscarora village. A small ravine succeeds, with a brook falling into a gulf, or deep break in the escarpment, where once stood a saw mill, and where may still be traced some vestiges of this early attempt of the first settlers to obtain a water power from a vernal brook. Immediately after crossing this little ravine, and rising to the general level of the plain, we enter the old fields and rock fortress of Kienuka, described in the following diagram.

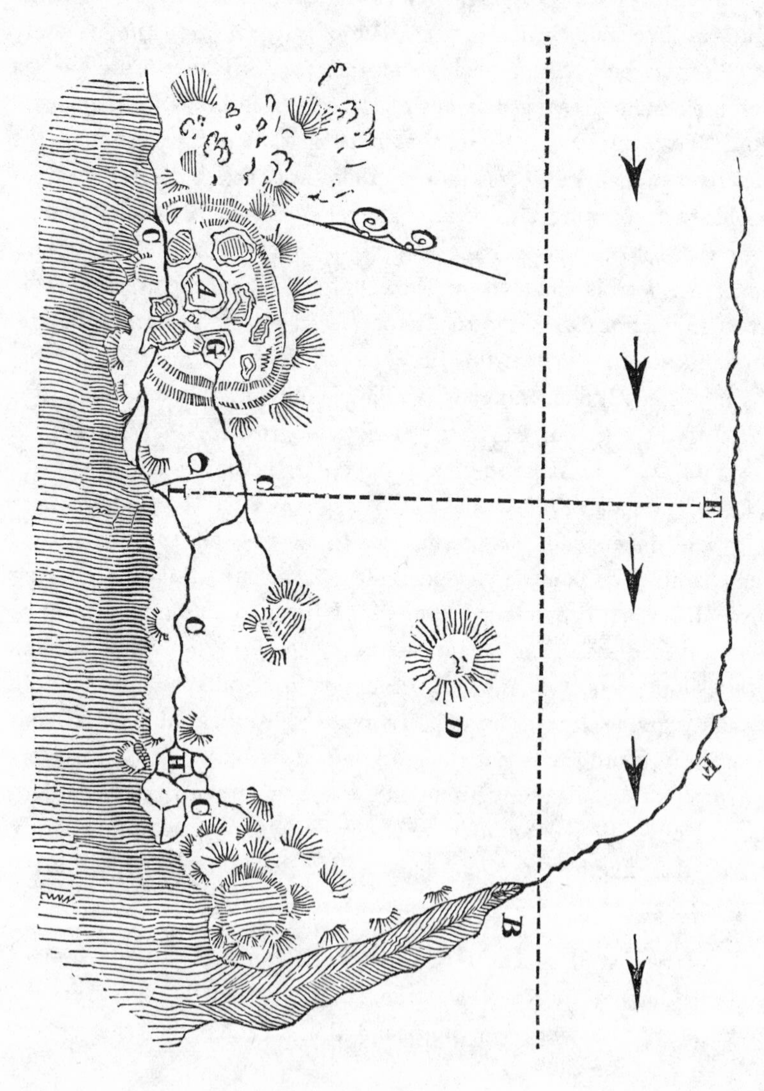

To obtain a proper conception of this plan, it is necessary to advert to geological events, in this part of the country, whose effects are very striking. The whole country takes an impress, in some degree, from the great throe which worked out a passage for the Niagara, through seven miles of solid rock, severing, at its outlet, the great coronal ridge, at its highest point of elevation. Nothing, we think, is more evident to the observer, in tracing out the Kienuka plateau, than the evidences which exist of Lake Ontario having washed its northern edge, and driven its waters against its crowning wall of limestone. The fury of the waves, forced in to the line of junction, between the solid limestone and fissile sandstone, has broken up and removed the latter, till the overlying rock, pressed by its own gravity, has been split, fissured or otherwise disrupted, and often slid in vast solid masses down the ragged precipice. Kienuka offers one of the most striking instances of this action. The fissures made in the rock, by the partial withdrawal of its support, assume the size of cavern passages; they penetrate, in some instances, under other and unbroken masses of the superior stratum, and are, as a whole, curiously intersected, forming a vast reticulated area, in which large numbers of men could seek shelter and security.

A. denotes the apex of this citadel of nature. At this point, heavy masses of the limestone, rest, in part, upon the fissures, and serve as a covering. From these primary fissures, others, marked C.C.C.C.C., proceed. The distance from G. to H. is 227 paces. The cross fissure at I., thirty-seven paces.

Most of these fissures which extend in the general parallel of the brink appear to have been narrow, and are now covered with the sod, or filled with earth and carbonaceous matter, which gives this portion of them the aspect of ancient trenches. D. denotes a small mound or barrow. E. F., a brook, dry at midsummer. B. the site of an abandoned saw-mill, at the head of an ancient lake inlet or gorge. The arrow head denotes the site of habitations, which are marked by remains of pottery, pipes, and other evidences of the ancient, rude arts of the occupants. The parallel dots at B. mark the road, which, at this point, crosses the head of the gorge. Trees, of mature growth, occupy some portions of the brink of the precipice, extending densely eastward, and obscure the view, which would otherwise be commanding, and fully justify the original name. Directly in front, looking north, at the distance of seven or eight miles, extends the waters of Lake Ontario, at a level of several hundred feet below. The intermediate space, stretching away as far as the eye can trace it, east and west, is one of the richest tracts of wheat land in the State, cultivated in the best manner, and settled compactly, farm to farm. Yet such to the eye is the effect of the reserved woodlands on each farm, seen at this particular elevation, that the entire area, to the lake shore, has the appearance of a rich, unbroken forest, whose green foliage contrasts finely with the silvery whiteness of the lake beyond. It requires the observer, however, at this time, to ascend the crown of the ridge, to realize this view in all its beauty and magnificence.

[*h*.] Site of an ancient battle-field, with vestiges of an entrenchment and fortification on the banks of the Deoseowa, or Buffalo creek.

The following sketch conveys an idea of the relative position of the several objects alluded to. Taken together they constitute the distinguishing feature in the archæology of the existing Indian cemetery, mission station, and council-house on the Seneca reservation, five or six miles south of the city of Buffalo. As such, the site is one of much interest, and well worthy of further observation and study. The time and means devoted to it, in the preparation of this outline, were less than would be desirable, yet they were made use of, under favorable circumstances, as the current periodical business and deliberations of the tribe brought together a large part of them, including the chief persons of education and intelligence, as well as many aged persons who are regarded as the depositories of their traditions and lore.

Tradition, in which all concur, points out this spot as the scene of the last and decisive battle fought between the Senecas and their fierce and inveterate enemies the KAH-KWAHS, a people who are generally but erroneously supposed to be the same as the Eries.* It is not proposed in this place, to consider the evidences on this point, or to denote the origin and events of this war. It is mainly alluded to as

* This is a French pronunciation of a Wyandot or Huron term. Vide Hennepin, Amsterdam, ed. 1698.

a historical incident connected with the site. It is a site around which the Senecas have clung, as if it marked an era in their national history; although the work itself was clearly erected by their enemies. It has been the seat of their government or council fire, from an early period of our acquaintance with them. It was here that Red Jacket uttered some of his most eloquent harangues against the steady encroachments of the white race, and in favor of retaining this cherished portion of their lands, and transmitting them with full title to their descendants. It was here that the noted captive, Dehewamis, better known as Mary Jemison, came to live after a long life of most extraordinary vicissitudes. And it is here that the bones of the distinguished ORATOR, and the no less distinguished CAPTIVE, rest side by side, with a multitude of warriors, chiefs and sages. Nor can we, on natural principles of association, call in question the truthfulness or force of the strenuous objections, which, for so many years, the whole tribe has opposed to the general policy of its sale. But these events are now history; the tribe has come into arrangements to remove to reservations owned by their brethren, in more westerly parts of the State, and there will soon be no one left whose heart vibrates with the blood of a Seneca, to watch the venerated resting places of their dead.

It was suitable, before the plough was put into these precincts, and the last trench and mound of the tribe were obliterated, that some memorial of the locality should be preserved, and I can only regret that the labor itself has not been better or more successfully accomplished.

ANCIENT WORK ON BUFFALO CREEK.

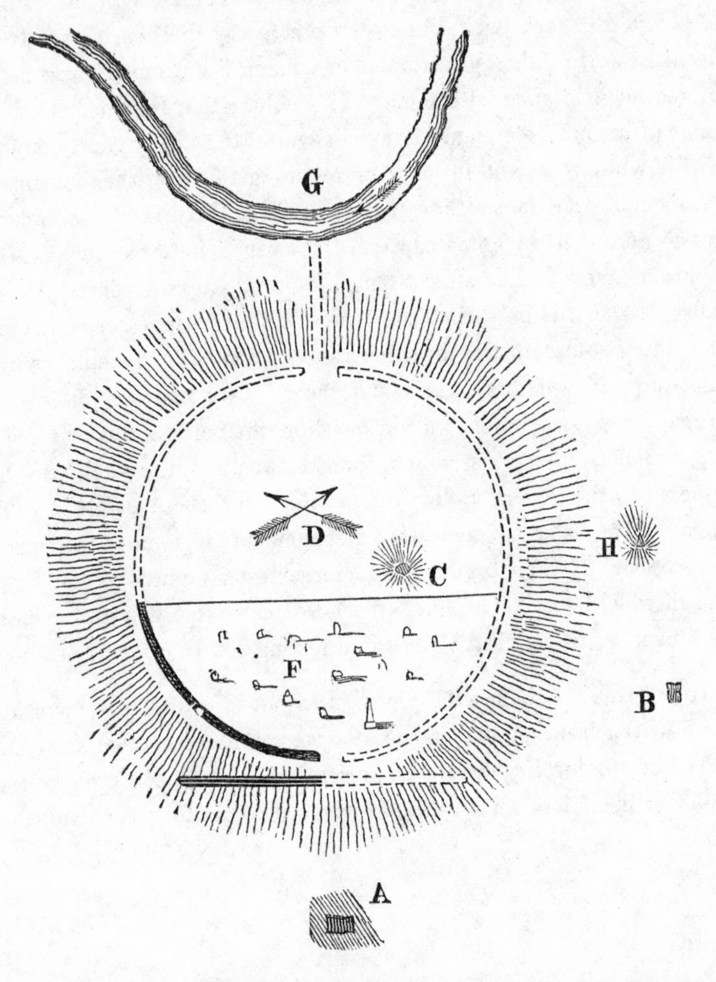

A. denotes the site of the mission house; B, of the council house; D, of the battle field, or that portion of it where the result was consummated; F, the grave yard. At C, there are still the remains of a mound, which tradition asserts was raised over the incinerated bodies of victor and vanquished slain in battle. These bodies were piled together, interspersed with the carcasses of deer and other game, which had been hunted with the special view, that it might be offered as a sacrifice with the bodies, or to appease their spirits in the land of the dead. In making partial excavations into this mound, which has been frequently plowed over in modern times, I procured several partially charred or blackened bones, supposed to represent parts of the human and brute species ; a proof, it would seem, of the truth of this curious part of the tradition.* Mixed in the funeral pile, there were set vessels of pottery, with drinks offered as libations to the dead. And it is certain, also, that pieces of reddish coarse pottery were obtained at the same time, in making these partial examinations.

The dotted lines are designed to show the probable figure and extent of the work, from the accounts of the Indians. That it was a circular work, appears to be denoted by the only parts of the wall yet remaining, which are drawn in black. The site itself was elevated moderately above the plain. There is no reason to suppose that this elevation of the surface was artificial. The relative position of the creek is denoted by G. H marks the position of a stone, which is connected with the history of their domestic arts, before the discovery of the country. It was not practicable to obtain accurate admeasurements of distances ; the design being merely to present a pencil sketch.

* The Indian name of Buffalo creek, which gives name to the city, has been variously written. In the treaty of 1784, at Fort Stanwix, it is called "Tehoseroron," which is the Mohawk term, the final *n* being probably designed to convey a nasal sound. The word, as pronounced to me by the late Mrs. Carr of Wellington square, Canada, who was a daughter of the celebrated Brandt, I have written TEHOSERORO, meaning Place of the Linden tree. The letters *d* and *t* are interchangeable between the Mohawks and Senecas. The latter, who at the same time do not use the letter *r*, and have some peculiarities in the use of the vowels, pronounce it in a manner which I thought should be written Deoseowa, as above. Mr. Wright, in his "Mental Elevator" and "Seneca Spelling Book,', makes it a word ot four syllables, and uses the sound of *y* as heard in "yonder," for the vowel *e* in his second syllable. Every practised ear is acute to satisfy its own requisitions of sound, which is not easy in unwritten languages ; and there is besides a marked difference in the pronunciation of Indians from different localities, or uttered under different circumstances. Mr. Ellicott, on his original plat of Buffalo, writes it "Tushuway." Others have spelt it still differently. The meaning of the word has excited but little difference of opinion. It denotes a locality of the linden or basswood tree, a species found upon the rich bottom lands of this stream, whose bark was highly valuable to these tribes for covering their lodges, and for the tough and fibrous inner coat, which at an early time served them to make both twine and ropes.

Whence then, it may be asked, is the origin of the word Buffalo, since it is not found in the Indian term? Tradition denotes that the range of this animal once extended to the banks of the great lakes. There was a current opinion among the early travellers along the shores of Lake Erie, that the bison had been seen and killed on this creek. Whether the impression arose from, or was traceable, in part or wholly, to a deception of certain hunters in bringing in "other flesh," under the denomination of Buffalo meat, as has been said, it would be difficult to determine. From whatever cause, it is certain that the stream acquired the popular name it now bears at an early day, whilst the aboriginal name was neglected.

V. ANCIENT STATE OF INDIAN ART.

To denote the state of art among the aboriginal race, it is necessary closely to examine such monuments of it, as exist. The word "monument" is used to denote any remains of art. Such are their relics in the form of worked shells and amulets, pottery, carved implements and utensils of stone, and other antiquarian remains found in their mounds, graves, fortifications, and other places of ancient occupancy in our latitudes. Of architectural ruins in stone, which constitute so striking a portion of aboriginal antiquities, in central and South America, particularly in the ruins of their temples and teocalli, (the only form of such architecture indeed, which survives,) we have no remains north of the latitude of the mouth of the Mississippi, unless they shall be disclosed in some of the large mounds yet unopened, or in portions of the country north of such a line, which yet remains unexplored, west of the extreme sources of the Red river and the Rio Del Norte.

From this inquiry, we may peremtorily exclude, all articles and remains of metal (not gold, silver or native copper) and all sculpture and inscriptions (not picture writing) which have been found and commented on, with an air of wonder, in various places, but which are one and all, undoubtedly of European, or to give the greatest scope to conjecture, of trans-atlantic origin. Such are, to begin with the highest object, the Grave creek inscription in apparently Celtiberic characters, the stone with a rude inscription in Roman letters and Arabic figures found in Onondaga county, and now deposited in the Albany Academy ; the amulets of coarse enamel colored pastes and glass, of the imperfect fabric of the 15th and 16th centuries, found in Indian graves ; or old village and fort sites, together with theflattened gun barrels, broken locks, artists' tools and other articles of iron, brass, or semi-vitrified earthenware, which are found over so considerable an extent of country in western New-York. The latter are undoubtedly, evidences of either earlier, or more systematic attempts to settle, if not to found colonies, amongst the Red Race from abroad, than we are yet prepared fully to comprehend. But there need be no question as to the general era and character of art to which they belong ; they are too clearly European in every instance to admit of scruple.

The introduction of the fabrics of European art, among the tribes of this continent, had the inevitable and speedy effect to destroy the prior Indian arts. It is astonishing to find how soon the aborigines of our latitudes, lost the art of making culinary vessels of clay ; of carving amulets and pipes out of steatites and other fissile mineral bodies ; of perforating, dissecting and forming sea shells into the various shapes of wampum, gorgets, pendants, necklaces, belt and pouch ornaments, and other ornamental fabrics. They no sooner obtained the light brass, copper, iron, and tin kettle, than they laid aside the more clumsy and frail Akeek, or clay pot ; their women relieved from the labor of selecting and tempering the clays, and forming it into pots and dishes, were advanced one step in the art of housewifery, and took the first lesson in European civilization.

The maker of arrow and javelin heads, for this was a distinct art, was superceded by the superior efficacy of fire arms ; and his red descendant at this day, as well as the gleaner of antiquities, is alike at a loss to find, where the ancient artist in chert and hornstone procured his materials of so suitable a quality and fracture, and how he obtained the skill to chip and form them into such delicate and appropriate patterns. The small and slender axe of iron, with a steel edge, and pipe-head, at once took the place of the crescent-shaped stone tomahawk, which had alone been appropriated to war ; while the larger half-axe, so called, supplanted the clumsy stone Agakwut before employed rather as a gouge to detach coal in the process of felling trees by fire, than an axe proper. By the application of the common lathe and turning chisel, those species of thick sea shells, which the natives had, with so much labor, converted into seawan and wampum, were manufactured with such superior skill, expedition and cheapness, (although this is an article which the trader always held comparatively high) that the old Indian art of the *wampum-maker*, sunk, like that of the *arrow-maker*, never to be revived. But of all, the ex changes made between civilized and savage life, the gift of the steel-trap, in replacing the Indian trap of wood, was the most eagerly sought, and highly prized by the hunter, although it hastened the period of the destruction of the whole class of furred animals, and thus in effect, brought to a speedy close the Indian dominion.

Pottery was an art known universally among all the tribes from Patagonia to the Arctic ocean, but was practised with very different degrees of skill. The northern tribes who bordered on the great lakes, and thence reached down to the Atlantic, made a rude article, which just answered the simple purposes of the culinary art. The clay, or argillaceous material used for it, was such as is common to diluvial and tertiary soils. It was tempered with silex, in the form of pounded quartz, or often quartz and feld-spar, as it exists in granite, in quite coarse particles. This mixture prevented shrinkage and cracks in drying, and enabled the mass to withstand the application of heat—an art which has resulted, and would very soon result, in any given case, from experience. There were no legs to the Indian *akeek*, or pot. It was designed to be used, to use a chemical phrase, as a sand-bath. Being set on the ashes, a fire was built around it. It might also admit of suspension, by a bark cord tied below the lip, which flared out well, and thus could be attached to the ordinary Indian cooking-tackle, namely ; a long-legged tripod, tied at the top with bark.

There is no evidence in the structure of any of this species of pottery, at least, in these latitudes, that it had been raised or formed on a potter's wheel. The fact that prepared clay placed on a revolving horizontal circle, would rise, by the centrifugal force, if resisted by the hand, or a potter's stick or former, was not known to these tribes ; although it is admitted to be one of the oldest arts in the world. Some skill was consequently required to form the mass and shape the vessel, without machinery. It was essential to its utility, and to prevent unequal shrinkage in drying, that the body should be of uniform thickness ; and this art was also, if we may judge from fragments, and one or two entire vessels examined, very well attained.

It is believed that this art, in this quarter, was in the hands of females; but every female or mistress of a lodge, was not adequate to it. It must have been the business of a class of persons in each village, who were professed potters. Tradition says that it was the practice to mingle some blood in wetting and tempering the clay.

It was impossible that this art, so rude and laborious, and so ill-suited to perform its offices when done, could survive and continue to be practised for any length of time after the tribes had been made acquainted with the products of the European potteries, rude as these were comparatively speaking, in the fifteenth and sixteenth centuries.

Architecture, as it existed in the north and west, was confined, we may suppose, to earthen structures, crowned with wood, in the shape of beams and posts. And it is only as it exhibited a knowledge of geometry, in the combination of squares and circles, to constitute a work of defence, that it is deserving of notice. The knowledge of the pyramid and its durability, is one of the most ancient geometrical discoveries in the world, and it is quite clear, in viewing the mounds and teocalli of North America, that the aborigines possessed, or had not forgotten it. In most of the works of defence, in the western country, the circular pyramid, or mound of earth of various sizes, formed a striking feature; whilst in relation to the mounds used for religious ceremonies, as we must suppose the larger mounds to have been, its completeness of plan and exact truncation, parallel to the plain or basis, denotes the prevalence among them, of this ancient architectural idea. We detect also, in a survey of the old works, the square, the parallelogram, the circle, and the ellipsis. And these figures were variously employed in the arrangement of masses of earth, to produce a rampart and a moat.

The domestic economy required implements to perform the arts which we express by the words sewing and weaving.

The awl and needle were made from various species of animal bones of the land and water. The larger awl used to perforate bark, in sewing together the sheething of the northern canoe, made from the rind of the betula, was squared and brought to a tapering point. A very close grain and compact species of bone was employed for the fine lodge awl used for sewing dressed skins for garments. After this skin had been perforated, a thread of deer's sinew was drawn through, from the eye of a slender bone needle. There was, besides this, a species of shuttle of bone, which was passed backwards and forwards, in introducing the bark woof of mats and bags; two kinds of articles, the work of which was commonly made from the scirpus læustris or larger bulrush. It was only necessary to exhibit the square and round awl, and grose and fine needle of steel, to supercede these primitive and rude modes of *seamstress-work* and *weaving*.

In an examination of Indian antiquarian articles, taken from the graves and mounds, there is some glimmering of the art of design. There is no other branch of art to which we can refer the numerous class of carved ornaments and amulets, or their skill in symbolical or representative drawing, evinced in their picture writing.

Amulets and neck, ear and head ornaments, constituted a very ancient and very important department in the arcanum of the Indian wardrobe. They were not only a part of the personal gear and decorations which our old British writers sometimes denote "braveries," but they were connected with his superstitions, and were a part of the external system of his religion. The aboriginal man, who had never laid aside his oriental notions of necromancy, and believed firmly in witchcraft, wore them as charms. They were among the most cherished and valued articles he could possibly possess. They were sought with great avidity, at high prices, and, after having served their office of warding off evil, while he lived, they were deposited in his grave, at death. Bones, shells, carved stones, gems, claws and hoofs of animals, feathers of carnivorous birds, and above all the skin of the serpent, were cherished with the utmost care, and regarded with the most superstitious veneration. To be decked with suitable amulets was to him to be invested with a charmed life. They added to his feeling of security and satisfaction in his daily avocations, and gave him new courage in war.

But if such were the influence of pendants, shells, beads and other amulets or ornaments, inspired by children who saw and heard, what their parents prized, this influence took a deeper hold of their minds at and after the period the virile fast, when the power of dreams and visions was added to the sum of their experimental knowledge of divine things, so to call them. To fix it still stronger, the Indian system of medicine, which admits the power of necromancy, lent its aid. And thus, long before the period which the civilized code has fixed on, to determine man's legal acts, the aboriginal man was fixed, grounded and educated in the doctrine of charms, talismans, and amulets.

To supply the native fabric in this particular branch, was more difficult. Christianity, in a large part of Europe, certainly all protestant Europe had, in 1600, religiously discarded all such, and kindred reliances on amulets, from its ritual and popular observances, where they had taken deep root during the dark ages; and hence the first English and Dutch voyagers and settlers who landed north of the capes of Florida, regarded the use of them as one of the strong evidences of the heathenishness of the tribes, and made light of their love of "beads and trinkets." It was necessary, however, to the success of their traffic and commerce—the great object of early voyages, that this class of articles should be noticed; and they brought from the potteries and glass-houses of Europe various substitutes, in the shape of white, opaque, transparent, blue, black, and other variously colored beads, and of as many diverse forms as the genius of geometry could well devise. We see, what it is somewhat difficult as an inquiry of art otherwise to reach, that they also brought over a species of paste-mosaic, or curious oval and elongated beads of a kind of enamel or paste, skilfully arranged in layers of various colors, which, viewed at their poles, represented stars, radii, or other figures. These were highly prized by the natives, (ignorant as they were of the manner of making them,) and were worn instead of the native amulets. In place of their carved pipes of steatite, or clay pipes ornamented with the heads of birds, men, or animals, they supplied them with a somewhat corresponding heavy, plain, or fluted pipe-bowl, which was designed, like the native article, to receive a large wooden stem, such as we see among the remote interior tribes, at the present day. The jingling ornaments of native copper or deer hoofs, were replaced from European work-shops, by the article of brass, called "hawks-bells," an article which, like that of wampum, still retains its place in the invoices of the Indian trade.

But by far the most attractive class of fabrics which the commerce of Europe supplied in exchange for their rich furs and peltries, was arm-bands, wrist-bands, ear-rings, gorgets, and other ornaments, both for the person and dress, of silver. This metal was esteemed, as it is at this day, above all others. Its color and purity led them to regard it as pre-eminently *the* noble metal, and its introduction at once superceded the cherished Nabikoagun Antique, and other forms of medals and gorgets made from compact sea-shells.

In this manner the introduction of European arts, one after another, speedily overturned and supplanted the ancient Indian arts, and transferred them, at the end of but a few generations, from useful objects to the class of antiquities. It is unnecessary to pursue the subject to the department of clothing, in which woollens, cottons, linens and ribbons, took the place of the dressed skins of animals and birds, and the inner barks of trees, &c. Such objects are no part of the antiquities to be studied here. They are wholly perishable, and if any thing is to be gleaned from their study in the unburied cities of Pompeii and Herculaneum, where stone and marble offered objects of temporary resistance to currents of flowing lava, they offer no facts to guide the pen of the antiquarian here. The European and the Indian fabrics of the 16th century have alike submitted to the inevitable laws of decomposition ; but were it otherwise, could we disinter from the Indian graves the first duffils, strouds, osnaburgs, and blankets, that were given to the race, they would only prove that the latter quickly laid aside the inferior when they could get the superior article. It would prove that guns and gunpowder, brass kettles and iron axes, had caused the manufacture of stone darts and clay kettles to be thrown aside and forgotten, and in like manner the labors of the spindle and loom had given the Indian, even before Columbus descended to his grave, a new wardrobe.

To denote what the Indian arts were, at the beginning of the 16th century, we must resort to their tombs, mounds, and general cemeteries. The melancholy tale that is told from the dust and bones of these sacred repositories is to be our teacher and schoolmaster. Its whispers are low and almost inaudible. There are pauses and lapses which it is difficult to make out. It requires great care—nice attention—examination and re-examination. We must not hastily compose the thread of the narrative. We must doubt and reject where doubt and rejection are proper. We must discriminate the various epochs of art from the objects disinterred. If objects of various ages lie in the same cemeteries we must not confound them. Carefully to labor, patiently to study, cautiously to conclude, is the province of the antiquarian; and if, after all, he has but little to offer, it is, perhaps, because there is but little to glean.

NOTE.

The following specimen of Iroquois picture writing should have been placed under the article "Onondagas," where the omission is supplied, by a head from an ancient pipe, hereafter described under the class of relics named Opoaguna. It represents the first Iroquois ruler, under their confederacy, named Atotarho.

VI. RELICS OF ABORIGINAL ART IN WESTERN NEW-YORK.

[Antique insignia, amulets, implements and ornaments.]

It will tend to render the work of antiquarian examination exact, and facilitate comparison, if names descriptive of the general classes and species of each object of archæological inquiry be introduced. No science can advance if the terms and definitions of it be left vague. The mere inception of this design is here announced; it is not proposed, at present, to do more than submit a few specimens from a large number of antiquarian articles, the result of many years' accumulation. The figures and descriptions introduced are confined exclusively to the geographical area under examination.

To establish the classes of articles, names are introduced from the Indian vocabulary. These are qualified by specific terms, adjective or substantive, from the same class of languages, or from the English; rarely from other sources. A nomenclature derived from such sources, appeared preferable for these simple objects of savage art, to one taken from the ancient languages, whose prerogative it has so long been to furnish terms for science and art.

AMERICAN ANTIQUITIES—Plate I.

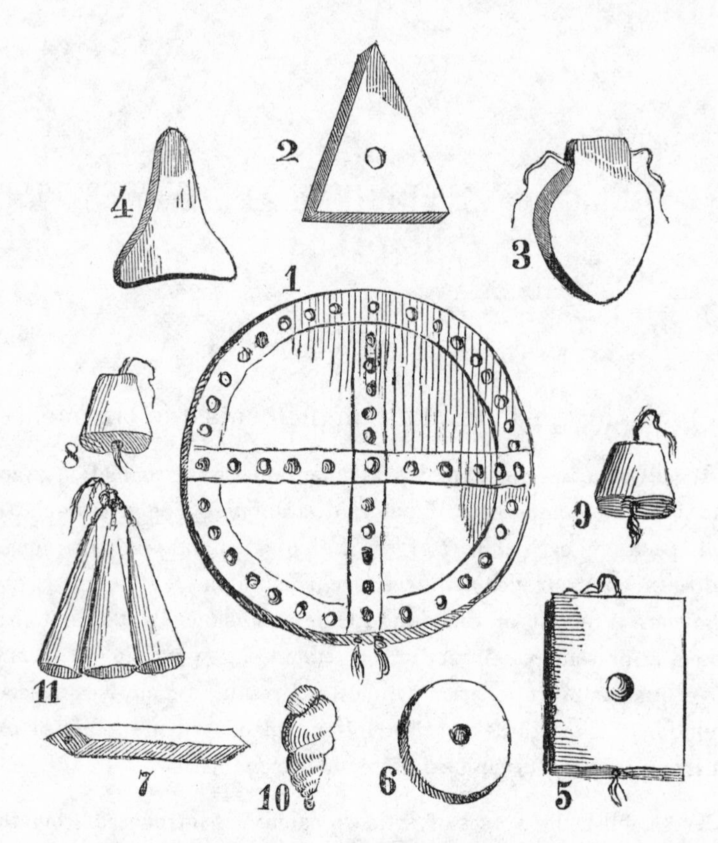

CLASS FIRST. NABIKOAGUNA.*

Objects of this kind were worn as marks of honor or rank. So far as known, they were constructed from the most solid and massy parts of the larger sea shells. Few instances of their having been made from other materials, are known, in our latitudes. The ruins and tombs of Central and South America have not been explored, so far as is known, with this view. Nor have any insignia of this character been found of stone.

Nabikoáguna Antique. Fig. I., Plate I. This article is generally found in the form of an exact circle, rarely, a little ovate. It has been ground down and re-polished, apparently, from the sea conch.

---

* From the Algic, denoting a medal, a breast-plate or collar.

Its diameter varies from three-fourths of an inch to two inches. Thickness, two-tenths in the centre, thinning out a little towards the edges. It is doubly perforated. It is figured on the face and its reverse, with two parallel latitudinal, and two longitudinal lines crossing in its centre, and dividing the area into four equal parts. Its circumference is marked with an inner circle, corresponding in width to the cardinal parallels. Each division of the circle thus quartered, has five circles with a central dot. The latitudinal and longitudinal bands or fillets, have each four similar circles and dots, and one in its centre, making thirty-seven. The number of these circles varies, however, on various specimens. In the one figured, they are fifty-two. The partial decomposition of the surface renders exactitude in this particular sometimes impossible. This article was first detected, many years ago, in a medal, one and a half inches diameter, found in an ancient grave on the Scioto, in Ohio, and was supposed to be a kind of altered enamel or earthern ware. The structure of the shell is, however, present in all cases, in its centre. Its occurrence, the present year, in the ancient fort grounds and cemeteries of Onondaga, identifies the epochs of the ancient Indian settlements of Ohio and western New-York, and furnishes a hint of the value of these investigations. A medium specimen was examined, in the possession of I. Keeler, jr., Jamesville, very much obliterated; another, of the minimum size, at James Gould's, Lafayette. The largest specimen seen, is one sent by I. V. V. Clarke, from Pompey and Manlius. The Indians have no traditions of the wearing of this species of shell medal, so far as known. It must be referred to the era preceding the discovery.

Nabikoáguna Iroquois. Fig. 2, annexed. This article consists of a metal, which is apparently an alloy. It is slightly ovate, and is perforated in the rim, so as to have been hung transversely. Its greatest diameter is two and four-tenth inches. There are no traces of European art about it, unless the apparent alloy be such. Locality, valley of Genesee river.

AMERICAN ANTIQUITIES—Plate II.

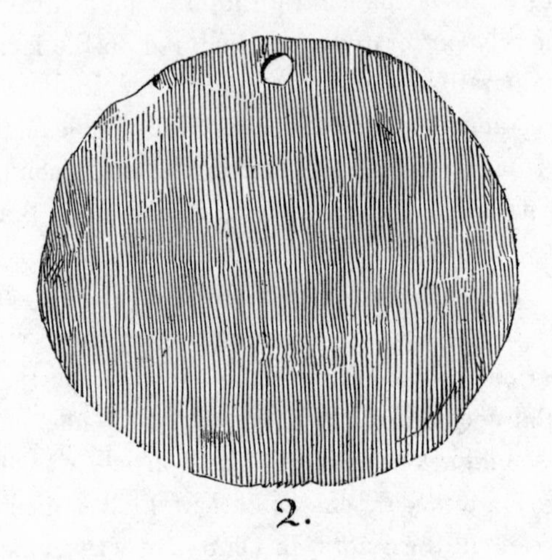

2.

Nabikoaguna Cameo, Fig. 3, 4. Plate III. This well sculptured article, was discovered in the valley of the Kasonda creek, Onondaga county. The material is a compact piece of sea shell. It still possesses, in a considerable degree, the smoothness and lustre of its original finish. Fig. 4 shews the prominence of the features in profile. At the angles of the temples are two small orifices, for suspending it around the neck. The entire article is finished with much skill and delicacy. [Mifflin Gould.]

AMERICAN ANTIQUITIES—Plate III.

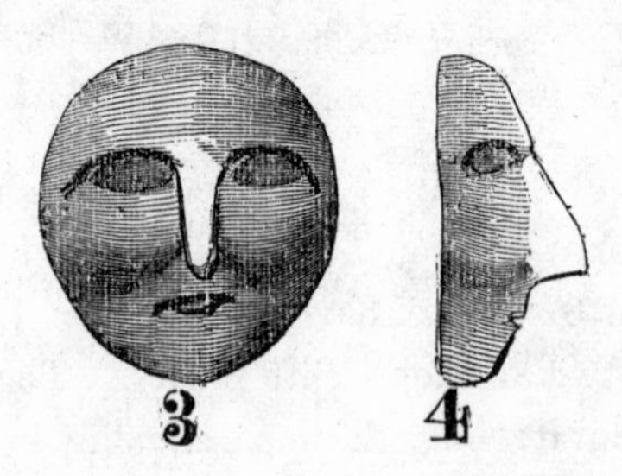

3 4

Nabikoáguna Mnemonic. Fig. 1, plate IV. This is the head of an infant represented in the fine red pipe-stone from the Missouri. Locality, site of the ancient fort of the Kasonda valley. [I. Keeler, junior.]

AMERICAN ANTIQUITIES—Plate IV.

1

CLASS SECOND.—MEDÄEKA.

This class comprises the amulets proper. All the objects of this class are supposed to have been worn on various parts of the person, as a defence against witchcraft, sorcery, or spells, or to propitiate good luck by superstitious means.

Medäeka Missouric. See Fig. 1, Plate V, with the illustration of the manner of its being worn on the breast. This article varies moderately in length, breadth and figure. It is generally the frustrum of an acute pyramid, perforated in its length, to admit being suspended from the neck, or ears. The figure exhibited is three inches in length by two-tenths in breadth at its superior, and nine-tenths at its inferior extremity. Sometimes, as in the figure given, it has a raised surface in the direction of the perforation. It is formed of the red pipe-stone of the Coteau Des Prairie, west of the Mississippi; and its disinterment from Indian graves in western New-York, denotes an early traffic or exchange of the article, or rather the material of its construction, with the tribes in that quarter. This stone is fissile, and easily cut or ground by trituration with harder substances to any figure. It bears a dull gloss, not a polish, which was produced by rubbing the surface with the equisitum, or rush, which has a silicious gritty surface. It is of the period anterior to the introduction of European arts. The specimen figured is from Onondaga county, [I. V. V. Clarke.] It occurred also at Oswego, in removing the elevation of the old fort. [J. McNiel.] Also, at Lower Sandusky, Ohio. [L. Cass.]

AMERICAN ANTIQUITIES.—Plate V.

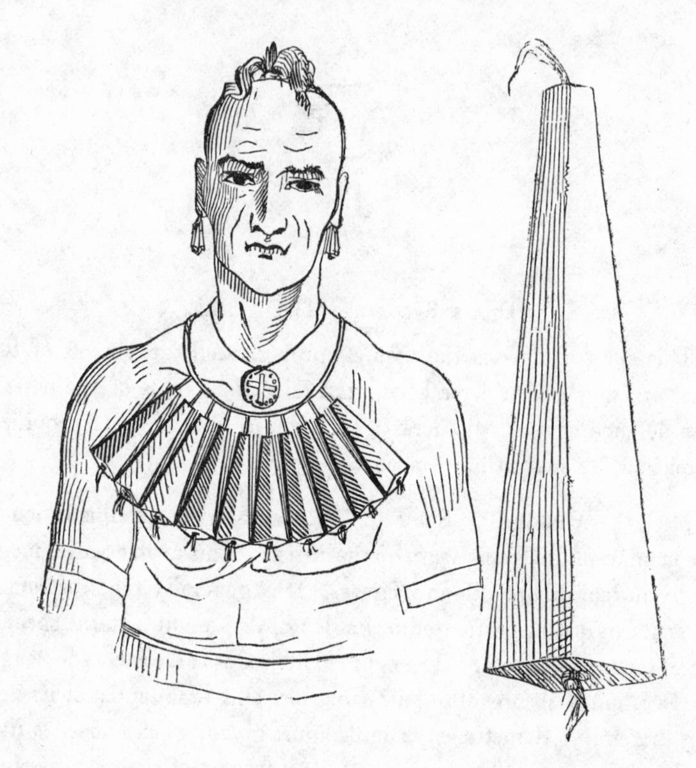

Medäeka Dental. Fig. 4, 5. Plate VI. Fossil specimens of the bear's tooth. A power against charms or spells was often attributed to amulets of this kind. The two species, very different in size, and of course the age of the animal, were obtained from a single grave. Valley of the Genesee river. [E. Trowbridge.]

Medäeka Okun. Fig. 3, Plate VI. This species is made from a compact kind of bone, squared and perforated. Valley of the Genesee river. [E. Trowbridge.] From an ancient grave.

AMERICAN ANTIQUITIES.—Plate VI.

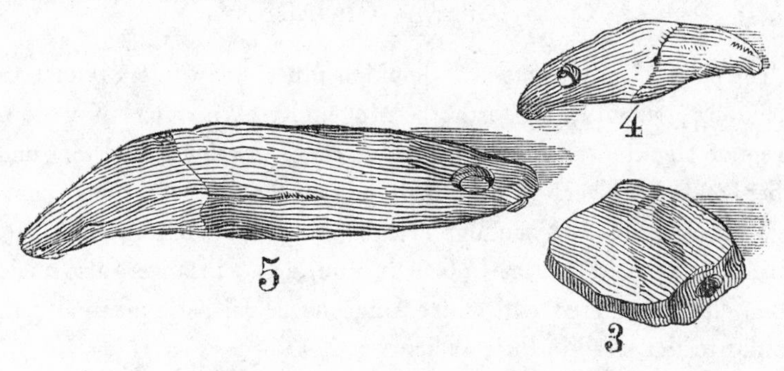

CLASS THIRD.—ATTAJEGUNA.*

Under this class are grouped a great variety of implements and instruments of utility, war, hunting and diversion. The material is chiefly stone. Without plates, however, it is impossible to give that exactitude to the description of this numerous class of antiquarian remains which is desired. But a single figure has been prepared—ATTAJEGUNA DEOSEOWA. This relic of Indian art was pointed out to me by Mr. Wright, missionary on the Seneca reservation, near the city of Buffalo. It consists of a block of limestone, having two spherical basin-shaped depressions. It is the tradition of this people that in this ancient mortar, the female potters of olden time pounded the stone material with which they tempered the clay for the ancient akeek or cooking vessel. The original stone had been broken. From the portion of which the annexed is a figure, the entire mass must have been one of considerable weight.

AMERICAN ANTIQUITIES.—Plate VII.

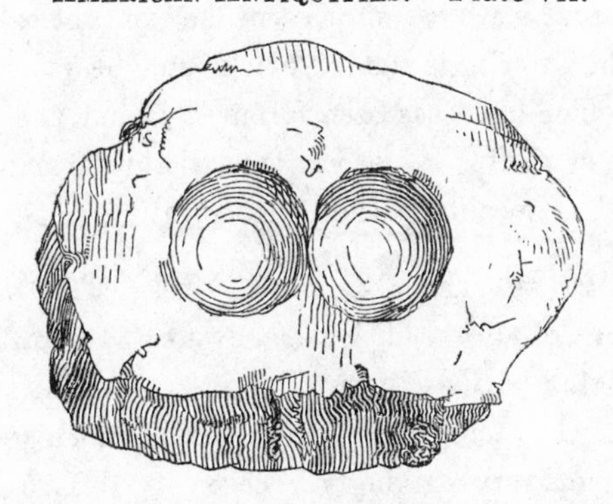

* From the Algonquin JEEGUN, an instrument, an implement, or any artificial contrivance, or invention.

CLASS FOURTH.—OPOAGUNA.

The class of antique pipes. Smoking pipes, constitute a branch of Indian art, which called forth their ingenuity by carvings of various forms of steatite, serpentine, indurated clay, limestone, sandstone and other bodies. A very favorite material was the red sedimentary compact deposit, found on the high dividing ridge between the Missouri and Mississippi, called the Coteau du Prairie. Pipes were also made from clay, tempered with some siliceous or felspathique material, similar to that used in their ancient earthenware.

OPOAGUNA ALGONQUIN.—Fig. 1. AM. ANT. Plate VIII.

1.

The composition of this pipe is a compact brown clay, tempered with a fine siliceous matter, and dried in the sun, not baked in a potter's oven. The exterior is stained black, and bears a certain gloss, not a glazing. The bowl has been formed by hand, and is rude. The principal point of skill is evinced in the twist ornamenting the exterior of the bowl. Locality, Genesee river valley.

OPOAGUNA AZTEEK. Fig. 3, plate VIII. The material is a species of Terra Cotta, or reddish earthenware. Its fracture discloses very minute shining particles, which appear to be mica. Probably the ingredient used to temper the clay, was pounded granite. The features resemble, very strikingly, those of Mexico and central America, figured by Mr. Catherwood & Stephens. Onondaga county.

AMERICAN ANTIQUITIES—Plate VIII.

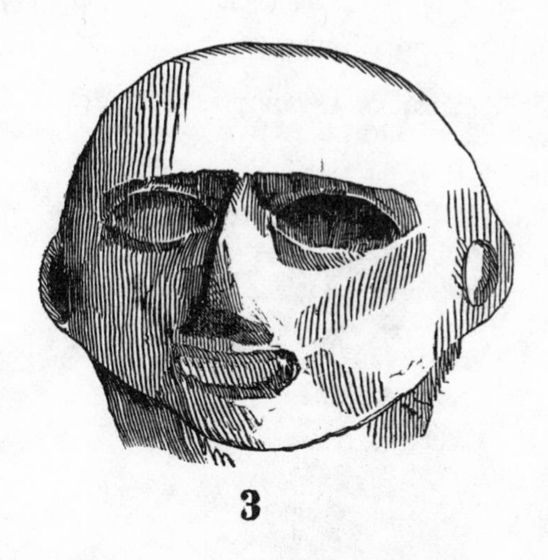

3

OPAGUNA IBERIC. Fig. 1. Plate IX. Material, a slate coloured ware. Features, thin and sharp. Neck, acute in front, with an angular line extending from the chin downwards. Onondaga.

AMERICAN ANTIQUITIES.—Plate IX.

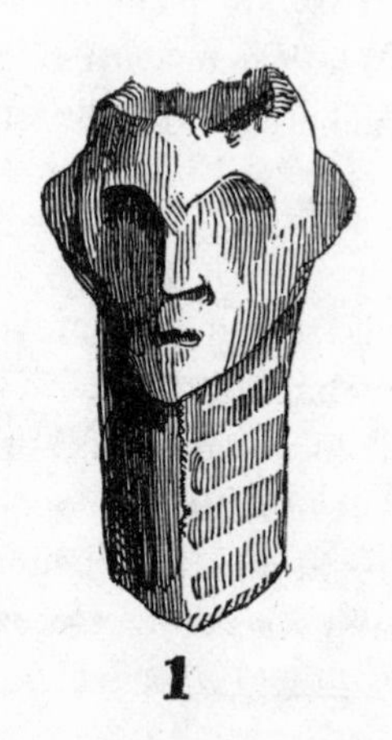

1

OPOAGUNA ETRUSCAN. Fig. 2. Plate X. Material similar to O. Azteek. Figure double headed—heads alike, placed back to back, like the Grecian deity Janus, connected by five parallel fillets,--bowl rudely formed, by hand. Onondaga.

AMERICAN ANTIQUITIES.—Plate X.

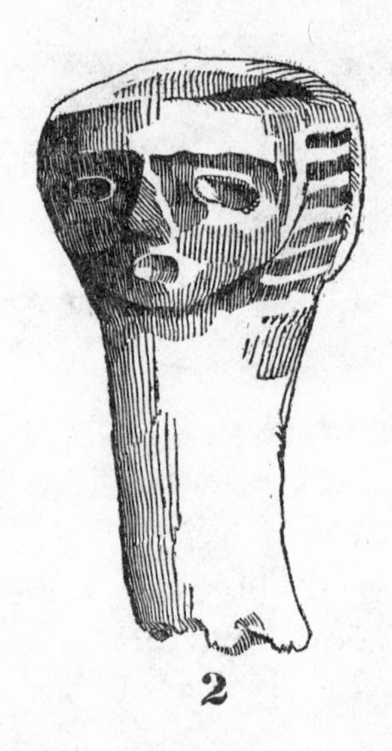

2

CLASS FIFTH.—MINACE.*

Articles of this kind hold the relative character of modern beads or necklace ornaments. They are made of shells, bones, fissile minerals, sometimes pieces of calcareous or fissile crystal. The substitutes of the European period are glass and pastes.

MINACE ALLEGHANIC. Fig. 6, Plate I. This article was first disclosed on opening the Grave Creek mound, in the Ohio valley, in 1839, and received the false designation of "ivory." It is figured and described in the first volume of the Transactions of the American Ethnological Society, published at New-York in 1845, where its character is determined. It has often the appearance of having been formed of solid masses of horn. It is believed to be, however, in any case, a product of massy sea-shell. Decomposition gives its sur-

* From Meen, a berry; and ace, a diminutive; hence minas or minace, a bead, or an ornament for the neck.

face a dead white aspect and limy feel. The powder scraped from the surface effervesces in acids. It is generally, not uniformly, an exact circle, and resembles extremely a very thick horn button-mould. It is characteristic of the orifice, that it appears to have been perforated with an instrument giving a spiral or circular line. This ancient ornament was also disclosed in my visit to the Beverly bone deposits of Canada in 1843. Its occurrence, in Onondaga, denotes the universality of the art, during the ante-European period.

Class Sixth.—PEÄGA.*

The ancient species of this article are numerous, and not exclusively confined to sea shells. The Indian cemeteries denote it in the form of bone and mineral.

Peäga Iowan. Fig. 7, Plate 2. The material in this species is the red pipe stone of the west, so much valued. It is perforated longitudinally, and was evidently worn about the neck and breast like the modern article of wampum.

Class Seventh.—MUDWÄMINA.

Ornament alone appears to have been the object of this numerous class of remains. Generally the object was the production of a jingling sound in walking. It was generally used to decorate some part of the dress. It assumed a great variety of shapes, and was made from as many species of material, including native copper. Another object was to inspire fear by the tread.

Mudwämina Miskwabic.† Fig. 11, Plate I. The article figured is three-fourths of an inch in length, bell shaped, and composed of native copper, beat very thin. Onondaga.

Mudwämina Ossinic.‡ Fig. 8, Plate 2. Material, red pipe stone, perforated. Onondaga.

Mudwämina Wassäabic. Fig. 9, Plate 2. Material, a crystal, perforated. Traces of its irridescence. Probably a crystal of strontian. Onondaga.

---

* From *Peag,* one of the sea-coast terms of the Algonquins, for wampum.

† Copper. ‡ Stone.

CLASS EIGHTH.—OTOAUGUNA.

The name is derived from *Otowug*, meaning implements of, or relating to the ear. It is a noun inanimate in *a*. Under this head all pendants and ornaments for the ear are comprised.

OTOAUGUNA STATUESQUE. Fig. 3, Plate IV. This pendant for the ear is made out of sea shell. It bears eight perpendicular and four transverse dots. Locality, old fort, site near Jamesville. Onondaga.

2

OTOAUGUNA PYRAMIDAL. Fig. 2, Plate I. This article varies in size, in the specimens examined, from nine-tenths to one and five-tenths inch, in the greatest length. It is an inequilateral triangle, generally, as here shown, varying to a very acute truncated prism reversed. Thickness from four to six lines. Perforated. Material, red pipe stone. Locality, Onondaga county.

OTOAUGUNA BIFURCATE. Fig. 4, Plate I. Length eight-tenths inch. Perforated. Red pipe stone. Onondaga county.

OTOAUGUNA QUADRALATERAL. Fig. 5, Plate 2. Material, red pipe stone. Onondaga county.

CLASS NINTH.—ÆS.*

The number and variety of sea and sometimes fresh water shells worn by the ancient aborigines, has not been ascertained, but is large. They are uniformly found to be univalves.

ÆS MARGINELLA. Fig. 10, Plate I. This species was first detected in the Grave Creek mound. It is a marginella. The figure is, incidentally, inexact. Onondaga.

---

* Æs, a generic name for a shell—Algonquin.

Class Tenth.—OCHALIS.*

This class of ornaments were worn as pendants from the inner cartilage of the nose. The material of nose-jewels in modern times, when worn, is, generally, silver or some metal. Anciently bone or shell were the chief substances.

Ochalis Ödä-ä.† Plate 1, Fig. 3. The material is a part of some massy species of sea shell. The outer coating is partially decomposed, exhibiting an opaque, limy appearance. Length, eight-tenths of an inch—rounded, heart-shaped. Onondaga. [J. V. V. Clarke.]

* From the Shawanoe word *Ochali*, a nose. † Heart-shaped, or like.

VII. ORAL TRADITIONS OF THE IROQUOIS—HISTORICAL AND SYMBOLICAL.

This department of the inquiry constitutes one of deep and varied interest. It is found, however, that no little time is required to study, compare and arrange such parts of the matter as have claims to be considered historical, whilst those which are symbolical or fictitious, take so wide a range as hardly to justify, in this report, the space which they would occupy. Specimens drawn from both classes of matter are introduced in the following papers, which, together with those inserted under the first head of "Minutes," will serve to convey a proper idea of this species of lore.

[*a.*] Ancient Shipwreck of a vessel from the old world on the coast.

Whilst the northern tribes lived under the ancient confederacy before named, on the banks of the St. Lawrence and its waters, and before they had yet known white men, it is affirmed that a foreign ship came on the northern coasts, but being driven by stress of weather, passed southward, and was wrecked in that quarter. Most of the crew perished, but a few of them, dressed in leather, reached the shore, and were saved with some of their implements. They were received by a people called the Falcons,* who conducted them to a mountain, where, however, they remained but a short time, for their allies, the Falcons, disclosed an unfriendly and jealous spirit, and threatened them. In consequence they immediately selected another location, which they fortified. Here they lived many years, became

* One of the totems and clans of the Iroquois, is the hawk, or falcon.

numerous and extended their settlements, but in the end, they were destroyed by furious nations.

This tradition is divested of some of the symbolic traits which it possesses in the original, and by which the narrators may be supposed to have concealed their own, acts of hostility or cruelty, in the extirpation of the descendants of the Europeans thus cast on their shores. To this end, they represent in the original, the saving of the crew to have been done through the instrumentality of carniverous birds, and attribute the final destruction of the colony to fierce animals. It is one of the well known facts of history that none of the vessels of Columbus, Cabot, Verrizani, Sir Walter Raleigh, or Hudson, were *wrecked* on the American coasts : and there is hence a bare presumption that some *earlier* voyage or adventure from the old world is alluded to.

Can we suppose that in this dim tradition there is light cast on the lost colony of Virginia, which was first left on the island of Roanoke? The Tuscaroras,* who preserve the tradition, came to western New-York from that quarter. They were a fierce, powerful and warlike nation, having in 1712 resolved on the massacre, on a certain day, of all the whites in the Carolinas. What is once done by natives, barbarous or civilized, is often the reproduction of some prior national act, and especially if that act had been attended with success ; and it is by no means improbable that in this desperate and bloody resolve of 1712, the Tuscaroras meant to repeat the prior tragedy of "Croatan."* Whether, however, the incident be of ante-Columbian or post-Columbian date, it is worthy preservation, and may be assigned its place and proper importance when we have gleaned more facts from the dark abyss of American antiquity.

[*b*.] Forays into the country of the Cherokees and Catawbas.

Nothing is more distinct or better settled in the existing traditions of the Iroquois, than their wars with some of the southern tribes,

* This tribe have also the clan of the hawk or falcon.

† Vide Hackluit.

particularly the Cherokees. I found this subject first alluded to among the Oneidas, who were hotly engaged in this southern war; afterwards among the Onondagas, the Senecas of Tonawanda, the Tuscaroras, and with still increasing particularity, among the Senecas of Buffalo, Cattaraugus, and Teonigono. But I was never able to fix the era of its commencement, or to find an adequate cause for it. It seems almost incredible that a war of this kind should have been carried on, at such a great distance from their central council fire at Onondaga, yet nothing is better established in their reminiscences.

They first came into contact, as Tetoyoah told me was his opinion, in the western prairies. The Iroquois are known to have hunted and warred far and wide in that quarter. The two nations seem to have been deeply and mutually exasperated. Tetoyoah spoke of an act of horrid treachery, the breaking of a peace pledge, and the murder of a peace deputation.

The war, however, instead of calling out the banded energies of the confederacy, appears to have been almost entirely one of a partizan character. It is memorable rather for partial enterprizes and personal exploits, than for exhibiting the grander features of the military policy of the Iroquois. Warriors tested their bravery and heroism by going against the Cherokees. There were, it seems, no great armies, no grand battles. All was left to individual energy and courage. The great object of every young Iroquois, as soon as he was old enough to take the war path, was to go against the Cherokees. A march from the Oneida stone, the Kasonda creek, or the Genesee valley, to the southern Alleghanies, was regarded as a mere excursion or scouting trip. This long journey was performed without provisions, or any other preparation than bows, arrows and clubs. The fewer there were in one of these partizan enterprizes, the greater was their chance of concealment and success. They relied on the forest for food. Thousands of miles were not sufficient to dampen their ardor, and no time could blot out their hatred. They called the Cherokees, by way of derision, WE YAU DAH, and O YAU DAH, meaning a people who live in caves. These are the terms I found to be in use for the Cherokee nation, in 1845.

[*c*.] Exploit of Hi-a-de-o-ni.

The following incident in the verbal annals of Iroquois hardihood and heroism, was related to me by the intelligent Seneca TETOYOAH, (William Jones of Cattaraugus) along with other reminiscences of the ancient Cherokee wars. The Iroquois thought life was well lost, if they could gain glory by it.

HI-A-DE-O-NI, said he, was the father of the late chief Young King. He was a Seneca warrior, a man of great prowess, dexterity, and swiftness of foot, and had established his reputation for courage and skill, on many occasions. He resolved, while the Senecas were still living on the Genesee river, to make an incursion alone into the country of the Cherokees. He plumed himself with the idea, that he could distinguish himself in this daring adventure, and he prepared for it, according to the custom of warriors. They never encumber themselves with baggage. He took nothing but his arms, and the meal of a little parched and pounded corn.* The forest gave him his meat.

HI-A-DE-O-NI reached the confines of the Cherokee country in safety and alone. He waited for evening before he entered the precincts of a village. He found the people engaged in a dance. He watched his opportunity, and when one of the dancers went out from the ring into the bushes, he despatched him with his hatchet. In this way he killed two men that night, in the skirts of the woods, without exciting alarm, and took their scalps and retreated. It was late when he came to a lodge, standing remote from the rest, on his course homeward. Watching here, he saw a young man come out, and killed him as he had done the others, and took his scalp. Looking into the lodge cautiously, he saw it empty, and ventured in with the hope of finding some tobacco and ammunition, to serve him on his way home.

* One table spoonful of this mixed with sugar and water will sustain a warrior twenty-four hours without meat.

While thus busied in searching the lodge, he heard footsteps at the door, and immediately threw himself on the bed from which the young man had risen, and covered his face, feigning sleep. They proved to be the footsteps of his last victim's mother. She, supposing him to be her son, whom she had a short time before left lying there, said, "My son, I am going to such a place, and will not be back till morning." He made a suitable response, and the old woman went out. Insensibly he fell asleep, and knew nothing till morning, when the first thing he heard was the mother's voice. She, careful for her son, was at the fireplace very early, pulling some roasted squashes out of the ashes, and after putting them out, and telling him, she left them for him to eat; she went away. He sprang up instantly, and fled; but the early dawn had revealed his inroad, and he was hotly pursued. Light of foot, and having the start, he succeeded in reaching and concealing himself in a remote piece of woods, where he laid till night, and then pursued his way towards the Genesee, which, in due time he reached, bringing his three Cherokee scalps as trophies of his victory and prowess.

Such are the traditionary facts which are yet repeated by the Iroquois, to console their national pride in their decline. The incident reminds one strongly of the class of daring personal deeds of the noted Adirondack PISKARET, as related by Colden; and it demonstrates how soon the daring traits of one ruling tribe may be adopted and even surpassed by another.

The Tonawandas, who are Senecas, appear to have preserved more distinct recollections of the origin of this war. HOHOEEYUH,* stated to me, as did TETOYOAH, that it originated from the contact of their hunting parties on the plains of the southwest. But the latter affirms, that the Cherokees were the original offenders, by robbing and plundering a Seneca hunting party, and taking away their skins. Retaliation ensued. Tragic scenes of surprise and treachery soon followed. The Five Nations took up the matter in all their strength. They, contrary to what is above intimated, raised large war-parties, and marched through the country to the Cherokee borders, and brought away scalps and prisoners. There are now, he added, descendants of the Cherokees in the third degree

---

* J. A. Sandford.

living on the Tonawanda reservation. Le Fort, an Onondaga chief, speaking on the same subject, said that there was, some years ago, a chief of pure Cherokee blood, by father and mother, living among them. He had been taken captive when a mere child. The fact being revealed to him after he had obtained the chieftaincy, he went to seek his relatives in the south, and to live and die among them; but after every inquiry, he was unable to find them. The memory of the event of his loss was forgotten. He lingered a time, and then came back to the Senecas, and died among them—an example of that severe principle in the policy of this people, which has been before referred to, under the term of WE HAIT WA TSHA, *i. e.* flesh cut in pieces, and scattered amongst the tribes.

Iroquois tradition on this subject is the same now that it was in 1794. During this year, the interpreters told Col. Timothy Pickering, who was a commissioner on the part of the United States, that there were then living, warriors of the Six Nations, who had marched the whole distance to the Cherokee county, and attacked the latter. In proof of the former wars, they showed him a chief, who was a native Cherokee, born in the Cherokee country, who had been captured when a boy, and invested with this honor in mature life by the Senecas.* While the foregoing tradition of living Iroquois is strengthened by this coincidence, we are, at the same time, furnished by the latter with a proof that the Iroquois policy was favorable to the rise of talent and bravery, and that whatever be the checks provided by the TOTEMIC SYSTEM, on the descent of chiefs, the elective feature was ever strongly marked upon their entire government and policy.

---

* Yates and Moulton, p. 232.

[*d.*] Embassy of Peace to the Cherokees, and Daring Feat of a Seneca.

In the course of the long and fierce war between the Six Nations and the Cherokees, it happened, said Oliver Silverheels, that eight Senecas determined to go on an embassy of peace. Among them was LITTLE BEARD, the elder, and Jack Berry. They met some Cherokees on the confines of the Cherokee territories, to whom they imparted their object. Intelligence of this interview was sent forward to their village, where the ambassadors were duly received, and after this preliminary reception, they were introduced to the ruling chiefs, and favorably received by the Cherokee council.

All but *one* of the Cherokee chiefs agreed to the terms of peace He also would consent, if, prior to the treaty, the eight Seneca delegates would first consent to go to war against their enemies, situated south of them. [Who their enemies were is not mentioned.] They consented, and set out with a war party. A fight ensued in which the leader of the Senecas, called AWL, was taken prisoner. The other seven escaped. The fate of Awl was decided in the enemies camp, where it was determined that he should be burned at the stake. Preparations were made for this purpose, but as they were about to bind him, he claimed the privilege of a warrior, to sing his death song and recite his exploits by striking the post. Pleased with the spirit of his request, and his noble air and words, his suit was granted, and they put a tomahawk into his hands, that he might go through the ceremony. He began by relating his exploits in the north. He recited his feats against the western Indians, adding, with the usual particularity, times and places, and the number of scalps taken. They were pleased and interested in these recitals, and quite forgot the prisoner, in the warrior. At last he came to the late battle, in which he was taken. He told how many of the Catabas, Apalaches, or Muscogees (if these were the tribes) he had killed. He kindled with redoubled ardor as he struck the post with his tomahawk, exclaiming, "so many of your own people, I have killed," and suiting his actions to his words, "so many I will yet kill." With this he struck down two men, bounded through the ring and ran. Consternation, for a moment, prevented pursuit, which gave him a start. Being swift of foot he outran his pursuers, eluded them in the woods, and reached the Cherokee camp, where he found and joined his seven companions.

They concluded the peace, and returned in safety to the Seneca country.

[e.] The Graveyard Serpent and Corn Giant.

Seneca tradition states that they formerly lived on the Chippewa river, near Niagara Falls, Canada. One year, while thus located, they were visited by a calamitous sickness, and their corn was blighted. Their prophet dreamt, one night, that a great serpent laid under the village, with his head to the graveyard, and that it devoured all the bodies buried. This gave a most offensive breath, which was the cause of the sickness.

He also dreamt that there was a great giant under the cornfield, who ate up the corn.

When he revealed these dreams to the chiefs, they determined to abandon the town, and immediately removed to Buffalo creek. The serpent soon followed them, and entered the mouth of the creek; but the Great Spirit, whose especial favorites they ever were, sent lightning to destroy it. The monster, however, proceeded up the stream, until the arrows from above fell so thick, that he was obliged to turn. His great size made him press against the shores, and break off the ground, and this is the cause of the expanse of the river three miles above its mouth. Before he reached the mouth of the stream, however, the arrows had cut him apart and thus they escaped this scourge.

When they went back to visit their old town on the Chippewa river, they found the giant who had eaten up the corn, hanging by one leg from the crotch of a high lodge pole, with his body on the ground. He was very meagre, and had very long and thin legs, with scarcely any flesh on them. [*W. I. C. Hosmer.*]

[If the above is to be regarded, as it clearly must, as an allegory of sickness and famine, it would have put Greek fancy to the task, to have concentrated the matter in a smaller compass, or to have exhibited it in a more striking light.]

[*f*.] Allusion to the siege of Fort-Stanwix and the Battle of Oriskany.

Seneca tradition is rife on this subject. Tetayoah says that they lost thirty-three chiefs in the battle of Oriskany.

Jacob Blacksnake adds, that he has seen a book in which it was stated that the Senecas had burned eight officers taken at this battle, in revenge for their losses. This he contradicts, on the authority of his father, Governor Blacksnake, who was there. The officers had been asked for after the battle, by the British; but they were refused, on account of their great losses. They were not, however, burned at the stake. It was decided that they should run the gauntlet, and they were killed by clubs, &c. in this ordeal.

[g.] Defeat of the Kah-Kwahs on Buffalo creek.

Some of the Senecas affirm, that it is ninety years since the battle with the Kah-Kwahs, on the site of the grave yard, on the Buffalo creek reservation, was fought. This would place the event in 1755, a date so modern, and so well known, in our colonial history, as to prove what a poor figure they make in attempts to adjust chronology. If 190 years [and, perhaps, such should be the tradition,] be taken, the event (allowing two years for their defence) would assume the precise time [1655] indicated for it, by one of Le Moyne's missionary letters, in which he says, that the war with the Eries had broken out afresh in 1653.

[*h.*] Era of the Confederation.

There is a tradition among portions of the Senecas, that the present confederation took place four years before Hudson sailed up the river bearing his name. This gives A. D. 1605. This question has been examined in its general bearings in a prior paper. All other authorities *indicate an earlier* date.

[*i.*] Some passages of the traditions of their wars with monsters, giants and supernatural phenomena.

It is proposed to narrate a few passages of their early wars with monsters and giants, the two prominent objects in the foreground of their traditions. If it be thought, in perusing them, that mythology and superstition mingle too freely with real events or actions, to which the mind makes no exception, that is a matter upon which we have nothing to offer. Let it rather be considered as a proof of the authenticity of the narrative; for certainly there could be no stronger indication of a contrary character, than to find the Indian narrator relating a clear, consistent chain of indisputable facts and deductions, to fill up the foreground of his history. What is said of such creations tallies admirably with their belief, at the present day, and harmonizes with itself, and with that state of proud heathendom, adventurous idolatry, and wild and roving independence in which they lived. Who but an Aonaod ? who but an Iroquois ? could enact such a part, or believe that his ancestors ever did ? To be great, and admired and feared, they roved over half America in quest of beasts and men. Surely, the man should be allowed to tell his own story in his own way, with all the witchcraft and spirit-craft he has a mind to bring to bear upon it.

No people in the world have ever, probably, so completely mingled up and lost their early history, in fictions and allegories, types and symbols, as the red men of this continent. Making no sort of distinction themselves, between the symbolic and the historical, they have left no distinctions to mark the true from the false. Their notions of a Deity, founded, apparently, upon some dreamy tradition of original truth, are so subtile and divisible, and establish so heterogenous a connection, between spirit and matter, of all imaginable forms, that popular belief seems to have wholly confounded the possible with the impossible, the natural with the supernatural. Action, so far as respects cause and effect, takes the widest and wildest range, through the agency of good or evil influences, which are put in motion alike for noble or ignoble ends—alike by men, beasts, devils or gods. Seeing some things mysterious and wonderful, he believes all things mysterious and wonderful; and he is afloat, without shore or compass, on the wildest sea of superstition and necromancy. He sees a god in every phenomenon and fears a sorcerer in every enemy. Life, under such a system of polytheism and wild belief, is a constant scene of fears and alarms. Fear is the predominating passion, and he is ready, wherever he goes, to sacrifice at any altar, be the supposed deity ever so grotesque. When such a man comes to narrate events, he stops at nothing, be it ever so gross or puerile. He relates just what he believes, and unluckily he believes every thing that can possibly be told. A beast or a bird, or a man, or a god, or a devil, a stone, a serpent, or a wizzard, a wind or a sound, or a ray of light—these are so many causes of action, which the meanest and lowest of the series, may put in motion, but which shall, in his theology and philosophy, vibrate along the mysterious chain through the uppermost skies; and life or death may, at any moment, be the reward or the penalty. If there be truth, mingled in the man's narrations, as there sometimes is, it must be judged of by the lights of reason, common sense, science, sound philosophy and religion. It is a gordian knot for the modern historian to untie; or it is a mass of traditionary chaff, from which we may, perhaps, winnow a few grains of wheat. Herodotus had, probably, just such materials to work upon, and he made the best possible use of them, by letting the events stand as they were given, without exercising any inductive faculty upon them, or telling us the why and the wherefore; or if he ever deviates from the rule, as in the case of the fishes descending the Nile, it is a species of labor which might as well have been omitted.*

* It was designed, when these preliminary remarks were penned, to add some wilder legends than are here presented, which are, at present, withheld.

By the figure of a long house, the Iroquois meant to denote the confederated frame work of the league ; by a great tree planted, they symbolized its deep seated natural power, one in blood and lineage, and its overshadowing influence and permanency. To assail such a combination of stout hearts, nature they thought must send forth the stoutest and most appaling objects of her creation.

The first enemy that appeared to question their power, or disturb their peace, was the fearful phenomenon of Ko-nea-rau-neh-neh, or the Flying Heads. These heads were enveloped in a beard and hair, flaming like fire ; they were of monstrous size, and shot through the air with the velocity of meteors. Human power was not adequate to cope with them. The priests pronounced them an emanation of some mysterious influence, and it remained with the priests alone, to exorcise them by their arts. Drum and rattle and incantation, were deemed more effective, than arrow or club. One evening, after they had been plagued a long time with this fearful visitation, the Flying Head came to the door of a lodge occupied by a single female and her dog. She was sitting composedly before the fire roasting acorns, which, as they become done, she deliberately took from the fire and eat. Amazement seized the flying head, who put out two huge black paws, from beneath his streaming beard. Supposing the woman to be eating *live* coals he withdrew, and from that time he came no more among them.*

The withdrawal of the Ko-nea-rau-neh-neh, was followed by the appearance of the great ONYARE,† or Lake Serpent, which traversed the country, and by coiling himself in leading positions near the paths, interrupted the communication between the towns. He created terror wherever he went, and diffused a poisonous breath.

While this enemy yet remained in the land, and they were councelling about the best means of killing him, or driving him away, the country was invaded by a still more fearful enemy, namely : the OT-NE-YAR-HEH, or Stonish Giants. They were a powerful tribe from the wilderness, tall, fierce and hostile, and resistance to them was vain. They defeated and overwhelmed an army which was sent out

---

*For a poetic use of this tradition of the Heads and Stonish Giants, see Hoffman's Wild Scenes, vol. 1, page 82. New-York edition of 1843.

† Mohawk.

against them, and put the whole country in fear. These giants were not only of prodigious strength, but they were cannibals, devouring men, women and children in their inroads.

It is said by the Shawnees, that they were descended from a certain family, which journeyed on the east side of the Mississippi, after the vine broke, and they went towards the northwest. Abandoned to wandering and the hardships of the forest, they forgot the rules of humanity, and began at first, to eat raw flesh, and next men. They practiced rolling themselves in the sand, and by this means their bodies were covered with hard skin, so that the arrows of the Iroquois only rattled against their rough bodies, and fell at their feet. And the consequence was, that they were obliged to hide in caves, and glens, and were brought into subjection by these fierce invaders for many winters, (or years.) At length the Holder of the Heavens, visited his people, and finding that they were in great distress, he determined to grant them relief, and rid them entirely of these barbarous invaders. To accomplish this, he changed himself into one of these giants, and brandishing his heavy club, led them on, under the pretence of finding the Akonoshioni. When they had got near to their strong hold at Onondaga, night coming on, he bid them lie down in a hollow, telling them that he would make the attack at the customary hour, at day-break. But at day break, having ascended a height, he overwhelmed them with a vast mass of rocks, where their forms may yet be seen. Only one escaped to carry the news of their dreadful fate, and he fled towards the north.

They were thus relieved, and began to live in more security, but the great ON-YAR-HE, or Lake Serpent, was yet in the country. Alarmed by what Tarenyawagon had done to relieve his people, and fearing for himself, he withdrew to the lakes, where he and his brood were destroyed with thunder bolts, or compelled to retire to deep water.

The Five Families were so much molested with giants and monsters, that they were compelled to build forts to protect themselves. The manner of doing it was this : they built fires against trees, and then used their stone axes to pick off the charred part ; in this way, by renewing the fire, they soon felled them ; and the fallen trunks were burned off in suitable lengths, in the same way, and then set up according to the size and plan of the fort, a bank of earth being piled outside and inside. They left two gates, one to get water, and the other as a sally port. [D.]

For some time after the great ON-YAR-HE had left the country, they had peace ; but in after years a still more terrific enemy came. It had a man's head on the body of a great serpent. This terrific foe took his position on the path between the Onondagas and Cayugas, and thus cut off all intercourse between their towns, for this was also the great thoroughfare of the five families, or nations. The bravest warriors were mustered to attack him with spears, darts and clubs. They approached him on all sides with yells. A terrible battle ensued ; the monster raged furiously, but he was at last pierced in a vital place, and finally killed. This triumph was celebrated in songs and dances, and the people were consoled. They hunted again in peace, but after a time rumors began to be rife of the appearance of an extraordinary and ferocious animal in various places, under the name of the great O-YAL-KHER, or mammoth bear. One morning, while a party of hunters were in their camp, near the banks of a lake, in the Oneida country, they were alarmed by a great tumult breaking out from the lake. Going to see the cause of this extraordinary noise, they saw the monster on the bank rolling down stones and logs into the water, and exhibiting the utmost signs of rage. Another great animal of the cat kind, with great paws, came out of the water, and seized the bear. A dreadful fight ensued ; in the end the bear was worsted and retired, horribly lamed. The next day the hunters ventured out to the spot, where they found one of the fore legs of the bear. It was so heavy that two men were required to lift it, but they found it was palateable food and made use of it, for their warriors believe that it inspires courage to eat of fierce and brave animals.

After a while, a great pestiferous and annoying creature of the insect tribe, appeared about the forts at Onondaga, in the guise of the GE-NE-UN-DAH SAIS-KE, or huge musqueto. It first appeared in the Onondaga country. It flew about the fort with vast wings, making a loud noise, with a long stinger, and on whomsoever it lighted, it sucked out his blood and killed him. Many warriors were killed in this way, and all attempts made to subdue it were abortive, till Tarenyawagon, or the Holder of the Heavens, was on a visit one day to the ruler of the Onondagas. The giant musquito happened to come flying about the fort, as usual at this time. Tarenyawagon attacked it, but such was its rapidity of flight that he could scarcely keep in sight of it. He chased it around the border of the great lakes, towards sun-setting, and round the great country at large, east and west. At last he overtook it and killed it near Gen-an-do-a, or the salt lake of Onondaga. From the blood flowing out on this occasion, the present species of small musquitoes originated.

VIII. TOPICAL INQUIRIES.

The state of the book trade, and the importation of books into this country, but a few years ago, were such as to offer but scanty advantages to the pursuit of historical letters. There were but few libraries deserving of notice, and these were placed at remote points, spread over a very extensive geographical area, where access became often difficult or impossible. By far the largest number of American libraries were limited to a few thousand volumes, often a few hundreds only, and these were chiefly made up of common or elementary works on arts, sciences and general literature. Writers were compelled to consult works at second hand, and could seldom get access to scarce and valuable originals ; and the difficulties of making original inquiries into archæology, antiquities, philology, and other more asbtruse, or less popular topics, increased at every step, and were in fact insurmountable to men of ordinary means. This state of things will sufficiently account for the low state of historical letters up to within a comparatively short period, without impugning the judgment or sagacity of early observers, on our local and distinctive history ; and offers also a rational plea why the aboriginal branch of our antiquities, and the just expanding science of ethnology, has been left enshrouded in so much darkness and historical mystery. We have, in fact, not had the means of making such inquiries. The libraries at Harvard, the public collection set on foot by Franklin at Philadelphia, the library of Congress, and that of the New-York Historical Society, and perhaps the growing library of the State Capitol at Albany, are some of the chief collections yet made in the Union ; and these might be conveniently stowed away, *en masse*, in one corner of the " Bibliotheque Royal " at Paris, without exciting notice.

[a.] Who were the Eries?

Louis Hennepin, who was a Recollect, remarks in the original Amsterdam edition of his travels of 1698, that Canada was first discovered by the Spanish, alluding doubtless to the voyage of Cortereal and that it received its first missionaries under the French, from the order of Recollects. These pioneers of the cross, according to this author, made themselves very acceptable to the Hurons or Wyandots, who occupied the banks of the St. Lawrence, and who informed them that the Iroquois pushed their war parties beyond Virginia and New-Sweden, and other parts remote from their cantons. They went, he says, in these wars, near to a lake, which they called Erige or Erie.* Now, if they went "beyond Virginia and New-Sweden," they were very remote from Lake Erie, and the assertion implies a contradiction or some ignorance of the geography of the country. This name in the Huron language, he informs us, signifies the Cat, or Nation of the Cat—a name, he says, which it derived from the fact that the Iroquois in returning to their cantons, brought the Erige or Erike, captives through it. The Canadians softened this word to ERIE. It would appear then, that the Eries either did not occupy the immediate banks of the lake, or else they lived on the upper or more remote parts of it. To be brought captives through it, they must have been embarked at some distance from its lower extremity. This vague mode of expression leaves a doubt as to the actual place of residence of this conquered and, so called, extinct tribe. Whether extinct or not, is not certain. The name is only a Wyandot name. They had others.

From inquiries made among the Senecas, they are, some believe, the same people whom this nation call KAH-KWAHS. But we do not advance much by changing one term for another. The inquiry returns, who were the Kah-Kwahs? Seneca tradition affirms that they lived on the banks of Lake Erie, extending eastward towards the Genesee river, and westward indefinitely; and that they were finally conquered in a war, which was closed by a disastrous battle, the locality of which is not fixed; after which they were chased

---

* Vide Appendix.

west, and the remnant driven down the Alleghany river. [See the subsequent paper *d.*]

Cusick, the Tuscarora archæologist, who writes the word "Squawkihows," intimates that these were an affiliated people, and that the remnant after their defeat, were incorporated with the Senecas. [D.]

Colden states that after the war with the Adirondacks broke out, say at the end of the 16th century, the Iroquois, to try their courage, went to war against a nation called Satanas,* who lived on the banks of the lakes, whom they defeated and conquered, which raised their spirits so much, that they afterwards renewed the war against the Adirondacks and Hurons† on the St. Lawrence, and finally prevailed against them. [Hist. Five Nations, p. 23, Lond. ed. 1767.]

Satanas, it appears from the same author, is a name for the Shaouanons, Shawanoes, or Shawnees, as the term is variously written; a tribe, it may be further remarked, who are called *Chât* by the modern Canadian French.

A letter of the missionary Le Moyne, published in the Missionary "Relacions," and hereto appended, proves that the war with the Eries, whatever may have been its origin or former state, had newly broken out in 1653, and there are references of a subsequent date to denote that by the year 1655, this war had terminated in the disastrous overthrow of this people. They appear to have been then located where the existing traditions of the Senecas place them, namely, west of Genesee river, and at or near Buffalo. We may suppose that up to this period, the Senecas were limited to the eastern banks of the Genesee. And it was probably the results of this war that transferred their council fire from the present site of Geneva or Canandaigua to the Genesee valley.

---

* This word appears to be an English *soubriquet*, derived from the Dutch language, and is from Satan, a synonyme for Duivel. [See Jansen's new Pocket Dictionary, Dortracht 1831.] The plural inflection in *a*, if this derivation be correct, is duplicated in its meaning, by the corresponding English inflection in *s*, a practice quite conformable to English orthœpy, which puts its vernacular plural to foreign plurals, as Cherubims for Cherubim, &c.

† Called Quatoghies by the Iroquois.

When La Salle reached the Niagara river in 1679, but twenty-four years after the close of this Erie war, he found the entire country on its eastern or American banks in the possession of the Senecas. [J.] The history and fate of the Eries was then a tradition.

We may here drop the inquiry to be resumed at a future period.

[*b*.] Building of the first vessel on the upper lakes.

The enterprise of Sa Salle, in constructing a vessel above the falls of Niagara, in 1679, to facilite his voyage to the Illinois and the Mississippi, is well known ; but while the fact of his having thus been the pioneer of naval architecture on the upper lakes, is familliar to historical readers, the particular *place* of its construction, has been matter of various opinions. Gen. Cass in his historical discourse, places it at Erie ; Mr. Bancroft in his history, designates the mouth of the Tonawanda. Mr. Sparks in the biography of Marquette, decides to place it on the Canadian side of the Niagara. These variances result in a measure from the vague and jarring accounts of the narrators, whose works had been consulted in some instances in abridged or mutilated translations, and not from doubt or ambiguity in the missionary "Letters."

Literary associations in America, who aimed to increase the means of reference to standard works, began their labors in feebleness. The New-York Historical Society, which dates its origin in 1804, and has vindicated its claims to be the pioneer of historical letters in America, published Tonti's account of the Chevalier La Salle's enterprise, in one of the volumes of its first series. It is since known, however, that this account was a bookseller's compilation from, it is believed generally correct sources, but it was disclaimed by Tonti. It is at least but an abreviation, and cannot be regarded as an o.iginal work.

In 1820, the American Antiquarian Society published in their first volume of collections, an account of Hennepin discoveries, which is known to bibliographers to be a translation of a mere abridgment of the original work, reduced to less than half its volume of matter. There was also an edition of this author, published in London in 1698; but still clipped of some of its matter, or otherwise defective; the tastes and wants of an English public being constantly consulted in the admission of continental books of this cast. The original work of Hennepin was published in French, at Amsterdam in 1698. Being of the order of Recollects, and not a Jesuit, there was much feeling and prejudice against him in France, of which Charlevoix, the accomplished historian of New-France, partook in no small degree. Yet whatever may have been the justice or injustice of these impeachments of the missionary's veracity, there could be no motive for disagreement in a fact of this kind.

Hennepin was the camp missionary of the party on the way to Illinois, and the companion of La Salle and Tonti on the occasion. By adverting to his narrative, in the appendix, the most satisfactory and circumstantial details on this subject will be found. The vessel, according to him, was built "two leagues above the falls," that is, about three miles above the present site of fort Schlosser, on Cayuga creek. There is no stream, at this distance, on the Canadian side. They reached the spot on the 22d of January, set up the keel on the 26th, and, after laboring all winter, amidst discouragements, during which the Senecas threatened to burn it, at one time, and refused to sell corn to support the workmen, at another, it was launched in the spring, and named the Griffin, "in allusion to the arms of the Count de Frotenac, which was supported by two griffins." The figure of a griffin adorned the prow, surmounted by an eagle, the symbolic type of the embryo power, which was destined, in due time, to sway the political destinies of the continent. There were seven small cannon, and thirty persons, including the crew. With great difficulty, and by the use of the *cordelle*, they ascended the rapids, the present site of Black-Rock, and finally, after many delays, they set sail, freighted with merchandize, on the 7th of August, 1679, just six months and twelve days after they had laid the keel. Thus the honor of furnishing the first vessel on our great chain of inland lakes, above the falls, is due to the present area of Niagara county, New-York. How this initiatory step has been followed up, in the course of one hundred and sixty-seven years, until these lakes are whitened by the canvass of the republic, and decorated with its self-moving palaces of wood and iron, under the guise of steamboats, it would be interesting to note. But we have no statistics of this kind to turn to. As an increment in such an inquiry, I subjoin, in the appendix, lists kept at my office, in the west, of the various species of vessels, which entered and departed from the remote little harbor of Michilimackinac, during the sailing seasons of 1839 and 1840, respectively.

[c.] Who were the Alleghans ?

This is an inquiry in our aboriginal archæology, which assumes a deeper interest, the more it is discussed. All the republic is concerned in the antiquarian knowledge and true etymology and history of an ancient race, to whom tradition attaches valor and power, and who have consecrated their name in American geography upon the most important range of mountains between the valley of the Mississippi, and the Atlantic. But the inquiry comes home to us with a local and redoubled interest, from the fact, that they occupied a large portion of the western area of the State, comprising the valley of the Alleghany river to its utmost source, and extending eastwardly an undefined distance. Even so late as 1727, Colden, in his history of the Five Nations, places them under the name of "Alleghens," on his map of this river. It is not certain that they did not anciently, occupy the country as far east and south as the junction of Allen's creek, with the Genesee. A series of old forts, anterior in age to the Iroquois power, extends along the shores of lake Erie, up to the system of water communication which has its outlet into the Alleghany through the Conewongo. There are some striking points of identity between the character of these antique military works, and those of the Ohio valley, and this coincidence is still more complete in the remains of ancient art found in the old Indian cemeteries, barrows and small mounds of western New-York, extending even as far east as the ancient Osco, now Auburn.

The subject is one worthy of full examination, who this ancient race were ? whence they came ? and whither they went ? are inquiries fraught with interest. We should not be led astray, or thrown off the track of investigation by the name. All the tribes, ancient and modern, have multiform names. This one of the Alleghans, probably fell upon the ears of the first settlers, but it is far from certain that it was their own term, while it is quite certain that it was not of the vocabulary of the bold northern race, the Iroquois, who impinged upon them. It has the character of an Algonquin word. Their descendants, whoever their ancestors were, may yet exist, under their own proper name, in the far west. The Iroquois, who pushed their conquests down the Alleghany and Ohio rivers after them, did not found a claim to territory further south on the Ohio river, than the mouth of the Kentucky. They pushed their war parties to the Catawba and Cherokee territories across the Alleghanies, and as far west as the Illinois. They swept over the whole region included between lakes Ontario, Erie and Huron, north. In the latter case we know it was a war against the tribes of the Algonquin stock, including one branch of another, and that their own generic stock, namely, the Quatoghies or Hurons.

The following communication on this subject, addressed to the Secretary of the Maryland Historical Society, is added in this connection. Although written to vindicate a question of antiquarian research, in a sister society, and partaking perhaps a little of a polemic cast, the facts are of permanent interest, and are thrown together in a brief and concentrated form.

New-York, *May 28th*, 1845.

GENTLEMEN :*

My attention has been called by a literary friend, to your notice of Mr. Brantz Mayer's report on the subject of a national name, or distinctive synonyme for our country. Mr. Mayer having chosen to reflect upon the antiquarian value of the historical research involved in the inquiry, I feel called upon, as a member of the committee of the New-York Historical Society, before whom this question was discussed, to say a few words in reply.

" The following quotation from my 'Glossary of Anglo-Indian Words,' will best set forth my personal connection with the subject

* Addressed to the Editors of the New-York Evening Post and National Intelligencer.

as a member of the society, and a humble laborer in the field of aboriginal antiquities, who is ready at all suitable times, to give authority for the use of whatever Indian terms he may employ.

" *Alleghan*, an obsolete aboriginal noun proper, applied adjectively both in French and English, to an ancient and long extinct people in North America, and likewise to the most prominent chain of mountains within the regions over which they are supposed to have borne sway."

Our authorities respecting the ancient Alleghans, are not confined to the very late period, *i. e.* 1819,* which is alone quoted, and exclusively relied on by the learned secretary of the Maryland Historical Society. Nor do they leave us in doubt, that this ancient people, who occupy the foreground of our remote aboriginal history, were a valiant, noble and populous race, who were advanced in arts and the policy of government, and raised fortifications for their defence. (N. Y. Hist. Col. vol. 2, p. 89, 91.) While they held a high reputation as hunters, they cultivated maize extensively, which enabled them to live in large towns; (Davies' Hist. Car. Isds.) and erected those antique fortifications which are extended over the entire Mississippi valley, as high as latitude 43°, and the lake country, reaching from Lake St. Clair (Am. Phil. Trans.) to the south side of the Niagara ridge (the old shore of Lake Ontario) and the country of the Onondagas and Oneidas (Clinton's Dis. N. Y. Hist. Soc. vol. 2.) Towards the south, they extended as far as the borders of the Cherokees and Muscogees.† From the traditions of Father Raymond, they were worshippers of the sun, had an order of priesthood, and exercised a sovereignty over a very wide area of country. (His. Carib. Isds. Paris, 1658. London ed. of 1666, p. 204, et seq.)

At what era the Alleghan confederacy, thus shadowed forth, existed and fell in North America, we do not know. Our Indian nations have no certain chronology, and we must establish data by contemporaneous tradition of the Mexican nations, or by internal antiquarian evidence.

---

* Trans. Hist. and Lit. Com. Am. Phil. Soc. Vol. 1, Philadelphia, 1819.
† Seneca tradition, N. Y. Hist. Col. vol. 2.

The "Old Fort" discovered by Dr. Locke in Highland Co. Ohio in 1838, denoted a period of 600 years from its abandonment,* that is, 284 years before Christopher Columbus first sailed boldly into the Western ocean. The trees on Grave Creek mound denote the abandonment of the trenches and stone look-outs in that vicinity to have been in 1338. (Trans. Am. Ethnological Society, vol. 1, N. Y. 1845.) The ramparts at Marietta had a tree decayed in the heart, but the concentric outer circles, which could be counted, were 463. (Clinton's Dis.) The live oaks on the low mounds of Florida, where one of the Algonquin tribes, namely, the Shawnees, aver that they once lived and had been preceded by a people more advanced in arts (Vide Arch. Am. vol. 1.) denote their abandonment about 1145. But even these data do not, probably reach back sufficiently far, to denote the true period.

If we fix upon the twelfth century as the era of the fall of the Alleghan race, we shall not probably over estimate the event. They had probably reached the Mississippi valley, a century or two before, having felt, in their original position, west and south of that stream, the great revolutionary movements which preceded the overthrow of the Toltec and the establishment of the Aztec empire in Mexican America.

There are but two words left in our geography, supposed to be of the ancient Alleghan language. These are Alleghany, and Yioghiogany, the latter, being the name of a stream which falls into the Monongahela, on its right bank, about twenty miles above Pittsburgh.

Tradition, not of the highest character, gives us the words Talligeu, or Talligwee, as the name of this ancient nation, although it is nearly identical in sounds with the existing and true name of the Cherokees, which, according to the late Elias Boudinot, (a Cherokee,) is TSALLAKEE. Col. Gibson, a plain man, an Indian trader and no philologist, who furnished Mr. Jefferson with Indian vocabularies of the dialects of his day, to be used in answer to the inquiries of Catherine the Great, (vide Trans. Royal Academy, Petersburgh,) expressed an opinion that this ancient people did not use a T before the epithet, but were called Allegewee. Tradition has, however, strictly speaking, preserved neither of these terms, although both

* Cincinnati Gazette.

appear to have strong affinities with them. The word Alleghany has come down to us, from the earliest times, as the name of the great right-hand fork of the Ohio, and also as the name, from the same remote period of antiquity, of the chain of mountains of which the stream itself may be said to be the most remote northeasterly tributary. In this form it is evidently a local term, applied geographically, according to the general principles of the Indian languages, like *hanna* in the Susquehanna, and *hannock* in the Rappahannock, which appear to denote, in each case, a river, or torrent of water. By removing this local inflection, we have Alleghan as the proper term for the people, and I have felt sustained, by this inductive process, in regarding Alleghan as the original cognomen of the "*mound builders*" of North America.

Having thus given my views with respect to the particular word which awakened this discussion, permit me now to turn to the other matters, so confidently brought forward by the secretary of the Maryland Historical Society.

The Iroquois affirm that they formerly lived in the area of the Cherokee country. (Clin. Dis. N. Y. H. Soc., vol.) Captain Smith met a war party of this nation, in exploring one of the rivers of Virginia in 1608. So late as the era of the settlement of North Carolina, they brought off to the north the last of their cantons, in the tribe of the Tuscaroras. They sold the lands as far south as Kentucky river. (Imlay's Hist. Kent.) They *quitclaimed* the soil in northern Virginia and Maryland, and they quite forbid all sales of land by the Delawares. All authorities, indeed, concur in showing the track of their migration, prior to 1600, to have been from the south to the north and northeast. Affiliation of language is also thought to denote their origin in the south. (Vide Gallatin, 2 vol. Archa. Amer.) The Hurons, who are of the same stock, affirm that they were originally the first of all the nations, and call the Lenapees, who have assumed the same distinction, *nephews*, denoting inferiority in the chronological and ethnological chain. In this term of nephews, so applied to the Delawares, all the Iroquois tribes concur. (Vide Oneota.)

Algonquin tradition, recorded by Mr. Heckwelder in the Am. Phi. Trans. in 1819, on the part of the Lenapees, denotes that a confederation of these two stocks, namely, the political uncles and nephews, defeated the Alleghans, and drove them from the country. This tradition is referred to a time when the Delawares or Lenapees, were shorn of all power and consequence, "having been degraded," according to their phrase, to assume the petticoat, and found a refuge in a new country, to them, on the Muskingum, where they were taken under the care, as they had previously been east of the mountains, of the Moravian brethren. In their reminiscences they would consequently be prone to give prominence to such events as would reflect the most favorable lights on their history. They are speaking of events which we see by the preceding references, must have transpired 500 or 600 years before, and in a very distant quarter of the Union. Yet they add some particulars which written history alone could preserve ; and they ascribe to themselves such a degree of foresight, prudence, wisdom, valor and sense of Christian justice, as no Indian tribe in America ever evinced. These traditions are recorded by Mr. Heckewelder in a spirit of Christian kindness on his part, but he does not vouch for them ; they are to be judged, like other traditions, by their probabilities and their conformity to other and known traditions. It is on this account that I have adduced the preceding data. Every Indian nation is prone to exalt itself, and if we would admit fully the claims of each, the rest would be sorry persons indeed.

The first thing to be borne in mind is, that the tradition is a very ancient one, and must have come down shorn of many particulars, which there appears to have been great carefulness to re-state. The scene also is remote from the place of narration. No such fact as the principal one of the crossing, on which great stress is laid by Mr. Mayer, on the part of the Maryland Historical Society, could have taken place in the Ohio valley, or within one thousand miles of Pittsburgh, where alone, it must be remembered, we have any evidence in the existing names of the country of the residence of the Alleghans.

The Algonquins, (we include the Lenapees in their proper groupe,) attempting to cross the Mississippi, into the territories of a foreign nation, with a large body of men, are defeated and driven back. They show themselves pacifically, in a moderate number, and the foreigners say, come ! but turning out a multitude, are assailed. Whether this was an original stratagem, or an after thought, we are left to infer, but in either case, it would be quite conformable to Indian policy. For the sake of clearness, we will locate this event in the section of this great river, between the Chickasaw bluffs and Natchez, its probable site. On this defeat they form an alliance with their uncles, the Iroquois, who were already east of the Mississippi, and were located north of the Alleghans. A long war begins, in the course of which the latter erect the fortifications which have excited so much curiosity in the Mississippi and Ohio valleys, and after proving themselves valient men, are finally overpowered and driven off. The Lenapees are in 1819 the historians of their enemies, and berate them as faithless. The Maryland Historical Society, twenty-six years later, endorse the whole story, and pronounce the Alleghans pusillanimous, not so much it would seem for their heroic struggle and defence, as for the cause of it, namely, not letting the Algonquin hordes march into or through their country, as the superior forecast and judgment of the latter might, on further progress, dictate.

Does any sound historian? does any one acquainted with Indian life, character or history, as it exists, and has always existed in North America, believe that the pacific and Christian request, put forth by Mr. Heckewelder, as the chronicler of his Delaware converts at Gnadenhutton, namely, that they might be allowed to explore a country east of them, to select it out and dwell therein, or that they had previously had the prudence, energy and forecast to send spies, like Moses, to spy it out—as if they were seeking a country for an agricultural settlement, with flocks and implements of husbandry—I repeat it, does any one, who reads this detailed part of the tradition as told to and believed by the good old missionary, credit a syllable of it? If he does, his good-natured credulity must be greater than that of the committee of the New-York Historical Society, whose suggestive report on the discussion of a distinctive national name has been the theme of so much misconception—may I not add, of so truly Pickwickian a degree of patriotism.

The truth is, this suggestion of a peaceful passage for the great Algonquin army, is to be found originally in the 20th chapter of Numbers, in the demand made, by divine direction, by the Jewish leader for a safe passport through the land of Edom, for the faithful performance of which there was a divine guaranty. And when the kind father had taught this historical lesson to his peaceable disciples on the banks of the Muskingum, he did not perceive, in afterwards putting down the traditions of his favorite Delawares, how completely they had adapted a sacred event to the exigencies of savage life, in a host of lawless invaders in the American wilderness, in the 12th century.

But we are not only to take this entire tradition of 1819, of an event happening 600 years before, in extenso, with all its moral exactness of motive, in the original actors, without any abatements or corrections required by other traditions or history, but the good father, whose moral excellence is pure and unimpeachable, but who was no philologist, aims to make the existing lexicography of the Delaware *prove* the tradition ; and we have, in a foot note, a forced etymology of the name of the river Mississippi, to demonstrate that this is a Delaware name. Now, the name of this river is not "Namaesa Sipu," that is, sturgeon, trout, or as he gives it, "fish river," but MISSI-SIPPI—a derivative from the adjective *great*, in an aboriginal sense, and sippi, a river. Mr. Gallatin (Archa. Am. vol. 2) is inclined to believe that it should be translated "the whole river," or a unity of waters, but neither he nor any other commentator, has been able to make "fish" out of "missi." The merest tyro in the Indian languages, must perceive that the etymology does not bear the meaning of Fish river, and if it did, it would prove, contrary to their reputation, that the Indians give the most inappropriate geographical names, of all men in existence. Fish river would be the most malappropriate name for the Mississippi. Its turbed waters and rushing channel, surcharged with floating trees, and subject to a thousand physical mutations every season, is absolutely forbidding to the larger number of species, and favorable only to the coarser kinds which are rejected from the table of the epicure.

A single remark more. The Delawares have never lived, or held an acre of land on the Mississippi, in its whole course between Itasca lake and the Balize. When Penn came to America, they lived on the Delaware, in central Pennsylvania. They were ordered to quit the sources of the Delaware river by the Iroquois in 1742, and go to

Wyoming or Shamoken.*. They found their way across the Alleghanies, in time to burn Col. Crawford at the stake,† and oppose the settlement of the Ohio valley, prior to the revolution ; they settled on the Muskingum, and after some afflictions and mutations, chiefly brought upon themselves, they accepted lands, and began to recross the Mississippi in 1818‡. They are now located on the west banks of the Missouri, on the Konza. Yet the etymology adverted to attributes to this tribe, not only the naming of the river upon which they never lived, and never held any lands, but presupposes, that the Illinois and other Algonquin nations living on its banks, above the influx of the Ohio and the Missouri, to whom, with the influence of the French, the actual name is due, preserved the Delaware term "Namæsa Sepu," although it is neither used by their descendants nor by Europeans.

[*d.*] War with the Kah Kwahs.

Some inquiries have been made in a prior paper, on the strong probabilities of this people, being identical with the Ererions or Eries. While this question is one that appears to be within the grasp of modern inquiry, and may be resumed at leisure, the war itself, with the people whom *they* call Kah-Kwahs, and *we* Eries is a matter of popular tradition, and is alluded to with so many details, that its termination may be supposed to have been an event of not the most ancient date. Some of these reminiscences having found their way into the newspapers during the summer§ in a shape and literary garniture, which was suited to take them from the custody of sober tradition, and transfer them to that of romance, there was the more interest attached to the subject, which led me to take some pains to ascertain how general or fresh their recollections of this war might be.

---

* Colden's Hist. Five Nations, vol. 1. p. 31.

† Metcalf's Indian Wars in the West.

‡ This is the first time that this tribe ever by history, or tradition, other than their own, saw this river.

§ See Buffalo Com. Adv. 12th July, 1845, article "Indian Tradition."

My inquiries were answered one evening at the mission house at Buffalo, by the Allegany chief, HA-YEK-DYOH-KUNH, or the Wood-cutter, better known by his English name of Jacob Blacksnake. He stated that the Kah-Kwahs had their chief residence at the time of their final defeat, on the Eighteen-mile creek. The name by which he referred to them, in this last place of their residence, might be written perhaps with more exactitude to the native tongue, Gah Gwah-ge-o-nuh—but as this compound word embraces the ideas of locality and existence along with their peculiar name, there is a species of tautology in retaining the two inflections. They are not necessary in the English, and besides in common use, I found them to be generally dropt, while the sound of G naturally changed in common pronunciation into that of K.

Blacksnake commenced by saying, that while the Senecas lived east of the Genessee, they received a challenge from the Kah-Kwahs, to try their skill in ball playing and athletic sports. It was accepted, and after due preliminaries, the challengers came, accompanied by their prime young men, who were held in great repute as wrestlers and ball-players. The old men merely came as witnesses, while this trial was made.

The first trial consisted of ball playing, in which, after a sharp contest, the young Senecas came off victorious. The next trial consisted of a foot race between two, which terminated also in favor of the Senecas. The spirit of the Kah-Kwas was galled by these defeats. They immediately got up another race on the instant, which was hotly contested by new runners, but it ended in their losing the race. Fired by these defeats, and still confident of their superior strength, they proposed wrestling, with the sanguinary condition, that each of the seconds should hold a drawn knife, and if his principal was thrown, he should instantly plunge it into his throat, and cut off his head. Under this terrible penalty, the struggle commenced. The wrestlers were to catch their hold as best they could, but to observe fair principles of wrestling. At length the Kah-Kwah was thrown, and his head immediately severed and tossed into the air. It fell with a rebound, and loud shouts proclaimed the Senecas victors in four trials. This terminated the sports, and the tribes returned to their respective villages.

Some time after this event, two Seneca hunters went out to hunt west of the Genesee river, and as the custom is, built a hunting lodge of boughs, where they rested at night. One day, one of them went out alone, and having walked a long distance, was belated on his return. He saw, as he cast his eye to a distant ridge, a large body of the Kah-Kwahs marching in the direction of the Seneca towns. He ran to his companion, and they instantly fled and alarmed the Senecas. They sent off a messenger post-haste to inform their confederates towards the east, and immediately prepared to meet their enemies. After about a day's march, they met them. It was near sunset when they descried their camp, and they went and encamped in the vicinity. A conference ensued, in which they settled the terms of the battle.

The next morning the Senecas advanced. Their order of battle was this. They concealed their young men, who were called by the narrator burnt-knives,* telling them to lie flat, and not rise and join the battle until they received the war cry, and were ordered forward. With these were left the rolls of peeled bark to tie their prisoners. Having made this arrangement, the old warriors advanced, and began the battle. The contest was fierce and long, and it varied much. Sometimes they were driven back, or faltered in their line—again they advanced, and again faltered. This waving of the lines to and fro, formed a most striking feature in the battle for a long time. At length the Senecas were driven back near to the point where the young men were concealed. The latter were alarmed, and cried out "now, we are killed!" At this moment, the Seneca leader gave the concerted war whoop, and they arose and joined in battle. The effects of this reinforcement, at the time that the enemy were fatigued with the day's fight, were instantaneously felt. The young Senecas pressed on their enemies with resistless energy, and after receiving a shower of arrows beat down their opponents with their war clubs, and took a great many prisoners. The prisoners were immediately bound with their arms behind, and tied to trees. Nothing could resist their impetuosity.

The Kah-Kwah chiefs determined to fly, and leave the Senecas masters of the field. In this hard and disastrous battle, which was

* A term to denote their being quite young, and used here as a cant phrase for prime young warriors.

fought by the Senecas alone, and without aid from their confederates, the Kah-Kwahs lost a very great number of their men, in slain and prisoners. But those who fled were not permitted to escape unpursued, and having been reinforced from the east, they followed them and attacked them in their residence on the Deoseowa (Buffalo creek) and Eighteen mile creek, which they were obliged to abandon, and fly to the Oheeo, [the Seneca name for the Alleghany.]

The Senecas pursued them, in their canoes, in the descent of this stream. They discovered their encampment on an island in numbers superior to their own. To deceive them, the Senecas, on putting ashore, carried their canoes across a narrow peninsula, by means of which they again entered the river above. New parties appeared to the enemy, to be thus continually arriving, and led them greatly to over-estimate their numbers.

This was at the close of day. In the morning not an enemy was to be seen. They had fled down the river and have never since appeared. It is supposed they yet exist west of the Mississippi.*

Two characteristic traits of boasting happened in the first great battle above described. The Kah-Kwah women carried along, in the rear of the warriors, packs of moccasins, for the women and children, whom they expected to be made captives in the Seneca villages. The Senecas, on the other hand, said, as they went out to battle, "let us not fight them too near for fear of the stench"—alluding to the anticipated heaps of slain.

[22nd *August*, 1845.]

---

* We may here venture to inquire, whether the Kah-Kwahs were not a remnant, or at least allies of the ancient Alleghans, who gave name to the river, and thus to the mountains. The French idea, that the Eries were exterminated, is exploded by this tradition of Blacksnake, at least if we concede that Erie and Kah-Kwah, were synonyms, which is questionable. A people who were called Ererions by the Wyandots, and Kah-Kwahs by the Iroquios, may have had many other names, from other tribes. It would contradict all Indian history, if they had not as many names as there were diverse nations, to whom they were known.

numerous and extended their settlements, but in the end, they were [illegible] by furious [illegible]

[illegible] which it [illegible] may be supposed [illegible] birds, and [illegible] It is [illegible] facts of history [illegible] the vessels [illegible] Hudson, were [illegible] from the old world is alluded [illegible]

Can we suppose there is in this tradition [illegible] cast on the lost colony of Virginia, which was first left on the island of Roanoke? The Tuscaroras, who preserve the tradition, came to western New York from that quarter. They were a fierce, powerful and warlike nation, who in 1712 resolved on the massacre, on a certain day, of all [illegible] in the Carolinas. What is once done by natives, barbarous or [illegible], is often the reproduction of some prior national act, and especially if that act had been attended with success; and it is by no means improbable that in this desperate and bloody resolve of 1712, the Tuscaroras meant to repeat the prior tragedy of "Croatan."* Whether, however, the incident be of ante-Columbian or post-Columbian date, it is worthy preservation, and may be assigned its place and proper importance when we have gleaned more facts from the [illegible] of American antiquity.

[illegible] the Cherokees and Ca[illegible]

[illegible] better settled in the existing traditions of the Iroquois, than their wars with some of the southern tribes,

---

* This tribe [illegible] the [illegible] of the hawk or falcon.

[illegible] Hakluyt.

IX. MISCELLANEOUS TRAITS.

A few traits are thrown in, under this head, in the shape of anecdotes, which are thought to be illustrative of Indian character.

[a.] Infant Atotarho of the Onondaga.

While I was engaged in taking the census of the Onondagas, at their council house, at the Castle, where a large number of all ages and both sexes were assembled, the interpreter, who spoke English very well, taking advantage of a pause in the business, said to me, pointing to a fine boy who sat on a bench, near a window, "that is our king!" I had, a short time before, requested that this boy should be sent for. His mother had now, unperceived by me, brought him, dressed out in his best clothes, and evinced, by the expression of her eyes and bearing, a conscious pride in bringing him to my notice. And truly, she had every reason to be proud of so finely formed, bright and well-looking a boy. In addition to these advantages, it is to be remembered that descent, amongst the Onondagas and the other Iroquois, is counted by the female, which constituted a further motive of satisfaction and pride to the mother, in showing her pretty Hux-sa-ha, or boy. She made no remark, however, on my noticing him, but sat with modesty and ease near him, but with an eye beaming with too much pride and self-complacence to be concealed.

The lad was but three years old, but tall for that age, and offered a fine model of form. I could not help noticing, what had often impressed me in similar instances, that the infusion of European blood, derived from his grandfather by the father's side, had served to heighten and improve physical development, and fulness and beauty of muscle. His eyes were full, large, black and sparkling. His dark hair also was a true trait of his race. His countenance was of a bright brown, showing the blood, and rather formed on the Grecian mould, with a good nose and pretty lips. Yet, over all, there was a physiological dash of the muscular expression, hue and air of the true Ko.ıcshioni.

There was nothing peculiar in his dress, which was of good materials and well made, agreeably to the nation's fashion for boys, except it might be the lining of the under brim of a light straw hat, which the mother had carefully decorated with a piece of light figured cotton goods, looking as if it had been cut from a printed handkerchief.

I did not think to ask the name of this promising young candidate for the seat and honors of the Atotarho, or chief magistracy of his nation. His father's name is Tso-ha-neeh-sa, which, according to the curious principles of naming persons, and the still more curious rules of the Indian syntax, means a road, the receding parallel lines of which intermingle by atmospheric refraction. This, apparently to them, mysterious uniting and separating of the lines in such a vista, is the idea described by this compound term. The boy, however, inherits, or has the right of inheritance of the Atotarho, not "a king," through the mother, who was a daughter of the principal Ho-ai-ne, or chief. This daughter was married to Ezekiel Webster, an American, a New-Englander, a Vermonter, I think, who either by freak, taste or fortune, wandered off among the Iroquois soon after the close of the American revolution, and finally fixed himself in the Onondaga valley, where he learned the language, established a trade in the gensing root, and became a man of note and influence in the tribe. He died in old age, and is buried in this valley, where he has left sons and daughters, all of whom, however, are recognized as members of the ancient Onondaga canton, or People of the Hills.

[*b*.] Red Jacket and the Wyandot claim to supremacy.

At a great council of the western tribes, assembled near Detroit, prior to the late war, the celebrated Seneca orator, Red Jacket, was present, when the question of the right of the Wyandots to light the council fire, was brought up. This claim he strenuously resisted, and administed a rebuke to this nation in the following terms :

"Have the Quatoghies forgotten themselves ? Or do they suppose we have forgotten them ? Who gave you the right in the west or east, to light the general council fire ? You must have fallen asleep, and dreamt that the Six Nations were dead ! Who permitted you to escape from the lower country ? Had you any heart left to speak a word for yourselves ? Remember how you hung on by the bushes. You had not even a place to land on. You have not yet done p——g for fear of the Konoshioni. High claim, indeed, for a tribe who had to run away from the Kadarakwa.*

"As for you, my nephews," he continued, turning to the Lenapees, or Delawares, "it is fit you should let another light your fire. Before Miqûon came, we had put out your fire and poured water on it; it would not burn. Could you hunt or plant without our leave ? Could you sell a foot of land ? Did not the voice of the Long House cry, go, and you went ? Had you any power at all ? Fit act indeed for you to give in to our wandering brothers—you, from whom we took the war-club and put on petticoats.†"

[*c*.] Anecdote of Brant.

When this chief was in London, he received ten pounds sterling, to be given, on his return to America, to any person or persons, among his people, whom he found to be doing most to help themselves. On coming to the Seneca reservation on Buffalo Creek, they had just finished the church, at an expense of seventeen hundred dollars. He gave the money to these Indians to buy stoves to warm it, which are still used for this purpose. He said he had seen no people who were doing so much to help themselves.‡

---

* Hon. Albert H. Tracy.

† For similar language to this, addressed to the Delawares, see Colden's Five Nations, for a speech of an Iroquois chief, in council, at Lancaster.

‡ Rev. A. Wright.

[*d*.] The County Clerk and the wolf-scalp.

A Seneca hunter killed a wolf just within the bounds of Cattaraugus county, close to the Pennsylvania line, and took the scalp to Meadville, Pennsylvania, for the bounty. Being questioned where the animal was killed, he honestly told the officer that he had come across it and shot it, as near as he could tell, within the territory of New-York, very near the state and county lines. On this, the clerk told him that it would be contrary to law to pay him the bounty. "That is a *bad* law!" replied the red man. "Why?" said the magistrate—"we cannot pay for scalps taken out of the county." "It is bad," replied the hunter, "because you require that the wolf should know the county lines. Had this wolf seen a flock of sheep just within the Pennsylvania lines, I dare say he would not have stopped for the county lines." On this, the magistrate paid him the bounty of five dollars.*

---

* N. T. Strong, Esq.

X. MORAL AND SOCIAL CONDITION AND PROSPECTS.

The gospel was preached to the Iroquois as well as to the several tribes of Algonquin origin, who lined the banks of the Hudson and the Delaware, early in the 17th century. The Reformed Church of Holland does not appear to have underrated its duties in this respect, while the Holland States, under a hereditary President or Stadtholder, were extending their civil jurisdiction and commercial enterprise on this continent, notwithstanding the want of any direct evidence, that the conversion of the Indians constituted a fixed part of the policy of the servants and governors of the West India Company, to whose lot it fell to introduce the arts and commerce of the mother country. It was the common impression of those times, not only in Holland, the centre of theological discussion, but in the reformed churches generally, that civilization and the arts must precede the introduction of Christianity among barbarous and idolatrous nations, and it was under such views, that the gospel was first carried to India and to Iceland by the pious zeal of the German reformers.

The impulse which had been imparted to the subject through the zeal and devotion of Xavier and Loyola, and the energetic spirit of making proselytes and converts, which characterized the particular order of the Romish church, which they founded, impressed the rulers of Spain, France and Portugal, with a deep sense of the importance of carrying the gospel to the aborigines of the countries which they discovered. Hence it was put forth, and really became one of the cardinal points of attention in their early attempts to found new colonies. And while the governors and servants of these countries did not prosecute the objects of trade and politics with less determination and success, nay, with a more unscrupulous disregard of the means, as the history of South America alone testifies, they carried missionaries in every early enterprise, and set forth to the world, the conversion of the native inhabitants as the great object of their aim, as it was indeed often the shield and cover to the reckless avarice and ambition of the Cortezes and the Pizarros who carried their flags.

It was not consonant to the genius of Christianity, as interpreted by Luther and his successors, to proceed in the work of spiritual conquest with so noisy and gorgeous a display, or with hand locked arm in arm with the State; and if the States of Holland did not put forth the object, in their first charters and commissions to the new world, it was, perhaps, because the Church was actuated in, and was guided by, the general policy of the Protestant European churches. England and Sweden, who planted colonies here, did the same.

It was not, indeed, until the new impulse which arose in the middle of the 17th century, and which brought Oliver Cromwell to the English throne, that different views and a deeper obligation of national duties in this respect began to prevail. And hence, when the English pilgrims, who had been sheltered awhile in the tolerant domains of Holland, set their faces towards the New World, it was with a pre-determination not only to carry out the principles of the gospel, in their own settlements, but to extend its benign influences among the aborigines. This was averred, and the well known prominency of the fact stamps the efforts to convert and civilize the North American Indians, with a moral force and grandeur, which cannot be claimed for England, in her royal capacity as administrator of patents and honors here, or for any other protestant king or potentate, who sent her poor, bold or enterprising children to the American wilds.

This much can be said, without disparagement to the piety of the Netherland church, which had her pastors and teachers at Manhattan, Fort Orange, and various other incipient points of her settlements at an early day. Whatever had been her policy, (and we have paid but little attention to this,) in sending teachers among the Mohegans, the Maquaas and other tribes who resorted to her forts and factories at Albany, and other points of early contact with these simple and warlike men; the English, after the conquest of 1664, appear to have followed in her footsteps, and pursued the same general, gradual and persuasive means, attaching high and deserved value at all points to the influence of European arts and the value of fixed industry.

Churches were founded at an early day, among the Mohawks at Caghnawaga, and at Dionderoga at the mouth of Schoharie Creek, better known as Fort Hunter, the latter of which received a present of a set of plate for the communion service, from Queen Ann.

Unfortunately for the conversion and civilization of the Indians, they had not a fixed population—they drew their supplies mainly from the chase, gave up a large portion of their time and means to war, and besides moving periodically, at least twice a year, *from* or *to* their hunting and planting grounds, they were in a general progress of recession before a civilized population. They shrank before the determined spirit of progress of civilized arts and industry, which elicited resources where the Indian had seen none, and made an industrious use of every acre of tillable ground. But while the silent influence of this progress did much to teach him, by denoting the use of tools and implements of art and agriculture, to improve him in his domicil and its fixtures, and his costume, and to harmonize and fix his mental habits and character, he was not proof against the leading temptation of the times, namely, the free and inordinate use of ardent spirits. From the partial paroxysms of this pernicious indulgence, he rose with less energy to pursue the chase, or follow the war path. The policy of land sales, the distribution of presents as boons from the crown, and the distribution of small sums of coin to the heads of families in the shape of annuities. A system founded in all but the last feature, under James VI, and confirmed under the old confederation, stepped in, as it were, to aid and reinforce him in his means of living, but which in effect, held him away from his hunting grounds, paralyzed his home industry, and supplied him new means of indulging his propensities for liquor and luxuries. That the gospel should not have made a very marked progress under these circumstances, is not surprising.

Some years before the breaking out of the American revolution, Mr. Kirkland planted the gospel standard among the Oneidas, at a time when the broad and sylvan fields and glades of Kun-a-wa-loa, or Oneida Castle, were still beyond the pale of European civilization.* And he is to be regarded as the apostle to the Iroquois. For many years, in perils and dangers, he preached the gospel to the Oneidas, at their once celebrated castle ; and by the purity, firmness and excellence of his character, won the confidence and the heart of their leading sachem. Skenandoah, gave his attention to this new scheme of acceptance with his Maker, admitted it, and became a consistent professor and practicer of its precepts, and of him, it can be confidently said, that he lived and died in the faith. To gain the influence of the most powerful man in the canton, was to gain the whole canton ; and when the war broke out, the tribe, wavering, as it did for a time, and assailed with all the arts of British intrigue and promise, so profusely put forth, adhered to the colonies. Kirkland, in the inception and progress of these movements, became the principal agent in disseminating the doctrines of peace and neutrality among the six cantons. Washington and the continental congress, reposed the highest trust in his virtue, judgment, and intelligence. He took from the lips of the father of his country, words of peace and good counsel, which coincided admirably, with the precepts of the gospel. He traversed the then wilderness of Genesee and Niagara on this mission, and has left enduring monuments of his faithfulness and zeal.

But the spirit of war prevailed—that spirit which the great body this people had so long served, under the guidance of their native priesthood. All but the Oneidas, some few of the Tuscaroras, who were then settled in their western precincts, and some one or two individuals, from St. Regis, joined the ranks of the mother country, under their bold and politic leader Brant. Seven years of battles, expeditions, ambushes, and murders, terminated not only in their political overthrow as a confederacy, but plunged many of them who had before listened to the voice of christianity, back into the arms of their native priests and forest habits. The Mohawks, part of the Cayugas, and some Onondagas and Tuscaroras, fled the country, and settled chiefly in Canada. The Oneidas, the body of the Onondagas and Senecas, and some parts of the Cayugas and Tuscaroras, remained. But they had fought for a phantom. All the rich promises of glory and conquest, emanating from Johnson Hall and

* Herkimer, the nearest point east, was about 40 miles distant.

fort Niagara, and the Canadas had failed ; and their delegates came to the treaty of Fort Stanwix in 1784, poor, crest fallen, and defeated. And by their first public act, after the drama of the revolution, they put their hands to a treaty, ceding away the larger portion of their ancient domain.

Thus they were thrown back an immeasurable distance in the work of civilization and christianity, and the effort to introduce the gospel was to be commenced almost anew.

Time will not permit any notice in detail, of this second period in their history. Kirkland, true to his original purpose, continued his ministry and useful labors, and died in the Oneida country. The venerable Skenandoah followed him at some few years later, and requested to be buried by his side. New missions were projected and carried into effect, at distinct times, among the remaining cantons. A review of these, it is impossible to make within the period allotted to this report ; and besides, were the time ample, the data furnished to me are not in all respects complete, and in some cases wholly deficient. Communications have been received from the Rev. Gilbert Rockwood and Rev. James Cusick of Tuscarora ; from the Rev. Asher Bliss at Cattaraugus, and from Rev. William Hall at Alleghany, which are printed in the appendix, and are referred to as giving the latest and most authentic information on the progress of christianity, letters, and morals among these respective tribes. So far as relates to the progress of this people in agriculture and the arts, the results of the census, hereto prefixed, although it denotes striking depopulation, afford the most definite, and at the same time, most favorable view of the remains of these cantons, which has, perhaps, ever been presented, of a whole Indian nation in America. The reluctance, which was felt in some quarters, has rendered it less complete than it might have been made. Still, with every proper abatement and qualification, applicable to the reservations as departmental bodies, and to the whole as a mass, there are strong encouragements to the friends of christianity to persevere. The seeds of industry are well sown ; letters have been generally introduced, and, in some instances, they have produced men of talents and intelligence, who have taken an honorable part in the professional and practical duties of life. Very gratifying evidences exist of the adoption, on a large scale, of the improved arts and conveniencies of polished life. In manners, costume and address, the Iroquois people offer a high example of the capacities and ready adoptive habits of the race. It only needs a reference to the statistical tables mentioned, to show that they are not behindhand in implements of husbandry, vehicles, work cattle, horses and the general features of their agriculture. They are abundantly able to raise sufficient for their own consumption, and some of the communities have a snrplus which is added to the productive resources of the State. From those who have done so well, and who have shown such unequivocal capacities for improvement, we may expect more. From the tree, which has produced blossoms, we may expect fruit; and from the bearing tree which has produced good fruit, we may expect more fruit. Under all circumstances, we may regard the problem of their reclamation as fixed and certain. They have themselves solved it. And whatever an enlightened people and legislature should do to favor them, ought not to be omitted. Churches and societies, who have granted their peculiar aids, should continue those aids; and the heart of the philanthropist and the statesman has cause to rejoice, that after all their wars and wanderings, mistakes and besetments, the Iroquois, made wise by experience, are destined TO LIVE. The results of the census, herewith submitted, demonstrate this. The time is indeed propitious for putting the inquiry, whether the Iroquois are not worthy to be received, under the new Constitution, as CITIZENS OF THE STATE.

RETURN

Of the Enumeration of the Indians on the several Reservations, with the other statistical information required by law to be obtained in the said Reservations.

1		2	3	4	5	6	7
RESERVATIONS.	Total Population.	Number of male persons in the Reservation.	Number of female persons in the Reservation.	Number of married females, under the age of 45 years, in the Reservation.	Number of unmarried females, between the ages of 16 and 45, in the Reservation.	Number of unmarried females, under 16 years of age, in the Reservation.	Number of marriages, during the year preceding, in the Reservation.
1. Oneida,	157	71	86	24	3	47	
2. Onondaga,	368	173	195	63	19	73	5
3. Tuscarora,	312	148	164	18	10	11	6
4. Buffalo,	446	200	246	73	47	61	3
5. Cattaraugus,	808	393	415	89	40	30	10
6. Cayugas on the Cattaraugus Reservation,	114	56	58	16	6	5	2
7. Alleghany,	783	390	393	127	33	168	6
8. Tonawanda,	505	224	281	101	45	69	4
9. St. Regis,	260	126	134	44	5	67	
Total,	3,753	1,781	1,972	555	208	531	36

RETURN OF ENUMERATION OF INDIANS—(CONTINUED.)

RESERVATIONS.	8 Number of births in the Reservation during the year preceding.		9 Number of deaths in the Reservation during the year preceding.		10 Number of persons in the Reservation born in the State of New-York.	11 Number of persons in the Reservation born in any of the other States of the Union.	12 Number of persons in the Reservation born in G. Britain or its possessions.	13 Number of children in Reservation between the ages of 5 & 16 years.	14 Number of children in the Reservation attending private or select unincorporated schools.
	Males.	Fema es.	Males.	Females.					
1. Oneida,	8	5	1	..	155	1	1	59	20
2. Onondaga,	6	10	11	12	364	..	1	169	40
3. Tuscarora,	5	5	1	3	286	..	30	63	43
4. Buffalo,	3	7	14	7	433	1	6	117	57
5. Cattaraugus,	17	11	11	13	789	..	7	121	86
6. Cayugas on the Cattaraugus Reservation,	4	1	3	3	114	..	..	21	14
7. Alleghany,	13	6	13	13	752	35	..	227	162
8. Tonawanda,	5	8	4	3	496	..	11	126	40
9. St. Regis,	..	7	5	3	125	..	135	81	
Total,	61	60	63	57	3,514	37	191	984	462

AGRICULTURAL AND HORTICULTURAL STATISTICS.

RESERVATIONS.	15	16		17		18		19	
	ACRES OF LAND.	BARLEY.		PEAS.		BEANS.		BUCKWHEAT.	
	Number of acres of improved land in the Reservation.	Number of acres of barley under cultivation.	Quantity of barley raised therefrom during the preceding year.	Number of acres of peas under cultivation.	Number of bushels raised.	Number of acres of beans.	Quantity raised.	Number of acres of buckwheat.	Quantity raised.
1. Oneida,	421	10	200	3½	35	3¼	11	2½	50
2. Onondaga,	2,043¼	2½	70	7¾	91	..	..	18	245
3. Tuscarora,	2,079½	20	430	5	65	..	..	3	
4. Buffalo,	1,914	..	....	18½	..	..	..	6½	420
5. Cattaraugus,	2,123	96¼	1,300	..	301	..	..	..	227
6. Cayugas on the Cattaraugus Reservation,	316	..	....	..	23	..	..	18¼	
7. Alleghany,	2,163½	6	35	18¼	90	..	..	5	112
8. Tonawanda,	2,216	42	550	30	200	1	15	8	
9. St. Regis,	591¼	¾	....	27	105	11	18		
Total,	13,867½	177¾	2,585	110	910	15¼	44	61¼	1,054

AGRICULTURAL AND HORTICULTURAL STATISTICS—(CONTINUED.)

	20		21		22			23	
	TURNEPS.		POTATOES.		WHEAT.			CORN.	
RESERVATIONS.	Number of acres of turneps.	Quantity raised.	Number of acres of potatoes.	Quantity raised.	Number of acres of wheat sown.	Number of acres of wheat harvested.	Quantity of wheat raised.	Number of acres of corn sown.	Quantity harvested.
1. Oneida,	..	..	32¼	841	14	13	325	60½	1,458
2. Onondaga,	¾	30	21	840	87¾	87¾	1,156	189½	4,492
3. Tuscarora,	2½	55	31	1,166	405½	..	4,897	152	3,515
4. Buffalo,	..	..	33	1,444	..	..	......	163½	2,925
5. Cattaraugus,	5¼	179	53¾	6,237	169½	..	1,822	473¼	7,966
6. Cayugas on the Cattaraugus Reservation,	..	..	38	955	14½	4	210	62½	1,970
7. Alleghany,	25¾	29	146½	3,638	46	..	503	407	8,565
8. Tonawanda,	3	60	40	1,150	200	..	2,400	170	3,950
9. St. Regis,	13/16	..	20⅝	410	42½	..	195	65½	658½
Total,	38 1/16	353	416⅛	16,681	979¾	104¾	11,508	1,743¾	35,499½

AGRICULTURAL AND HORTICULTURAL STATISTICS—(CONTINUED.)

RESERVATIONS.	24 RYE.		25 OATS.		26 NEAT CATTLE.				
	Number of acres of rye sown.	Quantity harvested.	Number of acres of oats sown.	Quantity harvested.	Number of neat cattle.	Under one year old.	Over one year old.	Number of cows milked.	Number of pounds of butter made during the preceding year.
1. Oneida,	..	..	28½	720	50	.	..	28	1,140
2. Onondaga,	..	..	107	2,110	189	..	..	82	1,150
3. Tuscarora,	..	..	205½	4,085	336	..	..	98	7,537
4. Buffalo,	..	..	115½	4,251	270	..	..	87	4,888
5. Cattaraugus,	..	..	58	8,922½	387	..	..	166	2,426
6. Cayugas on the Cattaraugus Reservation,	..	..	30	1,622	63	..	..	43	
7. Alleghany,	..	..	212¼	4,366	585	..	..	169	
8. Tonawanda,	4	60	100	2,500	305	..	..	88	3,200
9. St. Regis,	..	..	51	290	90	17	16	42	
Total,	4	60	907	28,866½	2,275	17	16	803	20,341

AGRICULTURAL AND HORTICULTURAL STATISTICS—(CONTINUED.)

	27	28		29	30	31	32
RESERVATIONS.	HORSES.	SHEEP.		HOGS.			
	Number of horses.	Number of sheep.	Number of fleeces.	Number of hogs.	Number of acres of meadow cut.	Number of ploughs.	Value of garden and horticultural products.
1. Oneida,	17	..	..	46	17	8	$173 00
2. Onondaga,	64	49	43	327	116¼	17	1,100 00
3. Tuscarora,	153	215	180	596	195	59	61 00
4. Buffalo,	123	41	30	369	174½	53	210 00
5. Cattaraugus,	223	365	168	882	201	87	399 75
6. Cayugas on the Cattaraugus Reservation,	39	40	30	109	50	17	37 00
7. Alleghany,	149	79	..	627	416½	80	557 00
8. Tonawanda,	130	50	40	390	180	60	300 00
9. St. Regis,	50	..	..	112	..	..	.....
Total,	948	839	491	3,458	1,350¼	381	$2,837 75

STATISTICS—(Continued.)

RESERVATIONS.	33			34	35	36	37
	LANDS LET TO OTHERS.						
	Number of acres let.	Annual value per acre received.	Total value of land let.	Number of bearing fruit trees of all descriptions.	Value of avails derived derived from the chase.	Number of persons who have attained the age of 80.	Number of persons who who possess no lands.
1. Oneida,	89	av. $2 91	$259 00	44	$85 00	2	10
2. Onondaga,	1,410½	2 63	2,404 00	640	131 25	3	21
3. Tuscarora,	183½	3 25	550 75	1,574	42 50	5	2
4. Buffalo,	533	....	....	259	61 00	4	13
5. Cattaraugus,	453	....	790 00	1,340	69 60	12	83
6. Cayugas on the Cattaraugus Reservation,	8	....	25 00	278	8 38	1	10
7. Alleghany,	238	....	686 68	1,483	427 00	15	15
8. Tonawanda,	600	2 50	1,500 00	1,250	50 00	25	6
9. St. Regis,	....	....	....	....	....	..	
Total,	3,515		$6,215 43	6,868	$874 73	67	160

STATISTICS—(CONTINUED.)

RESERVATIONS.	38										
	NUMBER OF PERSONS FROM OTHER TRIBES.										
	Cayugas.	Undetermined tribes.	Onondagas.	Oneidas.	St. Regis.	Stockbridge or Mohegans.	Cornplanter village in Pennsylvania.	Mohawks.	Lenapees or Delawares.	Tuscaroras.	Total.
1. Oneida,	..	..	..	..	1	4	..	1	1	.	7
2. Onondaga,	1	..	..	23	4	.	..	1	.	4	33
3. Tuscarora,	2	..	13	..	.	.	..	18	.	.	33
4. Buffalo,	21	..	6	19	.	.	..	2	.	.	48
5. Cattaraugus,	54	..	42	1	.	.	..	..	.	.	97
6. Cayugas on the Cattaraugus Reservation,	..	..	..	..	.	.	..	..	.	.	
7. Alleghany,	5	64	3	29	.	.	13	..	.	.	114
8. Tonawanda,	..	..	3	..	.	.	..	1	.	6	10
9. St. Regis,											
Total,	83	64	67	72	5	4	13	23	1	10	342

STATISTICS—(Continued.)

39

STATISTICS OF OCCUPATION.

RESERVATIONS.	Number of farmers.	No. of mechanics.	Number of lawyers.	No. of semi-hunters or who derive support in part from the chase.	Number of persons educated at colleges or academies.	No. of physicians.	No. ef teachers, catechists or ministers.	No. of interpreters or translators of the Iroquois.
1. Oneida,	18	1	.	6	.	.	.	3
2. Onondaga,	47	2	.	25	1	.	3	1
3. Tuscarora,	60	1	.	8	3	3	3	5
4. Buffalo,	23	1	1	6	5	1	1	7
5. Cattaraugus,	80	6	1	32	7	.	6	7
6. Cayugas on the Cattaraugus Reservation,	17	1	.	8	1	1	.	2
7. Alleghany,	96	6	.	46	1	1	2	7
8. Tonawanda,	30	2	.	20	2	1	2	3
9. St. Regis,								
Total,	371	20	2	151	20	7	17	35

RESERVATIONS.	40 STATISTICS OF MORALITY. Churches.	Number of persons who adhere to their native religion.	No. of church members of all denominations.	Number pledged to temperance.	Schools.	41 Aggregate population.	42 ANNUITIES. United States.	New-York.	U. S. Distribution—Share.	N. Y. Distribution—Share.
1. Oneida,	1	133	31	35	1	164	....			
2. Onondaga,	1	330	38	128	1	368	....	$2,430 00	......	$6 $60\frac{1}{3}$
3. Tuscarora,	2	249	63	231	2	312	....	....		
4. Buffalo,	1	436	5†	28	2	446	....	....	$4 80	
5. Cattaraugus,	1	768	40	75	4	808	$12,765*	500 00*	4 80	
6. Cayugas on the Cattaraugus Reservation,	.	97	16	15	1	114	....	600 00	4 80	
7. Alleghany,	1	603	117	158	2	783	....	....	4 80	
8. Tonawanda,	1	465	40	200	1	505	....	....	4 80	
9. St. Regis,	.	..	..	..	.‡	260	....	2,131 69	......	8 $19\frac{226}{266}$
Total,	8	3,081	350	870	14	3,760				
Deduct seven Oneidas,						7				
Total, as in first column,						3,753				

* These sums are the total of the annuities paid by the United States and the State of New-York to the Indians of the Tonawanda, Buffalo, Cattaraugus, including the Cayugas and Alleghany Reservations.

† Incomplete. ‡ The church of this tribe is north of the boundary line, in Canada.

NOTE.—It has not been ascertained in what manner the $500 and $600 annuities paid to the Senecas and Cayugas are divided among themselves—whether the Senecas receive any portion of that paid to the Cayugas, and the Cayugas any part of that paid to the Senecas.

DEAF AND DUMB, IDIOTS, LUNATICS AND BLIND.

I could not learn that there ever was a child born blind among the Iroquois. The traditions of the people do not refer to any instance of the kind. They believe none has occurred. It is certain, from inquiries made on the several reservations, that no such person now exists. Yet it is a subject which, from the importance of the fact in aboriginal statistics, deserves to be further investigated.

Among the Oneidas, prior to the removal of the principal body of this tribe to Wisconsin, there was one lunatic—a young man who was kindly taken care of, and who accompanied them on their removal to the west. There is also an instance of a deaf and dumb child, among those of the tribe who remain in the State. This person, who is a female, now under 12 years of age, was recently taken to the Onondaga reservation by her relatives, and is now at that location.

There is one idiot among the Onondagas, a young man under 21 years of age. He is supported by his relatives and friends.

I also found one idiot among the Tuscaroras.

My inquiries on the several reservations of the Senecas, at Tonewanda, Buffalo, Cattaraugus and Alleghany, did not result in detecting a single person who was either deaf and dumb, an idiot or a lunatic. As the Senecas are seven-fold more numerous than the highest in number among the other cantons, this result, if it should be verified by subsequent and fuller inquiries, after more thoroughly explaining the object of the information sought for to each band, would offer a remarkable exemption from the usual laws of population. There are no means of instruction for this class of persons on the reservations. The care of the three individuals above designated, calls for the same disproportionate tax on time, which is elsewhere necessary, and the admission of these persons to the State Lunatic Asylum, and the Deaf and Dumb Institute at New-York, free of expense, would seem to bè due to them.

Among the St. Regis, which is the only tribe I did not visit and take the enumeration of, it is not known whether there be any persons of either class.

One or two additional facts may be added to the preceding statistics in this connection.

I found three saw mills, with twenty-one gangs of saws, on the Alleghany reservation, and also two council houses and two public schools, constituting public property, belonging exclusively to this reservation, which were valued by the appraisers, under the treaty of 1842, at $8,219.00.

On the Cattaraugus reservation, there is the church, council house and farms, connected with the schools, being the property of the Indians and not the missionary society, which were valued together, by the same appraisers, at $3,214.50.

There is on the Buffalo creek reservation, a saw mill, valued at $404.75, a church built originally at an expense of $1,700, valued at $1,200, and a council house, valued at $75; making a total amount of public property, including all the preceding, of $13,113.25.

The total amount of private valuations on the Buffalo and Tonewanda reservations, under the treaty of 1842, was not exactly ascertained, but it is about $80,000. This is entirely Seneca property and funds. Its payment to individuals, in the sums awarded, is based on their removal to Cattaraugus and Alleghany, agreeably to the terms of the compromise treaty of 1842.

The Onondagas possess one saw mill, well built and in good repair, which is of some value to them, and might be rendered more so, under a proper system of management.

APPENDIX.

(A.)

Letter from the Secretary of State to Henry R. Schoolcraft, &c.

SECRETARY'S OFFICE,
Albany, *June* 25*th*, 1845.

HENRY R. SCHOOLCRAFT, Esq.

SIR—I have deemed it proper to appoint you to take the enumeration of the Indians residing on the following reservations, to wit: The Oneida, Onondaga, Tuscarora, and the Reservations of the Senecas, one or more in each of the counties of Allegany, Cattaraugus and Erie, and also of the Tonewanda Indians in the county of Genesee.

Your duties are summarily defined in the fifteenth section of the act of the Legislature, which authorizes me to make this appointment, and to which I invite your attention.

On calling at this office you will be furnished with the proper blanks to enable you to perform the duties of the important trust committed to your hands, which will indicate with sufficient precision the method of ascertaining the numbers, ages, sex, condition and classification of the remnants of this interesting race. You will find, on running through and examining the blanks for these returns, full scope for all the information that can be of any practical use.

I desire you will be very particular and minute in your inquiries in respect to every matter which relates to agricultural and statistical information, as well as of all other information called for by the returns, which will be furnished to you.

It is believed, from the information which has been received at this office, that there may be found, at the different reservations, Indians who were not originally of the tribe or stock to which they now profess, perhaps, to belong. You will, as far as may be in your power, and without exciting the jealousy and distrust of the Indians, endeavor to ascertain the number of their people, now living at the different reservations, who are not of the original stock or tribe with whom they are now sojourning.

It is important that you do not consolidate or bring into one return any more than the inhabitants of one reservation, and a sufficient number of blank returns will be furnished to enable you to accomplish this object without any difficulty, and you can use some one of the columns which will otherwise be found useless, to denote or mark the number who derive their subsistence from the chase.

It is expected that you will complete the enumeration, and file the several returns in the Secretary's office by the first day of September next, that I may be able to prepare abstracts and copies to be submitted to the Legislature at the next session.

You will no doubt experience some difficulties in the performance of the duties devolved upon you, owing to the jealousy of the Indians and the novelty of these proceedings; this, it is believed, being the first effort of the kind ever attempted by the State. You will assure our red brethren, that, in taking this enumeration of them, and making the inquiries into their present condition and situation, the Legislature, the Governor of the State, or any of the officers, have no other objects in view but their welfare and happiness.

The Indians within our State are under its guardian care and protection, and it is a high duty that is now to be performed of sending a competent and well qualified citizen to visit them, and inquire particularly into their situation. We have no connection with the government of the United States, or any land company, which prompts to these inquiries into their present social condition.

You will be at liberty to extend your inquiries to the early history and antiquarian remains of the Indians in the central and western parts of the State, but it is desired that these may be as brief as the nature of these inquiries will allow.

With these views of the subject I commit this important trust to your hands, confidently expecting and anticipating a very satisfactory result.

I have the honor to be, with great respect,
Your ob't ser't,
N. S. BENTON,
Secretary of State.

P. S. Please to advise me of your acceptance, and also state when you will probably call here to receive the blanks and commence your duties. N. S. B.

[*a.*] Fifteenth Section of an Act relative to the Census or Enumeration of the Inhabitants of the State, passed May 7, 1845.

§ 15. It shall be the duty of the secretary of state to appoint suitable persons to take the enumeration of the Indians residing on the several reservations in this state, who shall in respect to such reservations perform all the duties required of marshals by this act; and shall also return the number of acres of land cultivated by such Indians, and such other statistics as it may be in their power to collect, and as the secretary of state in his instructions shall prescribe; for which service they shall be paid out of the treasury upon the warrant of the comptroller such suitable compensation, not exceeding two dollars per day, as the secretary shall certify to be just. All expenses incurred by the secretary of state in executing this act shall be paid by the treasurer upon the warrant of the comptroller.

[*b.*] Attorneys or Agents of Indians appointed by the State.

Tribe,	Attorney or Agent.	Residence,	County.
Oneida Indians, ...	Spencer H. Stafford, Att'y,..	Vernon, ...	Oneida........
Seneca Indians,.....	Cephas R. Leland, do....	Hanover, ...	Chautauque...
Onondaga Indians,..	Wm. W. Teall, Agent,.....	Syracuse, ...	Onondaga....

[*c.*] Reservations

CATTARAUGUS COUNTY:

Reservation on the Allegany river,

Oil Spring reservation.

ERIE COUNTY:

Buffalo creek reservation,

Part of Cattaraugus reservation,

ALLEGANY COUNTY:

Part of Oil Spring reservation in this county,

GENESEE COUNTY:

The Tonawanta reservation is principally in this county,

ONONDAGA COUNTY:

Onondaga reservation.

NIAGARA COUNTY:

Tuscarora Indian reservation,

ONEIDA COUNTY:

Oneida reservation.

(B.)

Extracts from a Rough Diary of Notes by the way.

Such parts only of these notes and memorandums are retained, as have been referred to, as original materials, of which there is some particular fact or statement, which has not been exhausted. Sometimes the note itself was chiefly of a mnemonic character, and designed to recall further particulars entrusted to the memory.

MEMORANDA, NEW-YORK, JULY 1.

ANTIQUITIES OF NEW-YORK.

Localities to be examined, namely:

1. POMPEY, Onondaga.
   Vestiges of a town, 500 acres.
   Three circular walls, or elliptical forts, 8 miles apart.
   These formed a triangle, enclosing the town.

2. CAMILLUS, Onondaga.
   Two forts.
   One 3 acres on a high hill.
   East, a gate, west, spring 10 rods off.
   Shape elliptical.
   Ditch deep.
   Wall 10 feet high.
   Second fort, half a mile distant.
   Lower ground.
   Constructed like the other.
   About half as large.
   Shells, testaceous animals—plenty.
   Fragments, pottery.
   Pieces of brick.
   "Other signs" of ancient settlement, found by first settlers. [Clinton.]

3. EAST BANK OF SENECA RIVER.
   Six miles south of Cross and Salt lakes.
   Forty miles south of Oswego.
   Discovered 1791, New-York Magazine, 1792 with picture writing, on a stone 5 feet by 3½, and 6 inches thick, evidently sepulchral.

Two hundred and twenty yards length.
Fifty-five yards breadth.
Bank and ditch entire.
Two apertures middle of parallelogram, one towards the *water*, other *land*.
Second work, half a mile south.
Half-moon.
Outwork.
Singularity, extremities of the crescent from larger fort.
Bank and ditch of both, large old trees.
Pottery well burned, red, indented.
East, these works traced 18 miles east of Manlius square.

4. Oxford, Chenango county.
East banks Chenango river.
Great antiquity.
North to Sandy creek, 14 miles from Sackett's Harbor, near one which covers 50 acres.
Fragments of pottery.
West in great numbers.

5. Onondaga Town.

6. Scipio.

7. Auburn, two forts.

8. Canandaigua, three forts.

9. Between Seneca and Cayuga lakes—several.

10. Ridgeway, Genesee:
Several forts and places of burial.

11. Allen's Residence, 1788.
Two miles west.
A flat.
Deserted Indian village.
Junction of Allen's creek with Genesee.
Eight miles north of Kanawageas.
Five miles north of Magic Spring.
Six acres.
Six gates.
Ditch eight feet wide.
Six feet deep.
Circular on three sides.
Fourth side, a high bank.
A covered way, near two hundred years old.
Second, half a mile south, on a greater eminence.
Less dimensions.

But deeper ditch.
More lofty and commanding.

12. JOAIKA :
Twenty-six miles west of Kaneawgeas.
Six miles further.
Tegatainedaghgwe, or double-fortified town.
A fort at each end.
First about four acres.
Two miles distant another.
Eight acres.
Ditch about first five or six feet deep.
Small stream one side.
Traces of six gates.
Dug way to the water.
Large oaks two hundred years old or more.
Remains of a funeral pile—bones.
Mound six feet by twenty—thirty diameter—(sixty to ninety.)

13. PATH TO BUFFALO CREEK :
Heights—fortified.

14. WEST OF TONAWANDA :
Still another.

15. ON BRANCH OF THE DELAWARE :
A fort one thousand years old, by trees.

16. SOUTH SIDE OF ERIE :
Cattaraugus creek to Pennsylvania line, fifty miles.
Two to four miles apart—some half a mile.
Some contain five acres.
Wall and breast-works of earth.
Appearance of ancient beds of creeks.
[Note the geological change.]
Lake Erie retired from two to five miles.

17. FURTHER SOUTH :
A chain of parallel forts.
Two table grounds.
Recession of lake.

All these vestiges denote long periods of time, and probably different eras of occupation. Who preceded the Iroquois? Who preceded their predecessors? Do these vestiges tell the story? How shall we study them? By antiquities; by language; by comparison with other races of America, Asia, Africa, Europe.

ALBANY, *July 5th.*—Examine the site of ancient Mohawk residence in 1609, on the island and its vicinity at the mouth of Norman's Kill. Look for their ancient burial places. Bones, pieces of pottery, and other objects of art may tell something bearing on their history.

Is the Oasis opposite the turnpike gate, the site of their ancient burial-ground? Is this the spot denoted by their name of Tawasentha, or is it to be sought in other places, at the mouth, or up the valley of this stream?

UTICA.—The Mohawk valley appears to have no monumental, or other evidences of its having been occupied by races prior to the Mohawks.

VERNON.—Who were the original race that first set foot in Oneida county? When did the Oneidas come? Where did they originate, and how? They are said to be the youngest of the Six Nations.

L. Hitchcock Esq. says that he was present, when a boy, some forty years ago, when the last executions for witchcraft among the Oneidas took place. The suspected persons were two females. The executioner was Hon Yost. They were dispatched unawres, by the tomahawk.

Sachan, a strong wind, or tempest, was the Oneida name for Col. L. S.

The principal tributary to the Oneida creek which traverses this rich grazing town, is called after the noted chief, (to adopt the common pronunciation,) SCANADO. It means a deer. The old orthography, for this word is Skenandoah.

Mr. Tracy, of Utica, whose authority on this point is good, gives Tegesoken, as the Indian name of Fish creek. It means, *between the months*.

Cowassalon creek, *i. e.*, bushes hanging over the water.

Canastota. One pitch pine tree.

Aontagillon. Brook of the pointed rock.

Kunyonskota. White creek (on Dean's patent.)

Kanaghtarageara. Place of washing the penis. This is a dark ravine. This word appears to be Mohawk.

Sa-da-quoit. Smooth pebbles in the bed of the stream—creek at New-Hartford. All these are in Oneida county.

Ot, Judge J. says, means water in the Oneida tongue.

Otsego, he adds, is from Ot, water, and Sago, hail, welcome, how d'ye do? This I don't believe. It is not in accordance with the Indian principles of combination.

ONEIDA LANGUAGE.

The Oneidas call a man, Lon gwee.
" a woman, Yon gwee.
" God, Lonee.
" Evil Spirit, Kluneolux.

Some of their words are very musical, as Ostia, a bone; ahta, a shoe; kiowilla, an arrow; awiali, a heart; loainil, a supreme ruler.

The French priests, who filled the orthography of this language with the letter R, committed one of the greatest blunders. There is no sound of R, in the language ; by this letter, they constantly represent the sound of L.

Oneida Castle, *July*.

In a conference with Abraham Denne, an aged Oneida, he stated that Brandt was brought up by his (Denne's) grandfather, at Canajoharie ; that he was a bastard, his mother Mohawk, and did not come of a line of chiefs. Says, that Scanado was a tory in the war, notwithstanding his high name ; that he acted against us at the seige of Fort Stanwix. The anecdote of an Indian firing from a tree, he places, while they were repairing the fort ; says that after the man got up, he drew up loaded rifles with a cord ; that both Scanado and Brant were present.

Says Scanado was adopted by the nation, when quite young ; came from the west ; does not know of what tribe, but showed himself smart, and rose to the chieftaincy by his bravery and conduct. Says, that the (syenite) stone on the hill, is the true Oneida stone, and not the white stone at the spring ; was so pronounced by Moses Schuyler, son of Hon Yost, who knew it forty years ago ; that the elevation gave a view of the whole valley, so that they could descry their enemies at a distance by the smoke of their fires ; no smoke, he said, without fire. They could notify also, from this elevation, by a beacon fire. The name of the stone is O-ne-a-ta ; auk, added, renders it personal, and means an Oneida. The word Oneida is an English corruption of the Indian.

Origin of the Oneidas.

Abraham Schuyler, an Oneida, says that the Oneidas originated in two men, who separated themselves from the Onondagas. They first dwelt at the outlet of Oneida lake. Next removed to the outlet of Oneida creek, on the lake, where they fortified. Williams says he was born there, and is well acquainted with the old fort. They then went to the head of the valley at the Oneida stone, from which they were named. Their fourth remove was to the present site of Oneida Castle, called a skull on a pole, where they lived at the time of the discovery of the country and settlement of the colony by the Dutch, (i. e. 1609 to '14.)

Site of the Oneida Stone, Stockbridge.

Etymology.

Asked several Oneidas to pronounce the name for the Oneida stone. They gave it as follows :

O-ni-o-ta-aug.
O-ne-u-ta-aug.
O-ne-yo-ta-aug.

The terminal syllable, *aug*, seems to be a local particle, but carries also with its antecedent *ta*, the idea of life or existence, people or inhabitants.

Onia is a stone. The meaning clearly is, People of the (or who have sprung from the) Place of the *Stone*.

Adirondak, Jourdain, pronounces Lod-a-lon-dak, putting l's for r's and a's. It means a people who eat trees—an expression ironically used for those who eat bark of trees.

For Cherokees, he gives We-au-dah.

For Delawares, Lu-na-to-gun.

What a mass of fog philologists are fighting with, who mistake, as the eminent Vater and Adelung have, in some cases done, the different *names* of the same tribes of American Indians for different *tribes*.

Antique Corn Hills.

Counted one hundred cortical layers in a black walnut—centre broke so as to prevent counting the whole number, but by measuring estimated one hundred and forty more. If so, the field was deserted in 1605.

The present proprietor of the farm comprising the Oneida stone, spring, butternut grove, &c. is Job Francis., He first hired the land of Hendrick's widow; afterwards he and Gregg were confirmed by the State.

The white stone at the spring, a carbonate of lime, is not the *true* Oneida stone.

The Oneida stone is a *syenite*—a boulder.

Onondaga Castle.

Abraham Le Fort says, that Ondiaka was the great chronicler of his tribe. He had often heard him speak of the traditions of his father. On his last journey to Oneida he accompanied him. As they passed south by Jamesville and Pompey, Ondiaka told him that in ancient times, and before they fixed down at Onondaga, they lived at these spots. That it was before the Five Nations had confederated; but while they kept up a separate existence, and fought with each other. They kept fighting and moving their villages often. This reduced their numbers, and kept them poor and in fear. When they had experienced much sickness in a place, they thought it best to quit it and seek some new spot where it was hoped they should have better luck. At length they confederated, and then the fortifications were no longer necessary, and fell into disuse. This is the origin, he believes, of these old works, which are not of foreign origin.

Ondiaka told Le Fort that the Onondagas were created by Ha-wä-ne-o, in the country where they lived. That he made this entire "island" HA-WHO-NAO, for the red race, and meant it for them alone. He did not allude to, or acknowledge any migrations from foreign lands.

Their plan, after the confederation was to adopt prisoners and captives, that fragments of tribes who were parted amongst them and thus lost. They used the term We-hait-wa-tsha, in a figurative sense, in relation to such tribes. This term means a body cut and quartered and scattered around. So they aimed to scatter their prisoners among the other nations. There is still blood of the Cherokees in Onondaga. A boy of this nation became a chief among the Cherokees.

I called Le Fort's attention to the residence of the Moravian missionary, Zœisberger. He said there was no tradition of such residence—that the oldest men remembered no such mission ; that they were ever strongly opposed to all missionaries after the expulsion of the Jesuits, and he felt confident no such person, or any person in the character of a preacher, had lived at Onondaga Castle ; that there must be some mistake in the matter.

ONONDAGA. [Jackson's.]

Ondiaka told Le Fort that the Onondagas formerly wandered about, without being long fixed at a place, frequently changing their villages from slight causes, such as sickness, &c. They were at war with the other Iroquois bands. They were also at war with other tribes. Hence forts were necessary, but after they confederated, such defensive works fell into disuse. They lived in the present areas of De Witt, Lafayette, Pompey and Manlius, along Butternut creek, &c. Here the French visited them, and built a fort, after their confederation.

Ephraim Webster stated that the Indians were never as numerous as appearances led men to think. This appearance of a heavy population happened from their frequent removals, leaving their old villages, which soon assumed the appearance of ancient populous settlements.

He told Jas. Gould, that being once on a visit to Canada, he became acquainted with a very aged Indian, who, one day, beginning to talk of the Onondaga country, told him that he was born near the old church, near Jamesville, where there was a very populous village. One evening, he said, he stepped out of his lodge, and immediately sank in the earth, and found himself in a large room, surrounded by three hundred witches and wizzards. Next morning he went to the council, and told the chiefs of this extraordinary fact. They asked him whether he could not identify them. He said he could. They then accompanied him on a visit to all the lodges, when he pointed out this and that one, who were immediately killed. Before this inquiry ended, and the delusion was stayed, he says that three hundred persons were killed.

Nothing is more distinct or better settled in the existing traditions of the Iroquois, than their wars with the Cherokees. I found this alluded to at Oneida, Onondaga, &c., in the course of their traditions, but have not been able to trace *a cause* for the war. They seemed to have been deeply and mutually exasperated by perfidy and horrid treachery in the course of these wars, such as the breaking of a peace pledge, and murder of deputies, &c. Their great object was, as soon as young men grew up, to go war against the Cherokees. This long journey was performed without provisions, or any other preparation than bows, clubs, spears and arrows. They relied on the forest for food. Thousands of miles were not sufficient to dampen their ardor, and no time could blot out their hatred. The Oneidas call them *We au dah.*

Jeremiah Gould went with me to view the twin mounds. They exhibit numerous pits or holes, which made me at once think of the Assenjigun, or hiding pit of the western Indians. Gould, in answer to my inquiry, said that it was a tradition which he did not know how much value it was worth, that the Tuscaroras were brought from the south by the Oneidas, and first settled in this county. They warred against the Onondagas. The latter, to save their corn, buried it in these mounds or hills, then hid by the forest. In one of these excations, dug into forty years ago, they found a human skull and other bones belonging to the human frame.

James Gould went with me over the stream (Butternut) to show me a mound. It is apparently of geological formation, and not artificial. Its sides were covered with large trees, the stumps of which remain. There was a level space at the top, some four or five paces in diameter, trees and bushes around. The apex, as paced, measures one way 17, the other 12 paces; is elongated. It seemed to have been the site of the prophet's lodge. Near it is the old burying ground, on an elongated ridge, where the graves were ranged in lines.

Pottery.—Webster gives the Indian tradition of this ancient art thus. The women made the kettles. They took clay and tempered it with some siliceous or coarse stone. This they first burnt thoroughly, so as to make it friable, (probably they plunged it while hot into water,) and then pounded it, and mixed it with blood.

Charred corn, &c.—In Ellisburgh is found much charred corn beneath the soil, and numerous remains of occupancy by the natives. Is this the evidence of Col. Van Schaack's expedition into the Onondaga country during the revolutionary war? His battle with the Indians, tradition here says, took place near Syracuse. Bones, supposed to be of this era, were discovered, in ditching the swamp near Cortland House.

KASONDA.

Mr. I. Keeler says that he cut a large oak tree, near the site of the old fort, two and a half feet through. In re-cutting it, at his door, a bullet was found, covered by 143 cortical layers. It was still some distance to the centre. If this tree was cut in 1810, the bullet was fired in 1667. Consult " Paris Documents," 1666, treaty with the Onondaga Iroquois.

The Goulds say that the fort was a square, with bastions, and had streets within it. It was set round with cedar pickets, which had been burnt down to the ground. Stumps of them were found by the plough.

Nearly every article belonging to the iron tools of a blacksmith shop have been ploughed up at various times—an anvil, horn, vice screw, &c. ; Indian axes, a horse shoe, hinges, the strap hinge. A pair of these hangs the wicket gate to his house.

A radius of five to six miles around the old fort would cover all the striking remains of ancient occupancy in the towns of De Witt, Lafayette and Pompey.

Webster told the Goulds that the French who occupied this fort, and had the nucleus of a colony around it, excited the jealousy and ire of the Onondagas by the hostility of some western tribes in their influence. Against these the Onondaga warriors marched. The French then attacked the red men, &c. This led to their expulsion and massacre. All were killed but a priest who lived between the present towns of Salina and Liverpool. He refused to quit peaceably. They then put a chain around a ploughshare, and heating it, hung it about his neck ; he was thus, with the symbol of agriculture, tortured to death. His hut was standing when the county was settled.

The attempt to settle western New-York by the French was in the age of chivalry, (the 16th century,) and was truly Quixotic.

TRADITION.

Pompey and its precincts were regarded by the Indians as the ground of blood, and it brought up to their minds many dark reminiscences, as they passed it. Some twenty years ago, there lived an aged Onondaga, who said that many moons before his father's days, there came a party of white men from the east in search of silver. From the heights of the Onondaga hills, they descried the white foam of Onondaga lake, and this was all the semblance they ever found of silver. One of the men died, and was buried on Pompey hill, and his grave was marked by a stone.* The others built a fort on the noted ground, about a mile east of Jamesville, where they cultivated the land; but at length the Indians came in the night, and put them all to death. But there was a fearful and bloody strife, in which the Indians fell like leaves before the autumn wind. This spot is the field of blood.

L. Birdseye.

AURORA : August. See Rev. Mr. Mattoon.

Vestiges of the Cayugas—villages—orchards—old forts. Get a vocabulary of their language from Canada. Get diagram of forts.

---

* QUERY.—Is not this the inscription stone now deposited in the Albany Academy ?

Karistagea, or Steeltrap, thought to have been unfairly dealt with at his death. Buried in the road.

Fish Carrier's Reserve at the bridge. Four miles square.

Red Jacket born on the opposite banks of.the lake at Canoga.

Historical reminiscences of Mr. Burnham. Letter stating the first settlements on the Military Tract at Aurora.

Address before the G. O. I. Folly of keeping the society secret.

Horticultural meeting. Dr. Thompson. Mr. Thomas.

Anniversary of Academy. Salem Town.

Intelligence, moral tone, hospitality of the place.

Cars at Cayuga bridge.

Logan was the son of a Cayuga.

Did the Cayugas conquer the Tutelos of Virginia, and adopt the remnant?

Cayugas scattered among the Senecas, in Canada and west of the Mississippi. How many left? What annuities.

GENEVA: Ancient site of the Senecas. Origin of the word Seneca. Is it Indian or not Indian?

Examine old forts said to exist in this area. Are there any vestiges of Indian occupancy at the "Old Castle"—at Cashong—Painted-Post—Catherinestown—Appletown?

CANANDAIGUA: In visiting Fort-hill on the lake, see what vestiges. Another site bearing this name, exists to the north of Blossom's. What antiquities? What traditions? Ask old residents. Enquire of Senecas west.

ROCHESTER: Nothing left here of the footprints of the race—all covered deep and high with brick and stone. Whole valley of the Genesee worthy examination, in all its length and branches. Wants the means of an antiquarian society to do this.

Truly the Iroquois have had visited upon them the fate with which they visited others. They destroyed and scattered, and have, in turn, been destroyed and scattered. But their crime was the least. They destroyed as *heathens*, but *we* as *christians*. In any view, the antiquarian interest is the same—the moral interest, the same.

The Iroquois had noble hearts. They sighed for fame. They took hold of the tomahawk as the only mode of distinction. They brought up their young men to the war dance. They carefully taught them the arts of war. We have other avenues to distinction. Let us now direct their manly energies to other channels. The hand that drew a bow, can be taught to guide a plough. Civilization has a thousand attractions. The hunter state had but one. The same skill once devoted to war would enable them to shine in the arts of peace.

Why can not their bright men be made sachems of the pen, of the press, of the pulpit, of the lyre?

BATAVIA, *July*.—There are still traces of a mound on Knowlton's farm, a mile from Batavia, up the Tonewanda. Bones and glass beads, have been ploughed out of it. Other traces of former aboriginal occupancy exist in the vicinity, a stone pestle, axes, &c. having been found.

The Indian name of Batavia is Ge-ne-un-dah-sais-ka, meaning musquito. This was the name by which they knew the late Mr. Ellicott.

The Tonewanda falls 40 feet at a single place, within the Indian reservation. It heads on high ground about 40 miles above Batavia. On the theory of the former elevation of lake Erie, Buffalo itself would be the highest ground, between Batavia and the lake, in a direct line. Attica, is perhaps more elevated in that direction.

TONEWANDA RES. [Winsor & Richards.]

NAME OF SENECAS.

The Senecas call themselves NUN-DO-WAW-GAW, or people of the hill. The term Seneca is taken from the lake, on the banks of which they formerly lived, and had their castle. It is *not* a name of Indian origin. They are called NUN-DO-WAW-GAW, from the eminence called Fort-Hill, near Canandaguia lake. [Ho-ho-ee-yuh, or J. A. Sanford.]

CHEROKEES.

They call the Cherokees O-YAU-DAH, which means a people who live in caves. Their enmity against this people, the tradition of which is so strong and clear, is stated to have originated from the contact of war and hunting parties, in the plains of the southwest. The Senecas affirm that the Cherokees robbed and plundered a Seneca party and took away their skins. Retaliation ensued. Tragic scenes of treachery and surprise followed. The Five Nations took up the matter in all their strength, and raised large and strong war parties, who marched through the country to the Cherokee borders, and fought and plundered the vilages, and brought away scalps and prisoners. There are now, (1845) descendants of Cherokees in the third degree, living on the Tonewanda reservation. [Ho-ho-ee-yuh.] Some years ago, a chief of this blood, pure by father and mother, lived among them, who had been carried off captive when a boy. The fact being revealed to him, after he had obtained the chieftaincy, he went south to seek his relations and live and die among them, but he was unable to find them. He came back to the Senecas, and died among them. [Le Fort.]

TONEWANDA.

The most curious trait, of which we know but little, is that respecting TOTEMS.

Asked the chief called Blacksmith, his name in Seneca. He replied, De-o-ne-hoh-gah-wah, that is, a door perforated, or violently broken through, not opened. Says he was born on the Tonewonda reservation, and wishes to die there ; will be 60 years old, if he lives till next winter, 1846.

Says the Senecas call the Fort Stanwix or Rome summit, De-o-wain-sta, meaning the place where canoes are carried across the land from stream to stream ; that is, a carrying place.

Says, Te-to-yoah, or Wm. Jones of Cattaraugus, can relate valuable Seneca traditions.

He says there are eight Seneca clans ; they are the Wolf, Bear, Turtle, Deer, Plover, Beaver, Hawk and Crane. He is of the Wolf clan. This was also Red Jacket's clan.

These clans may be supposed to have arisen from persons who had greatly distinguished themselves at an early period as founders, or benefactors, or they may have held some such relation to the original nation, as the Curatii and Horatii, in Roman history. It is not only the Iroquois, who ascribed this honor to the clans of the Bear, the Turtle and the Wolf. They are equally honored among most of the Algonquin tribes.

Osteological Remains.

In the town of Cambria, six miles west of Lockport, (1824,) a Mr. Hammon, who was employed with his boy in hoeing corn, observed some bones of a child, exhumed. No farther thought was bestowed upon the subject for some time, for the plain on the ridge was supposed to have been the site of an Indian village, and this was supposed the remains of some child, who had been buried there. Eli Bruce, hearing of the circumstancc, proposed to Mr. H. that they should repair to the spot, with suitable instruments, and endeavor to find some relics. The soil was a light loam, which would be dry and preserve bones for centuries without decay. A search enabled them to come to a pit, but a slight distance from the surface. The top of the pit was covered with small slabs of the Medina sandstone, and was twenty-four feet square, by four and a half in depth—the planes agreeing with the four cardinal points. It was filled with human bones of both sexes and all ages. They dug down at one extremity and found the same layers to extend to the bottom, which was the same dry loam, and from their calculations, they deduced that at least four thousand souls had perished in one great massacre. In one skull, two flint arrow heads were found, and many had the appearance of having been fractured and cleft open, by a sudden blow. They were piled in regular layers, but with no regard to size or sex. Pieces of pottery were picked up in the pit, and had also been ploughed up in the field adjacent. Traces of a log council house were plainly discernable. For, in an oblong square, the soil was poor, as if it had never been cultivated, till the whites broke it up ; and where the logs of the house had decayed, was a strip of rich mould. A maple tree, over the pit, being cut down, two hundred and fifty concentric circles were counted, making the mound to be anterior to as many years. It has been supposed by the villagers that the bones were deposited there before the discovery of America, but the finding of some metal tools with a French stamp, places the date within our period. One hundred and fifty persons a day visited this spot the first season, and carried off the bones. They are now nearly all gone, and the pit ploughed over. Will any antiquarian inform us, if possible, why these bones were placed here ! To what tribe do they belong ? When did such a massacre occur ?

None of the bones of the men were below middle size, but some of them were very large. The teeth were in a perfectly sound state.

Present Means of living on the Reservation.

1. Rent of land from twelve shillings to three dollars per acre.
2. Sale of timber, fire wood, hemlock bark, staves, saw-logs.
3. Fishing and hunting. Very little now.
4. Raise corn, cattle, horses, hogs, some wheat, &c. &c., cut hay. Young men hire themselves out in harvest time.

Bones.

At Barnegat is an ancient ridge, or narrow raised path, leading from the river some miles, through low grounds ; it is an ancient burial ground, on an island, in a swamp.

Bones of the human frame, bone needles, and other ancient remains, are ploughed up at an ancient station, fort or line, in Shelby.

A human head, petrified, was ploughed up by Carrington, sen., in a field in Alabama, Genesee county, and is now in the possession of Mr. Grant, at Barnegat.

Petrified tortoises are said to be ploughed up in many places.

Opinion of a Chief of the Word Seneca.

De-o-ne-ho-ga-wa is the most influential chief of the Tonewandas. He is of the Wolf tribe—born on the forks of the Tonewanda, and is 59 years old. Being interrogated as to the Seneca history, he says, that the tradition of the tribe is clear—that they lived on the banks of the Seneca and Canandaigua lakes. They were called Nun-do-wau-onuh, or People of the Hill, from an eminence now called Fort Hill, at the head of Canandaigua lake. They are now called, or, rather, call themselves, Nun-do-wau-gau. The inflection onuh, in former times, denoted residence, at a hill ; the particle agau, in the latter, is a more enlarged term for locality, corresponding to their present dispersed condition.

The word Seneca, he affirms, is not of Indian origin. While they lived in Ontario, there was a white man called Seneca, who lived on the banks of the lake of that name. Who he was, where he came from, and to what nation he belonged, he does not know. But wherever he originated, he was noted for his bravery, wisdom and strength. He became so proverbial for these noble qualities, that it was usual to say of such, and such a one, among themselves, he is as brave as Seneca, as wise as Seneca, as noble as Seneca. Whether the lake was called after him, or he took his name from the lake, is not known. But the name itself is of European origin. The tribe were eventually called Senecas from their local residence. The idea, he says, was pleasing to them, for they thought themselves the most brave and indomitable of men. Of all the races of the Ongwe-Honwe, they esteemed themselves the most superior in courage, endurance and enterprize.

He refers to Te-to-yoah of Cattaraugus for further information.

On reference to Te-to-yoah, some time afterwards, he had no tradition on this particular subject. The probability is, that Blacksmith meant only to say, that the name was not Seneca. So far is true. What he says of a great man living on Seneca lake, &c., in older times, is probably a reproduction, in his mind, of an account of Seneca, the moralist, which has been told him, or some Indian from whom he had it, in days by-gone.

As the name of Seneca is one of the earliest we hear, after 1609, it was probably a Mohawk term for that people. It is spelt with a *k* in old French authors.

LEWISTON. [Frontier House.]

The Tuscarora clans are the following:

The Turtle.

The Wolf.

The Bear.

The Beaver.

The Snipe, or Plover.

The Eel. This is not an Iroquois totem.

The Land Tortoise.

They have lost the Falcon, Deer and Crane, perhaps in their disastrous wars of 1713. By this it appears they have lost one clan entirely—probably in their defeat on the Taw river, in N. Carolina. Two others of the clans are changed, namely, the Falcon and Deer, for which they have substituted the Land Tortoise and Eel.

Descent is by the chief's mother and her clan, her daughter or nearest kin, to be settled in council. The adoption of chiefs was allowed, where there was failure of descent.

Curious barrow, or mound, on Dr. Scovill's place—to be examined. Two others, near the old mill and orchard.

Old fort of KIENUKA, to be visited.

Get vocabulary of Tuscarora, to compare.

This tribe has gone through a severe ordeal, their history is full of incident. The following list shews their number in North Carolina, and all other Indians of that colony in 1708.

Tuscaroras, living in 15 towns,	1,200 men.
Waccons, in 2 towns,	120
Maramiskeets,	30
Bear Rivers,	50
Hatteras,	16
Neus, in 2 towns,	15
Pamlico,	15
Meherrin,	50
Chowan,	15
Carried forward,	1,511

Brought forward, ...	1,511
Paspatank, ...	10
Poteskeets of Carrituk, ...	30
Nottoways, ...	30
Connamox, in 2 towns, ...	25
Jaupim, ...	2
	1,608

Visited James Cusick, the brother of DAVID, the Indian archæologist, preacher to the Tusks, pictures in the house, old deeds from Carolina.

Sunday. Attended Mr. Rockwood's meeting, admirable behavior of all, dress well, good singing. W. Chew interprets.

Females, however, adhere to their ancient costume.

Women more pertinacious in their social habits and customs than men.

Tuscaroras raise much wheat, cattle, horses, quite in advance of the other tribes in agriculture.

They own the fee simple of about 5,000 acres, besides their reservation, which they purchased from the Holland Company.

NIAGARA FALLS.

This name is Mohawk. It means, according to Mrs. Kerr, the Neck, the term being first applied to the portage, or neck of land, between lakes Erie and Ontario.

BUFFALO.

Whence this name? The Indian term is Te-ho-so-ro-ro in Mohrwk, and De-o-se-o-wa in Seneca. Ellicott writes it Tu-she-way. Others, in other forms. In all, it is admitted to mean the place of the linden, or bass-wood tree.

There is an old story of buffaloes being killed here. Some say a horse was killed by hungry *Frenchmen*, and palmed off for buffalo meat at the camp. How came a horse *here*?

A curious bone needle was dug up this year, in some excavations made in Fort Niagara, which is, clearly, of the age prior to the discovery.

Bones and relics must stand for the chronology of American antiquity.

America is the tomb of the red man. All the interest of its anti-Columbian history, arises from this fact.

ERIES.

By Father Le Moyne's letter of 1653, [vide Relacions,] the war with the nation of the Cat or Eries was then newly broke out. He *thanks* the Onondagas, Senecas, Cayugas and Oneidas, for their *union* in this war.

On the 9th August, 1653, we heard a dismal shout, among the Iroquois, caused by the news, that three of their men had been killed by the Eries.

He condoles with the Seneca nation, on the capture of their great chief, Au-ren-cra-os, by the Eries.

He exhorts them to strengthen their "defences" or forts, to paint their warriors for battle, to be united in council.

He required them never to lay in ambush for the Algonquin or Huron nations, who might be on their way to visit the French.

We learn, from this, that the Eries or Cat nation, were not of the Wyandot or Huron, nor of the Algonquin nations. It would seem that these Eries were not friends of the French, and that by exciting them to this new war, they were shielding their friends, the Algons and Hurons, from the Iroquois club and scalping knife. That they were the same people called the "Neuter Nation," who occupied the banks of the Niagara, there is but little reason to believe. The Senecas called them Gawgwa or Kah-Kwah.

Cusick states that the Senecas fought against a people, west of the Genesee river, called Squakihaw, *i. e.* Kah-Kwah, whom they beat, and after a long seige took their principal fort, and put their chief to death. Those who recovered were made vassals and adopted into the tribe.

He states that the banks of the Niagara river were possessed by the Twa-kenkahor, or Missasages, who, in time, gave it up to the Iroquois peaceably. Were not these latter the Neuter Nation ?

To discuss the question of the war with the Eries, it is necessary to advert to the geographical position of the parties. The Senecas, in 1653, as appears by French authorities, lived in the area between the Seneca lake and the Genesee river. The original stock of the Five Nations appears to have entered the area of western New-York in its central portions ; and, at all events, they extended west of the Genesee, after the Erie war, and possessed the land conquered from the latter.

Mission Station, Buffalo Reservation.

Seventy-four Seneca chiefs attended the general council held here. Putting their gross population at 2,500, this gives one chief to every thirty-three souls. This makes them "captains of tens."

The Seneca language has been somewhat cultivated. Mr. Wright, the missionary, who has mastered the language, has printed a spelling book of 112 pages, also a periodical tract for reading, called the "Mental Elevator." Both valuable philological data.

The Senecas of this reservation are on the move for Cattaraugus and Alleghany, having sold out, finally, to the Ogden company. They leave their old homes and cemetery, however, with "longing, lingering looks."

Here lie the bones of Red Jacket and Mary Jemison.

Curious and interesting reminiscences the Senecas have. Jot down their traditions of all sorts. Can't separate fiction from fact. They must go together; for often, if the fiction or allegory be pulled up, the fact has no roots to sustain itself.

KAH-KWAHS, ERIES, ALLEGHANS,—who were they?

Mr. Wright showed me an ancient triturating stone of the Indians, in the circular depressions of which they reduced the siliceous material of their ancient pottery.

The Seneca language has a masculine, feminine and neuter gender. It has also an animate and inanimate gender, making five genders.

It has a general and dual plural.

It abounds in compound descriptive and derivative terms, like the Algonquin.

They count by the decimal mode. There are names for the digits to ten. Twenty is a compound of two and ten, and thirty of three and ten, &c.

The comparison of adjectives is effected by prefixes, not by inflections, or by changes of the words, as in English.

Nouns have adjective inflections as in the Algonquin. Thus *o-a-deh* is a road, *o-a-i-yu* a good road. The inflection, in this last word, is from *wi-yu*, good.

IRVING, CATTARAUGUS CREEK.

It is a maxim with the Iroquois, that a chief's skin should be thicker than that of the thorn locust, that it may not be penetrated by the thorns.

Indian speakers never impugn each other's *motives* when speaking in public council. In this, they offer an example.

Mr. Strong says, Silversmith of Onondaga, has the tradition of the war with the Eries.

INDIANS IN CANADA.

It is observed by a report of the Canadian Parliament, that the number of Indians now in Canada is 12,000. Of these, 3,301 are residing in Lower Canada, and the remainder 8,862, in Canada West. The number of Indians is stated to be on the increase, partly from the access of births over the deaths, and partly from a numerous immigration of tribes from the United States. This report must be taken with allowances. It is, at best, but an estimate, and in this respect, the Canadians, like ourselves, are apt to over estimate.

The Indian is a man who has certainly some fine points of character; one would think a man of genius could turn him to account. Why then are Indian tales and poems failures? They fail in exciting deep sympathy. We do not feel that he has a heart.

The Indian must be *humanized* before he can be loved. This is the defect in the attempts of poets and novelists. They do not show the reader that the red man has a feeling, sympathising heart, and feeling and sympathies like his own, and consequently he is not interested in the tale. It is a tale of a statue, cold, exact, stiff, but without *life*.

It is not a man with man's ordinary loves and hopes and hates. Hence the failure of our *Yamoydens*, and *Ontwas*, and *Escallas*, and a dozen of poems, which, although having merits, slumber in type and sheepskin, on the bookseller's shelf.

Horts' Corners, Catt.

One seems here, as if he had suddenly been pitched into some of the deep gorges of the Alps, surrounded with cliffs and rocks and woods, in all imaginable wildness.

Cold spring, Allegany river. [Sep. 3.]

Reached the Indian village on the reservation at this place, at 9 clock in the morning.

Indians call the place Te-o-ni-gon-o, or De-o-ni-gon-o, which means Cold Spring.

Locality of the farmer employed by Quakers, at the mouth of a creek, called Tunasassa; means a clear stream with a pebbly bed.

Allegany river they call Oheo, making no difference between it, and the stream after the inlet of the Monongahela.

Gov. Blacksnake absent; other chiefs, with his son Jacob meet in council; business adjusted with readiness.

Allegany river low; very different in its volume of water and appearance from what it was 27 years before, when I descended it, on my way to the West.

Lumbering region; banks lined with shingles, boards, saw logs. Indians act as guides and lumbermen.

Not a favorable location for the improvement of the Senecas. Steal their timber; cheat them in bargains; sell whiskey to them.

Had the imaginative Greeks lived in Allegany county, they would have pictured the Genesee and Allegany rivers, as two girls, who having shaken hands, parted, the one to skip and leap and run eastward to find the St. Lawrence, and the other to laugh through the Ohio valley, until she gradually melted into the ocean in the gulf of Mexico.

Napoli Centre.

The counties of Cattaraugus, Chautauque and Allegany, and part of Wyoming and Steuben, constitute a kind of Switzerland. The surface of the country resembles a piece of rumpled calico, full of knobs and ridges and vallies, in all possible shapes and directions. It is on the average elevated. Innkeepers and farmers encountered on two trips over it, say that there is considerably more moisture in the shape of rain and dews and fogs, than in the Genesee country. It is less valuable for wheat, but good for corn, grass, and raising stock. Nothing can be more picturesque. The hills are often cultivated to their very tops. It is healthy. Such a region is a treasure in a State so level and placid as much of western New-York; and had it the means of ready access to markets, and to the Atlantic, it would, in a few years, be spotted with gentlemens seats from the seaboard. There are some remarkable examples of the east and west, and north and south fissures of rocks (a trait also noted at Anburn,) in these counties. At one place, the fissures are so wide, and the blocks of rock between so large, that the spot is sometimes called CITY OF ROCKS. The rock here is conglomerate, i. e. the bed of the coal formation; a fact which denotes the elevation of the country. It is to be hoped, when this country is further subdivided into counties and towns, that some of the characteristic and descriptive names of the aborigines will be retained.

LODI.

This bright, busy, thriving place, is a curiosity from the fact, that the Cattaraugus creek, (a river it should be called) splits in exactly, or nearly so, in two parts, the one being in ERIE, the other in CATTARAUGUS. Efforts to get a new county, and a county seat, have heretofore been made. These conflict with similar efforts, to have a county seat located at Irving, at the mouth of the creek.

IRVING, MOUTH OF CATTARAUGUS.

This is a fine natural harbor and port of refuge. Its neglect appears strange, but it is to be attributed to the influence of capitalists at Silver-Creek, Dunkirk, Barcelona, &c.

EIGHTEEN-MILE CREEK.

Here are vestiges of the Indians old forts, town sites, &c. Time and scrutiny are alone necessary to bring out its antiquities.

BUFFALO.

The Chief, Capt. Cole.—The noted Onondaga Chief, Capt. COLE, died at his residence, among his people, a few days since, aged about seventy-five years. This Indian was well known here, having, for many years, made his home upon the reservation adjoining the city. He took the field, in defence of the country, during the last war, under the late Gen. PORTER, who was often heard to speak of his bravery and usefulness, in the various battles along the Niagara frontier.

COLE was of the "old school" of his race—a primitive, unadulterated Indian, equally uncontaminated in mind as in habits, by intercourse with the whites. Probity and justice were the leading features of his character; and to direct these he had an intellect which won for him a high control and extended influence among his tribe.

Some years since COLE was selected by our townsman, young WILGUS, as the finest specimen he had ever met, of the race to which he belonged; and he immediately took means to secure him as a sitter. The result was the half length portrait of the Chief which WILGUS executed, and which has been so often seen and admired alike by our citizens and by strangers.

An incident connected with the history of this piece, seems appropriate here, as illustrative of its excellence. When WILGUS left for

Porto Rico, where he now is, he took the portrait of Cole with him. It was seen, upon that island, by a gentleman from Amsterdam, who declared it the first piece he had seen which gave him the slightest ideas of the peculiar characteristics of the Indian race; and he became so interested in the picture that he asked and obtained permission to take it with him, to Europe, for the inspection of his friends. The piece was, by him, carried to Amsterdam, where the admiration of it was universal, and where it would have been retained, at almost any price, had it been for sale. But it was not: the gentleman had promised to return the painting safe to Buffalo; and he has done so, it having arrived here this spring; and it now stands, unostentatiously enough, in the bookstore of the artist's father, upon Main-street.

Batavia.

The Tonewandas at length consent to have their census taken.

Auburn.

Go with Mr. Goodwin to visit Oswaco lake—Gov. Throop's place—Old Dutch Church overlooking the lake, &c.

Fort-Hill.—Extensive vestiges of an elliptical work—Curious rectangular fisures of the limestone rock on the Owasco outlet—north and south.

The Indian name of the place, as told by an Onondaga chief—Osco; first called Hardenburgh's Corners, finally named after Goldsmith's "Deserted Village"—so that the poet may be said to have had a hand in supplying names for a land to which he once purposed to migrate.

It would have pleased "poor Goldsmith" could he have known that he was the parent of the name for so fine a town—a town thriving somewhat on the principle laid down in the concluding lines of the poem—

> "While self-dependent power can time defy,
> As rocks resist the billows and the sky."

Syracuse.

Pity a better name could not have been found for so fine, central, capital a site. The associations are now all wrong. What had Dionysius or Archimedes to do here? It was Atotarho Garangula, Dekanifora, Ontiyaka, and their kindred, who made the place famous. Onondaga would have been a far better appellation. The Indians called the lake and its basin of country together Gan-on-do-a. Salt Point, or the Saline, sounded to me as if, abating syllibants, it might be written Ka-ji-ka-do.

Utica.

There was a ford in the Mohawk here. It was the site of Fort Schuyler—a fort named after Major Schuyler, a man of note and military prowess in the olden time, long before the days of General Philip

Schuyler. Some philological goose, writing from the Canadas, makes Utica an Indian name!

Mouth of the Norman's Kill, or Tawasentha, Albany.

Mr. Brayton says, that in digging the turnpike road, in ascending Kiddenhook hill, on the road to Bethlehem, many human bones, supposed to be Indian, were found. They were so numerous that they were put in a box and buried. This ancient burial ground, which I visited, was at a spot where the soil is light and sandy. On the hill, above his house, is a level field, where arrow-heads have been found in large numbers.

Mr. B., who has lived here sixteen years, does not know that the isolated high ground, east of the turnpike gate, contains ancient bones—has not examined it with that view. Says Mr. Russell, in the neighborhood, has lived there fifty years, and will ask him.

Nothing could be more likely, than that this oasis on the low land should have served as the cemetery for the Mohawks, who inhabited the island, where the Dutch first landed and built a fort in 1614.

The occupancy of this island by the Indians could never have been any thing but a *summer residence*, for it is subject to be inundated every year by the breaking up of the river. This was probably the cause why the Dutch almost immediately abandoned it, and went a little higher, to the main land, where Albany now stands. The city, however, such are the present signs of its wealth and progress, has extended down quite half way to the parallel of the original site of "Het Casteel" under Christians, and should these signs continue, within twenty years South Pearl-street will present lines of compact dwellings and stores to the bridge over the Tawasentha, and Kiddenhook be adorned with country seats.

New-York.

Whatever else can be done for the red race, it is yet my opinion, that nothing would be as permanently beneficial, in their exaltation and preservation, as their admission to the rights and immunities of citizens.

Indian Election.

At a council of the Six Nations of Indians, held upon the Tonawanda Reservation, on Wednesday, Oct. 1st, there were present the Mohawks, Onondagas and Senecas, confederate brothers on the one part, and the Oneidas, Cayugas and Tuscaroras, brothers on the other part.

The Masters of the grand ceremonies were Deatgahdos, Hahsant (Onondagas) and Oahgwashah, (Cayuga.) The speakers were Hahsauthat, (Onondaga,) Shosheowaah, (Seneca,) and Oaghwashah, (Cayuga.)

After the grand ceremonies were performed, the folllowing were appointed Grand Sachems, Sachems and Chiefs.

Desha-go-gaah-neh was appointed Grand Sachem, in place of Ganoh-gaith-da-wih, deceased.

Ga-noh-la-dah-laoh was appointed Grand Sachem, in place of Gahno-gaih, deceased.

Deyawa-dah-oh was appointed Grand Sachem in place of Ganyodaiyuh, deposed.

The above are Seneca Indians.

Of the Onondagas—O-jih-ja-do-gah was appointed Grand Sachem in place of Hononiwedoh,) Col. Silversmith, an Onondaga resident among the Senecas) deposed.

So-dye-a-dolik was appointed Chief of the Onondagas, in place of Sha-go-ga-eh, (Button George,) deposed.

Deyushahkda was appointed Sachem of the Tuscaroras, and Ga-yah-jih-go-wa was appointed a Chief as runner for De-yushahkdo.—*Buff. Pilot.* W.

Sketches of an Indian Council.

A grand council of the confederate Iroquois was held last week, at the Indian Council House on the Tonawanda Reservation, in the county of Genesee. Its proceedings occupied three days—closing on the 3d instant. It embraced representatives from all the Six Nations—the Mohawk, the Onondaga, the Seneca; and the Oneida, the Cayuga and the Tuscarora. It is the only one of the kind which has been held for a number of years, and is, probably, the last which will ever be assembled with a full representation of all the confederate nations.

With the expectation that the council would commence on Tuesday, two or three of us had left Rochester so as to arrive at the Council House Monday evening; but owing to some unsettled preliminaries, it had been postponed till Wednesday. The Indians from abroad, however, had arrived at the Council Grounds, or in their immediate vicinity, on Monday; and one of the most interesting spectacles of the occasion, was the entry of the different nations upon the domain and hospitality of the Senecas, on whose ground the council was to be held. The representation of Mohawks, coming as they did, from Canada, was necessarily small. The Onondagas, with the acting Tod-o-dah-hoh of the confederacy, and his two counsellors, made an exceedingly creditable appearance. Nor was the array of Tuscaroras, in point of numbers at least, deficient in attractive and imposing features.

Monday evening we called upon and were presented to Blacksmith, the most influential and authoritative of the Seneca sachems. He is about 60 years old—is somewhat portly, is easy enough in his manners, and is well disposed and even kindly towards all who convince him that they have no sinister designs in coming among his people.

Jemmy Johnson is the Great High Priest of the confederacy. Though now 69 years old, he is yet an erect, fine looking, and energetic Indian, and is both hospitable and intelligent. He is in possession of the medal presented by Washington to Red Jacket in 1792, which, among other things of interest, he showed us.

It would be incompatible with the present purpose to describe all the interesting men who there assembled, among whom were Capt. Frost, Messrs. Le Fort, Hill, John Jacket, Dr. Wilson and others. We spent most of Tuesday, and indeed much of the time during the other days of the week in conversation with the chiefs and most intelligent Indians of the different nations, and gleaned from them much information of the highest interest in relation to the organization, government and laws, religion, customs of the people, and characteristics of the great men, of the old and once powerful confederacy. It is a singular fact, that the peculiar government and national characteristics of the Iroquois is a most interesting field for research and inquiry, which has never been very thoroughly, if at all, investigated, although the historic events which marked the proud career of the confederacy, have been perseveringly sought and treasured up in the writings of Stone, Schoolcraft, Hosmer, Yates and others.

Many of the Indians speak English readily; but with the aid and interpretations of Mr. Ely S. Parker, a young Seneca of no ordinary degree of attainment, in both scholarship and general intelligence, and who, with Le Fort, the Onondaga, is well versed in old Iroquois matters, we had no difficulty in conversing with any and all we chose to.

About mid-day on Wednesday, the council commenced. The ceremonies with which it was opened and conducted were certainly unique—almost indescribable; and as its proceedings were in the Seneca tongue, they were in a great measure unintelligible, and in fact profoundly mysterious to the pale faces. One of the chief objects for which the council had been convoked, as has been heretofore editorially stated in the American, was to fill two vacancies in the sachemships of the Senecas, which had been made by the death of the former incumbents; and preceding the installation of the candidates for the succession, there was a general and dolorous lament for the deceased sachems, the utterance of which, together with the repetition of the laws of the confederacy—the installation of the new sachems—the impeachment and deposition of three unfaithful sachems—the elevation of others in their stead, and the performance of the various ceremonies attendant upon these proceedings, consumed the principal part of the afternoon.

At the setting of the sun, a bountiful repast, consisting of an innumerable number of rather formidable looking chunks of boiled fresh beef, and an abundance of bread and succotash, was brought into the council house. The manner of saying grace on this occasion was indeed peculiar. A kettle being brought, hot and smoking from the fire, and placed in the centre of the council house, there proceeded from a single person, in a high shrill key, a prolonged and monotonous sound, resembling that of the syllable *wah* or *yah*. This was immediately followed by a response from the whole multitude, uttering in a low and profoundly guttural but protracted tone, the syllable *whe* or *swe*, and this concluded grace. It was impossible not to be somewhat mirthfully affected at the first hearing of grace said in this novel manner. It is, however, pleasurable to reflect that the Indian recognizes the duty of rendering thanks to the Divine Being in some formal way, for the bounties and enjoyments which He bestows; and were an Indian to attend a public feast among his pale faced brethren, he would be affected, perhaps to a greater degree of marvel, at witnessing a total neglect of this ceremony, than we were at his singular way of performing it.

After supper, commenced the dances. All day Tuesday, and on Wednesday, up to the time that the places of the deceased sachems had been filled, every thing like undue joyfulness had been restrained. This was required by the respect customarily due to the distinguished dead. But now, the bereaved sachemships being again filled, all were to give utterance to gladness and joy. A short speech from Capt. Frost, introductory to the enjoyments of the evening, was received with acclamatory approbation; and soon eighty or ninety of these sons and daughters of the forest—the old men and the young, the maidens and matrons—were engaged in the dance. It was indeed a rare sight.

Only two varieties of dancing were introduced the first evening—the trotting dance and the fish dance. The figures of either are exceedingly simple, and but slightly different from each other. In the first named, the dancers all move round a circle, in a single file, and keeping time in a sort of trotting step to an Indian song of yo-ho-ha, or yo-ho-ha-ha-ho, as sung by the leaders, or occasionally by all conjoined. In the other, there is the same movement in single file round a circle, but every two persons, a man and a woman, or two men, face each other, the one moving forward, the other backward, and all keeping step to the music of the singers, who are now, however, aided by a couple of tortoise or turtle shell rattles, or an aboriginal drum. At regular intervals, there is a sort of cadence in the music, during which a change of position by all the couples takes place, the one who had been moving backward taking the place of the one moving forward, when all again move onward, one-half of the whole, of course, being obliged to follow on by *advancing backwards!*

One peculiarity in Indian dancing would probably strongly commend itself to that class among pale faced beaux and belles denominated the bashful; though perhaps it would not suit others as well. The men, or a number of them, usually begin the dance alone; and the women, or each of them, selecting the one with whom she would like to dance, presents herself at his side as he approaches, and is immediately received into the circle. Consequently, the young Indian beau knows nothing of the tact required to handsomely invite and gallantly lead a lady to the dance; and the young Indian maiden, unannoyed by obnoxious offers, at her own convenience, gracefully presents her personage to the one she designs to favor, and thus quietly engages herself in the dance. And moreover, while an Indian beau is not necessarily obliged to exhibit any gallantry as towards a belle, till she has herself manifested her own good pleasure in the matter, so, therefore, the belle cannot indulge herself in vascillant flirtations with any considerable number of beaux, without being at once detected !

On Thursday the religious ceremonies commenced ; and the council from the time it assembled, which was about 11 o'clock, A. M., till 3 or 4 o'clock, P. M., gave the most serious attention to the preaching of Jemmy Johnson, the Great High Priest, and the second in the succession under the new revelation. Though there are some evangelical believers among the Indians, the greater portion of them cherish the religion of their fathers. This, as they say, has been somewhat changed by the new revelation, which the Great Spirit made to one of their prophets about 47 yeas ago, and which, as they also believe, was approved by Washington. The profound regard and veneration which the Indian has ever retained towards the name and memory of Washington, is most interesting evidence of his universally appreciated worth ; and the fact that the red men regard him not merely as one of the best, but as the very best man that ever has existed, or that will ever exist, is beautifully illustrated in a singular credence which they maintain even to this day, viz : that Washington is the only white man who has ever entered Heaven, and is the only one who will enter there, till the end of the world.

Among the Senecas, public religious exercises take place but once a year. At these times, Jemmy Johnson preaches hour after hour, for three days ; and then rests from any public discharge of ecclesiastical offices the remaining 362 days of the year. On this, an unusual occasion, he restricted himself to a few hours in each of the last two days of the council. We were told by young Parker, who took notes of his preaching, that his subject matter on Thursday abounded with good teachings, enforced by appropriate and happy illustrations and striking imagery. After he had finished, the council took a short respite. Soon, however, a company of warriors ready and eager to engage in the celebrated "corn dance," made their appearance. They were differently attired. While some were completely enveloped in a closely fitting and gaudy colored garb ; others, though perhaps without intending it, had made wonderfully close approaches to an imitation of the costume said to have been so fashionable in many parts of the State of Georgia during the last hot summer, and which is also said to have consisted simply of a shirt collar and a pair of spurs. But in truth, these warriors, with shoulders and limbs in a state of nudity, with faces bestreaked with paints, with jingling trinkets dangling at their knees, and with feathered war-caps waving above them, presented a truly picturesque and romantic appearance. When the center of the council house had been cleared, and the musicians with the shell rattles had taken their places, the dance commenced ; and for an hour and a half, perhaps two hours, it proceeded with surprising spirit and energy. Almost every posture of which the human frame is susceptible, without absolutely making the feet to be uppermost, and the head for once, to assume the place of *the understanding*, was exhibited. Some of the attitudes of the dancers, were really imposing, and the dance as a whole, could be got up and conducted only by Indians ! The women in the performance of the corn dance, are quite by themselves—keeping time to the beat of the shells, and gliding along sideways, without scarcely lifting their feet from the floor.

It would probably be well, if the Indian every where, could be inclined to refrain at least from the more grotesque and boisterous peculiarities of this dance. The influence of these cannot be productive of any good ; and it is questionable whether it will be possible, so long as they are retained, to assimilate them to any greater degree of civilization or to more refined methods of living and enjoyment, than they now possess. The same may be said of certain characteristics of the still more vandalic war dance. This, however, was not introduced at the council.

A part of the proceedings of Friday—the last day of the council, bore resemblance to those of thepreceding day. Jemmy Johnson resumed his preaching ; at the close of which the corn dance was again performed, though with far more spirit and enthusiasm than at the first. Double the numbers that then appeared—all hardy and sinewy men, attired in original and fantastic style, among whom was one of the chiefs of the confederacy, together with 40 or 50 women of the different nations—now engaged and for two hours persevered in the performance of the various, complicated and fatiguing movements of this dance. The appearance of the dusky throng, with its increased numbers, and, of course proportionably increased resources for the production of shrill whoops and noisy stamping, and for the exhibition of striking attitudes and rampant motions, was altogether strange, wonderful and seemingly super-human.

After the dance had ceased, another kind of " sport," a well contested foot race, claimed attention. In the evening, after another supper in the Council House, the more social dances,—the trotting, the fish—and one in which the women alone participated, were resumed. The fish dance seemed to be the favorite ; and being invited to join it by one of the chiefs, we at once accepted the invitation, and followed in mirthful chase of pleasure, with a hundred forest children. Occasionally the dances are characterised with ebullitions of merriment and flashes of real fun ; but generally a singular sobriety and decorum are observed. Frequently, when gazing at a throng of 60 or perhaps an hundred dancers, we have been scarcely able to decide which was the most remarkable, the staid and imperturbable gravity of the old men and women, or the complete absence of levity and frolicsomeness in the young.

The social dances of the evening—with occasional speeches from the Sachems and Chiefs, were the final and concluding ceremonies of this singular but interesting affair. Saturday morning witnessed the separation of the various nations, and the departure of each to their respective homes.

The writer would like to have said a word or two in relation to the present condition and prospects of the Indians, but the original design in regard to both the topics and brevity of this writing having been already greatly transcended, it must be deferred. The once powerful confederacy of the Six Nations, occupying in its palmy days the greater portion of New-York State, now number only a little over 3,000.* Even this remnant will soon be gone. In view of this, as well as of the known fact that the Indian race is every where gradually diminishing in number, the writer cannot close without invoking for this unfortunate people, renewed kindliness and sympathy and benevolent attention. It is true, that with some few exceptions, they possess habits and characteristics which render them difficult to approach; but still, they are only what the Creator of us all has made them. And, let it be remembered, it must be a large measure of kindliness and benevolence, that will repay the injustice and wrong that have been inflicted upon them. R. S. G.

Rochester, *Oct.* 7, 1845.

---

* **3,753, vide preceding census.**

(C.)

Letter from J. V. H. Clark to Henry R. Schoolcraft.

Manlius, *Oct.* 6*th*, 1845.

H. R. SCHOOLCRAFT, ESQ.,

DEAR SIR—Agreeable to your request I have been upon the grounds in our vicinity once occupied as forts and places of defence. So devastating has been the hand of time and the works of civilized men, that little can now be possibly gleaned by observation. Our main reliance in these matters must depend almost entirely upon the recollections of early settlers and traditions. Many of these accounts, as you are aware, are differently related by different individuals, and not unfrequently in material points contradictory. From careful investigation and inquiry I have been enabled to add a little to what I had previously gathered and referred you to, in the New-York Spectator. A locality in the town of Cazenovia, Madison co., near the county line, and on Lot 33, Township of Pompey, Onondaga co., called the "*Indian Fort*," was not described in that paper. It is about four miles southeasterly from Manlius village, situated on a slight eminence, which is nearly surrounded by a deep ravine, the banks of which are quite steep and somewhat rocky. The ravine is in shape like an ox-bow, made by two streams, which pass nearly around it and unite. Across this bow at the opening, was an earthen wall running southeast and northwest, and when first noticed by the early settlers, was four or five feet high, straight, with something of a ditch in front, from two to three feet deep. Within this enclosure may be about ten or twelve acres of land. A part of this ground, when first occupied in these latter times, was called the "*Prairie*," and is noted now among the old men as the place where the first battalion training (military) was held in the county of Onondaga. But that portion near the wall, and in front of it, has recently, say five years ago, been cleared of a heavy growth of black oak timber. Many of the trees were large, and were probably 150 or 200 years old. Some were standing *in* the ditch and others *on the top* of the embankment. There is a considerable burying place *within* the enclosure. The plough has already done much towards leveling the wall and ditch; still they can be easily traced the whole extent. A few more ploughings and harrowings and no vestige of it will remain. The specimens of dark brown pottery I send with this are from this locality. I picked them up at this visit. These specimens are somewhat numerous upon this ground now. Almost every variety of Indian relic has been found about here, but so fastidious are the holders of them, that I have not been able to procure any for you, and cannot, except *at a price*. However, they can be of little consequence, as they are described in the article above referred to. One fact, will, I think, apply to this locality, that does not belong to any other of the kind in this region, that I know of. Two cannon balls, of about 3 lbs. each, were found in the vicinity, showing that light cannon were used, either for defence, or in the reduction of this fortification. There is a large rock in the ravine on the south, on which are inscribed the following characters, thus, *IIIIIX*, cut three-quarters of an inch broad, nine inches long, three-quarters of an inch deep, perfectly regular, lines straight. Whether it was a work of fancy, or had significance, I know not. Perhaps you may determine.

On the site of the village of Cazenovia, I am told there was a fort or embankment; some persons say it was "*roundish*;" others that it was "*angular, with sides at right angles.*" Recollections respecting it are very imperfect. Many relics have been found here, indicating an earlier occupancy than those usually found in this county. This was on the Oneida's territory. There is a singular coincidence in the location of these fortifications which I have never observed until my recent visit. They are nearly all, if not quite all, situated on land rather elevated above that which is immediately contiguous, and surrounded, or partly so, by deep ravines, so that these form a part of the fortification themselves. At one of these (on the farm of David Williams, in Pompey,) the banks on either side are found to contain bullets of lead, as if shot across at opposing forces. The space between may be about three or four rods, and the natural cutting twenty or twenty-five feet deep. This only goes to show the care these architects had in selecting the most favorable situations for defence, and the fear and expectation they were in of attacks.

I do not believe any of the fortifications in this neighborhood are more ancient than the period of the French settlement of missionaries among the Onondagas, during the early part of the 17th century. But the more I investigate, the more I am convinced that there were many more of the French established here among the Indians, by far, than has been generally supposed, and their continuance with them longer.

The nature of the articles found, utensils of farmers and mechanics, hoes, axes, horseshoes, hammers, &c., go to prove that agriculture was practised somewhat extensively, as well as the mechanic arts. The Indian name by which it was anciently called, and is now, by the natives, I think goes to substantiate this fact: "Ote-que-sah'-ē-ēh," an open place with much grass, an opening, or prairie. The timber has a vigorous growth, and although in many places large, there is a uniformity in the size and age, which shows that it has all grown up *since* the occupancy; because under the trees are not only found the relics, but among them in many instances, corn hills can be traced in rows at considerable distances.

The presentation of medals, I believe to have been a very common custom among the missionaries and traders. Several have been found. A valuable cross of pure gold, sold for $30, was found on the farm of Mr. David Hinsdale, west part of Pompey. The significant "IHS" was upon it. Brass crosses are frequently found, and so are medals of the same metal. One recently found on the last named farm, about the size of a shilling piece. The figure of a Roman Pontiff in a standing position, in his hand a crosier, surrounded with this inscription, "*B. virg. sin. P. origi. con*," which I have ventured to write out, "*Beata virgo sine peccato originali concepta*," or as we might say in English, "the blessed virgin conceived without original sin." On the other side was a representation of the brazen serpent, and two nearly naked figures, looking intently upon it. This is by far the most perfect one I have seen. The letters are as perfect as if struck but yesterday. It was undoubtedly compressed between dies. It is oval in shape, and bored that it might be suspended from the neck. A silver medal was found near Eagle village, two miles east of this, about the size of a dollar, but a little thinner, with a ring or loop at one edge to admit a cord by which it might be suspended. On one side appears in relief, a somewhat rude representation of a fortified town, with several tall steeples rising above its buildings, and a citadel, from which the British flag is flying. A river broken by an island or two, occupies the foreground, and above, along the upper edge of the medal, is the name Montreal. The initials D. C. F., probably those of the manufacturer, are stamped below. On the opposite side, which was originally made blank, are engraved the words Canecya, Onondagoes, which are doubtless the name and tribe of the red ruler on whose dusky breast, this ornament was displayed. A valuable token of friendship of some British governor of New-York, or Canada, to an influential ally among the Six Nations. There is no date on this, or any of the medals. But this must be at least older than the revolution, and probably an hundred snows at least, have fallen on the field where the plough disinterred it, since the chief whose name it has preserved, was laid to rest with his fathers.

I have sent with this, such relics and Indian trinkets, as I could prevail upon our people here to part with. They are less than I expected to obtain. The gun lock, spear head, axe, piece of gun barrel, and lead ball, are all of the size and patterns usually found. They are from the farm of Mr. David Hinsdale, in the town of Pompey, west part. All the gun barrels, or parts of them, are found flattened similar to this. Not a perfect one has been found. The two parts of the axe, want about two inches between the broken portions to make the "*bit*" of the ordinary length. The stone axes, I thought might interest you. I have no doubt they were used in flaying animals slain in the chase, as well as in cleaving wood. I did intend to send you a beautiful gouge of hornblende, but to my surprise, it is not to be found; the like are frequently found here. It proves conclusively, that the natives were at an early day acquainted with the virtues of the maple, and possessed the art of making sugar. I have sent, as you will see, fragments of pipes of many varieties. The patterns are as various as the articles are numerous. The specimens of glass are different from any I have seen from any other quarter. I think some of the beads may have been used in rosarys, for the native proselytes. I have lately seen a fragment of a bell, which, when whole, would have weighed probably 200 lbs., the metal is very fine, and from appearance, this article must have been of considerable value ; time and exposure has not changed it in the least. When found, some 20 years since, it was broken up and the pieces found, enough to make it nearly entire.

I am aware, that I am corresponding with one far more experienced in these matters, than myself, and therefore, forbear obtruding my views and opinions further. If you have not a particular desire to place these things in your own cabinet, they might perhaps, be profitably disposed of, among the rare things of the New-York Historical Society. Dispose of them as you think best, I am sorry I could not obtain more.

I am, with sentiments of high regard,

Your ob't,

J. V. H. CLARK.

(D)

Letter from Mr. Cusick to Henry R. Schoolcraft.

August 4th, 1845.

It appears to me, very great difficulties are in the way of finding out and becoming acquainted with the discovery of all ancient traditions, and what original stock we came from. So far as our recollections extend according to our traditions of many centuries, the aborigines who inhabited the vast wilderness in this great continent, now North America, were guided and led by a certain man, who stood highest in dignity, and next to the Supreme Being, who is called THARONYAWAGO, that is to say, being interpreted, the Holder of Heavens. He was the great leader of the Red Men, and he regulated and taught how to divide the country and rivers, and mode of their living, and manners of costume and ceremonies, in many centuries. The Tuscaroras were descended from the Iroquois; they emigrated from the Five Nations to the Southern Country in North Carolina, and when the Iroquois used to send expeditions and war parties to go to war with other Indian tribes in that quarter, these parties went to the Tuscarora towns in North Carolina, and found a resting place and refreshment, and they used to be in the habit of intermarriage with each other, they have never been to war against each other, and they were always on terms of good friendship and connexion. And therefore we considered that the Tuscarora nation belonged to the Six Nations from ancient times. Before the discovery by Columbus the Tuscaroras consisted of six towns, and they were a most powerful nation, numbering more than twelve thousand warriors. But many combinations and causes fell upon the Tuscarora nation, and they became diminished in their numbers, by wars and pestilence, and were poisoned by ardent spirits. The Tuscaroras had many years of enjoyment and peaceful possession on the Roanoke river, until the Colony was planted near the settlement; something brought up disturbances, and their right was disputed to their territory. In 1712 the Indians of the Tuscaroras in North Carolina, with their accustomed secrecy, formed the design of exterminating in one night, the entire white population; the slaughter on the Roanoke was great, Capt. Barnwell appointed, and sent troops, who suddenly attacked the Tuscaroras, he killed 300, and took 100 prisoners, the survivors retreated to Tuscarora town, within a wooden breast-work, where at last they sued for peace.

The Tuscaroras, soon after abandoned their country, and united themselves with the Iroquois, and became the Sixth Nation. When we first came into this country, we lived with the Oneida nation, (now Oneida county,) and we called the Oneidas the Elder Brother, the second is the Cayugas, the youngest Brother Tuscaroras.

When the first missionary was sent to the Tuscarora nation, 1807, Eld. Elkanah Holmes, from the New York Missionary Society, labored several years with success, among them. This Mr. Holmes belonged to the Baptist Missionary Society. Afterwards, when Mr. Holmes was removed, another missionary was sent to the Tuscaroras by the American Foreign Mission, namely, the Rev. Mr. Grey, who remained until last war. After his dismissal in 1816, another missionary was sent by the Board of the New York Missionary Society, the Rev. James C. Crane. I will state briefly, those missionaries who afterwards came to the Tuscaroras, Rev. B. Lane, Rev. John Elliot, Rev. Joel Wood, Rev. Mr. Williams, the last who is now missionary, was the Rev. Gilbert Rockwood. In 1836, a portion of the Tuscarora nation thought expedient to become Baptists, according to the dictates of their own conscience, and free enjoyment of their religion in this republican government. And consequently a Baptist church was built and organized among the Tuscaroras; and they were called in council with several Baptist churches in this county. In 1838, they were admitted into the Niagara Baptist Association at Shelby. And have now in good standing fifty members of the church. In a ministerial council, June 14th, 1838, Mr. James Cusick was examined touching his Christian experience, and called to preach the gospel by Providence and the council; they decided on that question, and give him ordination as a native preacher, deciding that he was well qualified by a knowledge of theology. And now he has labored with several tribes among the Six Nations. Under his instrumentality, three Baptist churches have been formed, numbering 200 members, and he established a temperance society in 1830 of more than 100 members. In 1845 he established another temperance society among the Indians, numbering 50 members. Intemperance is one of the greatest and most destructive evils, and many more begin to be intemperate, especially among the young men. Among the females of the Tuscarora nation there is more virtue and sobriety and good morals than among the males. I hope the white citizens will try to assist them and promote the melioration of the Indian condition in order to qualify him for life and lead him to appreciate its true end, and to encourage intermarriages in their future generations and to advance in civilization, christianity, and industry.

From your respected friend,

JAMES CUSICK.

N. B. At the Rev. Mr. Vrooman's, in Queenston, you will find a copy of my late brother David's book on the Indians.

The following extracts are made from the curious publication referred to, in the preceding note. It appears to have been first printed at Lewiston, in 1825. As the work of a full blooded Indian, of the Tuscarora tribe, it is remarkable. In making these extracts, no correction of the style, or grammar is made, these being deemed a part of the evidence of the authenticity of the traditions recorded.

ACCOUNT OF THE SETTLEMENT OF NORTH AMERICA.

In the ancient days the Great Island appeared upon the big waters, the earth brought forth trees, herbs, vegetables, &c. The creation of the land animals: the Eagwehoewe people were too created and resided in the north regions; and after a time some of the people became giants, and committed outrages upon the inhabitants, &c.

Ancient Shipwreck.—After many years a body of Eagwehoewe people encamped on the bank of a majestic stream, and was named *Kanawage*, now St. Lawrence. After a long time a number of foreign people sailed from a port unknown; but unfortunately, before reached their destination the winds drove them contrary; at length their ship wrecked somewhere on the southern part of the Great Island, and many of the crews perished; a few active persons were saved; they obtained some implements, and each of them was covered with a leather bag, the big hawks carried them on the summit of a mountain and remained there but a short time. The hawks seemed to threaten them, and were compelled to leave the mountain. They immediately selected a place for residence and built a small fortification in order to provide against the attacks of furious beasts; if there should be any made. After many years the foreign people became numerous, and extended their settlements; but afterwards they were destroyed by the monsters that overrun the country.

Origin of the Five Nations.

By some inducement a body of people was concealed in the mountain at the falls named Kuskehsawkich, (now Oswego.) When the people were released from the mountain they were visited by TARENYAWAGON, i. e. the Holder of the Heavens, who had power to change himself into various shapes: he ordered the people to proceed towards the sunrise as he guided them and came to a river and named Yenonanatche, i. e. going round a mountain, (now Mohawk) and went down the bank of the river and came to where it discharges into a great river running towards the midday sun; and named Shaw-nay-taw-ty, i. e. beyond the Pineries, (now Hudson,) and went down the bank of the river and touched the bank of a great water. The company made encampment at the place and remained there a few days. The people were yet in one language; some of the people went on the banks of the great water towards the midday sun; but the main company returned as they came, on the bank of the river, under the direction of the Holder of the Heavens. Of this company there was a particular body which called themselves one household; of these were six families and they entered into a resolution to preserve the chain of alliance which should not be extinguished in any manner.

The company advanced some distance up the river of Shaw-na-taw-ty, (Hudson) the Holder of the Heavens directs the first family to make their residence near the bank of the river, and the family was named Te-haw-re-ho-geh, i. e. a Speech divided, (now Mohawk) and their language was soon altered; the company then turned and went towards the sunsetting and travelled about two days and a half, and come to a creek* which was named Kaw-na-taw-te-ruh, i. e.

* The creek now branches of the Susquehanna River at the head generally called Col. Allen's lake, ten miles south of the Oneida Castle.

Pineries. The second family was directed to make their residence near the creek, and the family was named Ne-haw-re-tah-go, i. e. Big Tree, now Oneidas, and likewise their language was altered. The company continued to proceed towards the sunsetting under the direction of the Holder of the Heavens. The third family was directed to make their residence on a mountain named Onondaga, (now Onondaga) and the family was named Seuh-now-kah-tah, i. e. carrying the name, and their language was altered. The company continued their journey towards the sunsetting. The fourth family was directed to make their residence near a long lake named Go-yo-goh, i. e. a mountain rising from water, (now Cayuga) and the family was named Sho-nea-na-we-to-wah, i. e. a great pipe, their language was altered. The company continued to proceed towards the sun-setting. The fifth family was directed to make their residence near a high mountain, or rather nole, situated south of the Canandaigua lake, which was named Jenneatowake and the family was named Te-how-nea-nyo-hent, i. e. Possessing a Door, now Seneca, and their language was altered. The sixth family went with the company that journeyed towards the sunsetting, and touched the bank of a great lake, and named Kau-ha-gwa-rah-ka, i. e. A Cap, now Erie, and then went towards between the midday and sunsetting, and travelled considerable distance and came to a large river which was named Ouau-we-yo-ka, i. e. a principal stream, now Mississippi; the people discovered a grape vine lying across the river by which a part of the people went over, but while they were engaged, the vine broke and were divided, they became enemies to those that went over the river; in consequence they were obliged to disperse the journey. The Holder of the Heavens instructs them in the art of bows and arrows in the time of game and danger. Associates were dispersed and each family went to search for residences according to their conveniences of game. The sixth family went towards the sunrise and touched the bank of the great water. The family was directed to make their residence near Cau-ta-noh, i. e. Pine in water, situated near the mouth of Nuse River, now in North Carolina, and the family was named Kau-ta-noh, now Tuscarora and their language was also altered; but the six families did not go so far as to loose the understanding of each other's language. The Holder of the Heavens returns to the five families and forms the mode of confederacy, which was named Ggo-nea-seab-neh, i. e. A Long House, to which are, 1st.—Tea-kaw-reh-ho-geh, 2d—New-haw-teh-tah-go ; 3d.—Seuh-nau-ka-ta ; 4th—Sho-nea-na-we-to-wah ; 5th.—Te-hoo-nea-nyo-hent.

(E.)

Letter from S. A. Goodwin to Henry R. Schoolcraft.

Auburn, Oct. 17, 1845.

My Dear Sir—I received yours of the 2d inst. in due course of post, and now send you, at the first practicable moment, a diagram and sketch of the "Old Fort." My engagements have been such as to prevent my going out to Geneva, and making a trip to the old fortification alluded to. As to the other one here referred to by McAuley, it is just back of my house, and as soon as I have time to make an examination I will drop you a line respecting it. I go to Rochester, to attend supreme court, to-morrow. I shall try, on my return, to stop at Geneva and get a sketch of that one.

Very truly your friend,
S. H. GOODWIN.

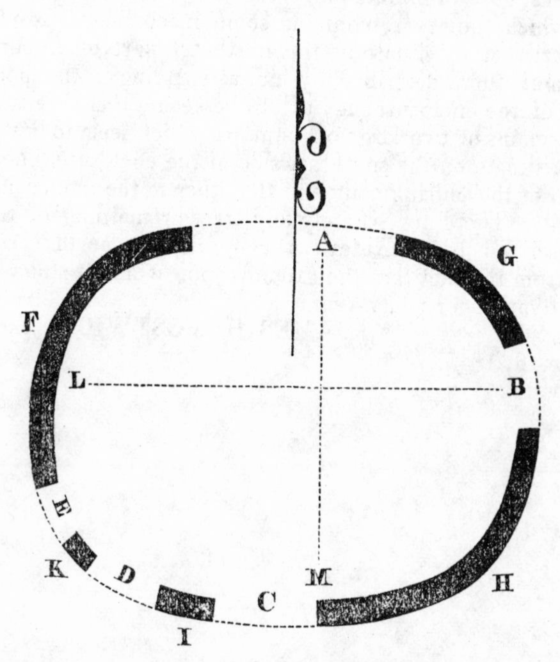

Diagram of an ancient fortification on Fort Hill, Auburn, N. Y.

This enclosure is situate on the highest point of land in the vicinity of Auburn, and is in the form of an ellipsis; and measures in diameter, from east to west, (from the outside of the base of the embankment) four hundred and sixteen feet, and from north to south, three hundred and ten feet; the circumference, twelve hundred feet; present height of the highest part of the embankment on the west side from the bottom of the ditch, four feet; the thickness at the base, fourteen feet; from the centre of the enclosure the ground has a gentle slope to the north, east and west, and is nearly level towards the south. The openings on the south, one of sixty and the other of seventy-eight feet, are directly opposite or against deep ravines separated by a narrow steep ridge, access through which would be difficult, being on an angle of nearly forty-five degrees. The opening on the north measures one hundred and sixty-six feet, opposite to which the ground continues to slope to the north for the distance of seventy feet, from which point the descent is very abrupt. The opening on the east measures sixty-six feet, opposite to which the ground continues on a gentle descent to the east for several hundred feet. The opening on the southwest measures fifty feet, and is opposite to a ridge gently descending to the southwest. There are no less than ten deep ravines and as many steep ridges surrounding and leading to this ancient fortification.

McAuley, in his history of the State of New-York, Vol. 2d, pages 111 and 112, gives a minute and interesting description of this fortification, which, however, contains some inaccuracies; and also of another fortification situate in the northeast part of Auburn. The large chesnut stump described by him as standing in the moat on the west side of the enclosure, is still to be seen; there are still to be seen the remains of two large oak stumps, which seem to have escaped his notice, situate on the southeast side of the enclosure, one of them on the top of the embankment, and the other in the ditch some twelve feet distant. There are scarcely any traces remaining of the fortification described by McAuley as being in the north east part of Auburn, from the fact that the ground upon which it stood has been under cultivation for many years.

JAMES H. BOSTWICK, *Surveyor.*

October 16, 1845.

(F.)

Letter from Frederick Follet to Henry R. Schoolcraft.

Batavia, Oct. 25, 1845.

DEAR SIR—My private and public duties together prevented my making a visit to "Fort Hill," until the 22d inst. and I proceed to give you my ideas of that formation.

The ground known as "Fort Hill" is situated about three miles north of the village of Le Roy, and ten or twelve miles northeast from Batavia, the capitol of Genesee county. The better view of "Fort Hill" is had to the north of it, about a quarter of a mile, on the road leading from Bergen to Le Roy. From this point of observation it needs little aid of the imagination to conceive that it was erected as a fortification by a large and powerful army, looking for a permanent and almost inaccessible bulwark of defence. From the centre of the "Hill," in the northwesterly course, the country lies quite flat—immediately north, and inclining to the east, the land is also level for one hundred rods, when it rises nearly as high as the "Hill," and continues for several miles quite elevated. In approaching the "Hill" from the north it stands very prominently before you, rising rather abruptly, though not perpendicularly, to the height of eighty or ninety feet, extending about forty rods on a line east and west, the corners being round or truncated, and continuing to the south on the west side for some sixty rods, and on the east side for about half a mile, maintaining about the same elevation at the sides as in front; beyond which distance the line of the "Hill" is that of the land around.

"Fort Hill," however, is not a work of art. The geological character of it shows it to be the result of natural causes. Nevertheless, there are undoubted evidences of its once having been resorted to as a fortification, and of its having constituted a valuable point of defence to a rude and half-civilized people.

It is probable that at a period of time very far distant, the ground about "Fort Hill" was, for some considerable distance around, entirely of the same level, and that by the action of water, a change took place, which brought about the present condition. The low land immediately in front to the north, is only the remains of a water course, which was made up of a stream coming down the gorge of the west side, and the present "Allen's creek," which flows through a portion of the gorge of the east side, the stream of the west having been a branch of that of the east side. Through the west gorge now flows, in the wet season, a moderate stream, coming from the lands above the gorge, and having an interrupted fall of some forty or fifty feet; while "Allen's creek" occupies a portion of the eastern gorge, much broader, at the extremity of which, some half a mile from the "Hill," there is a beautiful fall of eighty feet perpendicularly. The structure of the "Hill" bears out this construction; it being composed of the same rock—with the exception of the upper strata—as the falls. At the falls the upper strata of rock and that which forms the bed of the creek for some two miles or more east, is the *corniferous limestone*; underlaying which are *hydraulic* and *Onondaga limestones*. The two latter are only seen at "Fort Hill," covered by a few feet of soil and several small masses of stone, a part out of place, among which are a few of *Medina sandstone*. The strata are, therefore continuous from the falls, and at some former periods, extended over the gorges, and formed a regular and nearly level surface, the action of water having removed, which has left the broad and conspicuous point of "Fort Hill," as memorable monuments of the earlier condition of the country.

When "Fort Hill" was used as a fortification the summit was entrenched. Forty years ago an entrenchment, ten feet deep and some twelve or fifteen wide, extended from the west to the east end, along the north or front part, and continued up each side about twenty rods, where it crossed over and joining, made the circuit of entrenchment complete. At this day a portion of this entrenchment is easily perceived for fifteen rods along the extreme western half of the north or front part, the cultivation of the soil, with other causes, having nearly obliterated all other portions. It would seem that this fortification was arranged more for protection against invasion from the north than from any other quarter, this direction evidently being its most commanding position. Near the northwest corner have, at different times, been found collections of rounded stones of hard consistence, which are supposed to have been used as weapons of defence by the besieged against the besiegers.

Arrow-heads, made of flint or horn-stone, gouges, pestles, hatchets, and other weapons formed from stone, have been found about the "Hill" and throughout this section. Of the rarer articles, are pipes and beads, a few of the latter of which I have been able to obtain. The gouges, pestles and hatchets, are, I think, frequently made of compact limestone, probably what is now known in Mr. Hall's State report as the *one foot limestone* at Le Roy, though many of them seem to be formed of primitive rock, and very likely were worked out from boulders scattered about the country.

Skeletons found about "Fort Hill" and its vicinity sustain the impression that the former occupants of this "military station" were of a larger and more powerful race of men than ourselves. I learned that the skeletons generally indicated a stouter and larger frame. An humerus or shoulder bone of which preserved may safely be said to be one-third larger or stouter than any now swung by the living. A resident of Batavia, THOMAS T. EVERETT, M. D., has in his cabinet a portion of a lower jaw bone full one-third larger than any possessed by the present race of men, which was found in a hill near Le Roy, some two years since. From the same hill arrow-heads and other articles have been removed for many years.

The articles I send you are as follows :—No. 1, an Indian gouge, made of very hard stone, found at "Fort Hill;" No. 3, arrow-heads, of flint; No. 4, beads; No. 5, a bead, evidently formed from a tooth, as the enamel and other distinctive marks indicate; No. 6, a bead, apparently of bone.

No. 2 is a stone tomahawk, presented to me by JEROME A. CLARK, Esq., of this village. It was found on his premises half a mile south of this place. I herewith present it to you.

These articles I have sent to-day by a friend, and you will find them by calling at Tammany Hall. I have not yet been able to visit Tonawanda, but am in hopes to do so in a day or two.

Your ob't serv't,

FREDERICK FOLLETT.

(G.)

Letter from C. Dewey to Henry R. Schoolcraft.

FORT HILL.

This is celebrated as being the remains of some ancient work, and was supposed to have been a *fort*. Though the name is pronounced as if *hill* was the name of some individual, yet the place is a fort on a hill, in the loose use of the word. The name designates the place as *Fort*-hill, to distinguish it from the hills which have no fort on them. Neither is it *a hill*, except as you rise from the swale on the north, for it is lower than the land to which it naturally belongs.

As you pass towards Fort-Hill in the road from Le Roy village, which is about three miles to the south, you descend a little most of the distance to this place. The road passes a little west of the middle of the space nearly north and south.

The shape is quadrangular, and is shown in the diagram or ground plot.

On the right and east side is the deep water course of *Allen's Creek*, cut down through the rocks for a mile or more, perhaps one hundred and thirty feet deep; on the north is that of *Fordham's Brook*, of nearly the same depth, which drains a wide swale from the north and northwest; and on the west is a short and deep ravine, which is a water course in some seasons of the year, where the waters fall over a precipice a little south of the quadrangular space, or fortification. This ravine is not so deep as the water courses on the east and north. The descent is quite steep on these three sides. At the northeast Allen's Creek turns to the east and receives the waters from Fordham's Brook.

The quadrangular space, D, A, B, C, was enclosed by a trench, D A, nearly a north line on the east, by A B on the north, and B C on the west.

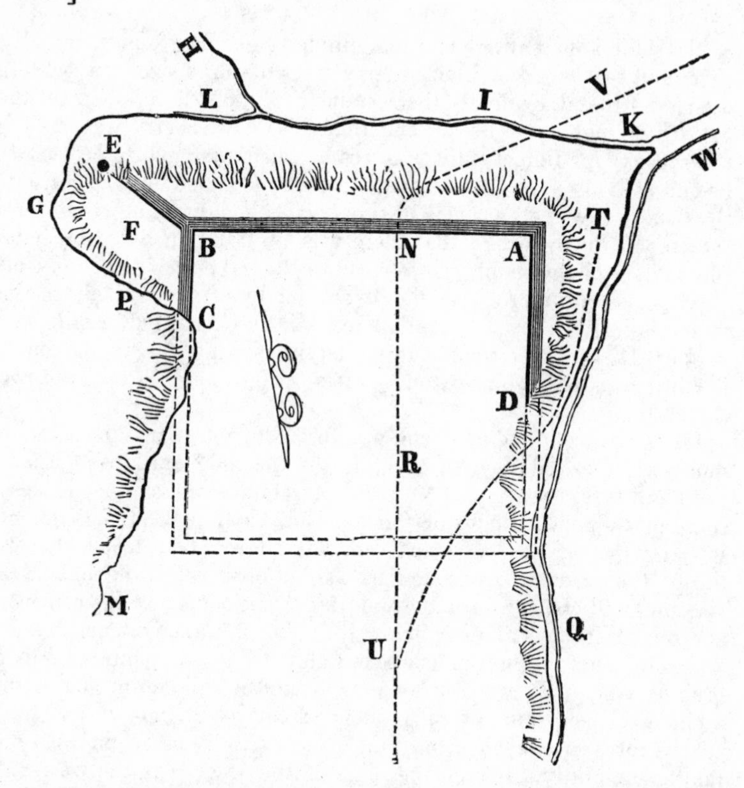

A B is the north trench about sixty rods long, and nearly east and west. A D is about thirty rods, and B C is fifteen rods, and terminates at the ravine at C. The trench D A, and A B lies on the brow of the descent to the streams below. At D the bend of the ravine stops the trench. At the northwest corner B, a trench is continued about 15° to the right and down the declivity 15 rods to a spring; 50 feet perhaps below A B, and B G is the brow of the descent west of the tιench at B, and G C is the edge of the ravine on the west. Q W is Allen's Creek on the east; H I K is Fordham's Brook on the north, and L P M is the water course on the west to the precipice at M, over which the water falls at some seasons, and the surface at M is only a few feet lower than the general level of the quadrangle. The space F was a burying ground, as bones, skulls, pipes, beads, have been ploughed up there. The road R N passes through the middle nearly of the space enclosed by the trench, and at N turns to the right to descend to the flat below; but formerly the road turned to the right at U and passed down at the right of the trench at D to T.

The place was pointed out to me by H. M. Ward, Esq., who was familiar with it when it was covered with the forest. He states that the trench must have been eight to ten feet deep and as many wide; that the earth was thrown either way, but much of it inwards; that the forest trees were standing in the trench and on the sides of it and of the same apparent age and magnitude as on the ground generally; that the heart-wood of black cherry trees of large size was scattered over the ground, evidently the remains of a forest anterior to the then growth of maple and beech, and that this black cherry was used by the settlers for timber; that the road, when first made, crossed the trench at N by a *bridge*; that the trench at D and A was cut down the bank a few feet, or else in time water had worn a passage from the trench downwards; that there was no tradition heard of among the Indians of the country, in respect to the use or design of the work.

The underlying rock is the hydraulic limestone of this section, which is fully exposed at the falls of Allen's Creek, half a mile south of Fort-Hill. This rock was struck in digging the trench on the north line in some places, and portions of it were thrown out with the earth.

Of the pipes found at F one was formed from granular limestone; one was of baked clay, in the form of the rude outlines of a man's head and face, nose, eyes, &c., and it reminds one of the figures in some of Stephens' Plates of the ruins of Palenque. It has the hollows for the ears to be fastened on, and shows no little effort. The top of the head is surrounded by a fillet or wreath, and behind are two more fillets. At the bottom of the neck is a similar ornament, and on the front is another below it. This is the most curious.

Another pipe is of reddish baked clay, with some pits or dots for ornament upon it, two rows of dots around it and another below like a chain suspended at several points and curved by its own weight.

The forest has been removed. Not a tree remains on the quadrangle, and only a few on the edge of the ravine on the west. By cultivating the land, the trench is nearly filled in some places, though the line of it is clearly seen. On the north side the trench is considerable, and where the road crosses it, is three or four feet deep at the sides of the road. It will take only a few years more to obliterate it entirely, as not even a stump remains to mark out its line.

From this view it may be seen or inferred,

1. That a real trench bounded three sides of the quadrangle. On the south side there was not found any trace of trench, palisadoes, blocks, &c.

2. It was formed long before the whites came into the country. The large trees on the ground and in the trench, carry us back to an early era.

3. The workers must have had some convenient tools for excavation.

4. The direction of the sides may have had some reference to the four cardinal points, though the situation of the ravines naturally marked out the lines.

5. It cannot have been designed merely to catch wild animals to be driven into it from the south. The oblique cut down to the spring is opposed to this supposition, as well as the insufficiency of such a trench to confine the animals of the forest.

6. The same reasons render it improbable that the quadrangle was designed to confine and protect domestic animals.

7. It was probably a sort of fortified place. There might have been a defence on the south by a *stockade* or some similar means, which might have entirely disappeared.

By what people was this work done ?

The articles found in the burying ground at F. offer no certain reply. The axes, chissels, &c. found on the Indian grounds in this part of the State, were evidently made of the greenstone or trap of New-England, like those found on the Connecticut river, in Massachusets. The pipe of limestone might be from that part of the country. The pipes seem to belong to different eras.

1. The limestone pipe indicates the work of the savage, or aborigines.

2. The third indicates the age of French influence over the Indians. An intelligent French gentleman says such clay pipes are frequent among the town population in parts of France.

3. The second and most curious seems to indicate an earlier age and people.

The beads found at Fort Hill are long and coarse, made of baked clay, and may have had the same origin as the third pipe.

Fort Hill cannot have been formed by the French, as one of their posts to aid in the destruction of the English colonies.

In 1689, or 156 years ago, the French in Canada made various attempts to destroy the English colony of New-York. If the French had made Fort Hill a post as early as 1660, or 185 years ago, and then deserted it, the trees could not have grown to the size of the forest generally in 1810, or in 150 years afterwards. The white settlements had extended only "twelve miles west of Avon" in 1798, and some years after 1800, Fort Hill was covered with a dense forest. A chesnut tree cut down in 1842, at Rochester, showed 254 concentric circles of wood, and must have been more than 200 years old in 1800. So opposed is the notion that this was a deserted French post.

Must we not refer Fort Hill to that race which peopled this country before the Indians, who raised so many monuments greatly exceeding the power of the Indians, and who lived at a remote era?"

H. R. SCHOOLCRAFT, Esq. : I forward you the observations on Fort Hill, for your use. My speculations are added for my pleasure, and you will use them as you please. In great haste, I am obliged to close.

Your obedient,

C. DEWEY.

[H.]

Letter from Rev. Gilbert Rockwood to Henry R. Schoolcraft.

Tuscarora Mision, August 1, 1845.

SIR :—In the following communication, you can make use of such statements as you may deem proper. If all the statements should not be necessary for your official objects, yet they may be interesting to you as an individual.

This mission was commenced about fifty years since, under the care of the "New-York Missionary Society." It was transferred to the "United Foreign Mission Society," in 1821, and to the "American Board of Com. for Foreign Missions," in 1826.

The church was organized in 1805, with five persons. The whole number of native members who have united since its organization is 123. The present number of native members is 53 ; others 5, total 58.

Between July 1st, 1844, and July 1st, 1845, there were only three admissions, two by profession and one by letter.

About one-third of the population attend meeting on the Sabbath. Their meeting house was built by themselves, with a little assistance from abroad.

They have also a school house, the expense of which was nearly all defrayed by themselves. There is but one school among them, which is kept the year through, with the exception of the vacations. The teacher is appointed by the American Board. The number of scholars the past year, is not far from 50.

I have been among these Indians now nearly eight years. I can see that there has been an advance, both in their moral and physical condition.

It is within the memory of many now living among them, when drunkenness was almost universal ; now, comparatively, few are intemperate. A majority of the chiefs, are decidedly temperance men, and exert a salutary influence. They have a temperance society, and hold frequent meetings. They utterly forbid the traffic in intoxicating drinks on their own soil.

The marriage relation is being better understood by them, and more appreciated. More of the young men and women, enter into the marriage relation, in the regular christian way, than a few years ago. Four couple have been regularly married the past year. Number of deaths, 8 ; an unusual number since I have been among them.

There is besides the church, above referred to, a Baptist church, organized a few years since, the particulars of which, I am unable to give. For any information you may wish respecting it, I would refer you to James Cusick, their minister.

On the whole, there is much to encourage the philanthropist and the christian in labors for the good and well being of the Indians here, although we meet with many obstacles and difficulties in the way.

They are becoming more and more industrious in their habits, as the appearance of their farms, and the amount of produce, and their personal appearance will testify.

With these brief statements, I subscribe myself,

Yours, truly,

GILBERT ROCKWOOD.

VOCABULARY OF THE TUSCARORA, FROM WILLIAM CHEW, WRITTEN OUT AND TRANSMITTED BY THE REV. GILBERT ROCKWOOD.

NOTE.—In affixing Indian words, to the following vocabulary, Mr. Chew, who speaks the English very well, has promised to act as your translator and interpreter. The principal thing to be guarded against, however, is inaccuracy in the definitions, both in English and Indian.

If there is no infinitive to verbs, as I suppose, insert the simplest existing form, as He loves, &c.

Is there any participle to Tuscarora verbs!

H. R. S.

To Mr. Rockwood.

TUSCARORA.

1	God..................	Ya wuhn ne yuh.
2	Devil.................	Oo na sa roo nuh.
3	Man	Ehn kweh.
4	Woman.............	Hah wuhn nuh.
5	Boy..................	Kun chu kweh'r.
6	Girl..................	Ya te ah cha yeuh.
7	Child....	Kats ah.
8	Father (my)..........	E ah kre ehn.
9	Mother (my)..........	E a nuh.
10	Husband (my)........	E na yah keah wuhn.te kehn rea nuhn.
11	Wife (my)............	(The same word as for my husband.)
12	Son (his).............	Trah wuhn ruh, nuh nuhn, a ne hah.
13	Daughter (his).........	Tra wuhn ruh, nuhn, kah-nuhn nuhn.
14	Brother (my).........	E ah ke ah t'keuh.
15	Sister (my)...........	Eah keah nuhn nooh'r.
16	An Indian............	Reuh kweh hehn weh.
17	Head.................	Yah reh.
18	Hair (his)............	Trah wuhn ruh, rah weh rah wuhn.
19	Face (his)............	" rah keuh seuh keh.
20	Forehead (his).........	" " keuh neuh keh.
21	Scalp "	" " nuh reh.

22 Ear	his	....	Trah wuhn ruh kunh nunh keh.
23 Eye	"	....	" " kah reuh keh.
24 Nose	"	....	" " cheuh seuh keh.
25 Nostril	"	....	" " cheuh kah reuh.
26 Mouth	"	....	" " skah reuh.
27 Tongue	"	....	" reuh toh neuh keh.
28 Tooth	"	....	" " rah tooh tseh.
29 Beard	"	....	" " sooh keh reh.
30 Neck	"	....	" " hah tseh.
31 Arm	"	....	" " neuh cheuh keuh
32 Shoulder	"	....	" " nunh neh.
33 Back	"	....	" " reuh wunh keh.
34 Hand	"	....	" " rah eh nunh keh.
35 Finger	"	....	" " rooh kweh.
36 Nail	"	....	" " skeuh kah reh.
37 Breast	"	....	" " ah sunh keh.
38 Body	"	....	" " keh s'heuh keh.
39 Leg	"	....	" " reuh seuh keh.
40	"	....	" "
41 Navel	"	....	" " ne seuh reuh keh
42 Thigh	"	....	" " te cheuh keh.
43 Knee	"	....	" " reuh kueh t'sunh [keh.
44 Foot	"	....	" rah rah neuh keh.
45 Toe	"	....	" " sooh kweh.
46 Heel	"	....	" " teh heuh cheh.
47 Bone	"	....	" " skeuh reh.
48 Heart	"	....	" " ra re ah seh.
49 Liver	"	....	" " rah t'wunh seh.
50 Windpipe	"	....	" " hunh t'seh.
51 Stomach	"	....	" " keh'r hah keuh.
52 Bladder	"	....	" " te ah neh.
53 Blood	"	....	" " t'kwah ra.
54 Vein	"	....	" " } nunh yah
55 Sinew	"	....	" " } t'seh.
56 Flesh	my	....	E kwa reh.
57 Skin	"	....	E ka nunh keh.
58 Seat	"	....	E ak tak.
59 Thighbone	"	....	E k'te chunh keh skenh reh.
60 Town	"	....	Kah tah nah yeuh.
61 Townsman	"	....	Kah koo tah nah keuh'f hah.
62 House		....	Yah keuh nunh.
63 Door		....	Oo chah reh.
64 Lodge		....	Wah k'tah nah yeuh noh'gh.
65 Smoke		....	Oo chah reh.
66 Chief		....	Ya koo wah nunh.
67 Warrior		....	Roo skeuh rah keh reh.
68 Friend		....	Enh nunh rooh.
69 Enemy		....	Yeuh chunh t'seh,
70 Kettle		....	Oo nunh weh.

71	Arrow................	Oo teh.
72	Bow.................	Nah chreh.
73	Warclub..............	Oo che kweh.
74	Spear................	Chu rets.
75	Axe.................	No keuh.
76	Knife................	Oo sah keuh neh.
77	Paddle...............	Kah weh t'chra.
78	Canoe...............	Oo nah keh.
79	Boat................	Oo hunh weh.
80	Ship................	Oo hunh weh koo.
81	Shoe................	Oo che koo ra
82	Leggin..............	Oo re streh.
83	Coat................	} Oo keh r'hoo t'chreh.
84	Shirt...............	} Oo keh r'hoo t'chreh.
85	Breachcloth..........	Ya hah'r hooh stoh
86	Belt or sash..........	Oo che hah t'chra.
87	Head dress...........	Hoh toh kweh.
88	Pipe................	Chah'rs hooh stoh.
89	Tobacco..............	Chah'rs hooh.
90	Pipe stem............	Oo treh neh.
91	Sky.................	Oo renh yah'rs.
92	Heaven..............	Oo reuh yah keuhf.
93	Sun................	He teh.
94	Moon...............	Ah t'seuh ye hah.
95	Star................	Oo ne senh reh.
96	Day................	A wunh neh
97	Night...............	A sunh neh.
98	Cloud...............	Oo roh'ts.
99	Light...............	Yu hooks.
100	Darkness.............	Yah weh toah yeuh.
101	Morning..............	Tsoo teh'r hunh.
102	Evening..............	Yah tsa t'henh hah.
103	Spring...............	Wah'r wooh stroh'gh.
104	Summer..............	Oo kenh hoh keh.
105	Autumn..............	Roh t'seh keh.
106	Winter...............	Kooh seh r'heuh.
107	Year................	Ah ooh streh.
108	Wind................	Oo reh.
109	Lightning............	Woh n'woh kah reh nah reek.
110	Thunder..............	He nunh.
111	Rain................	Wane too'eh.
112	Snow...............	Oo neets reh.
113	Hail................	Wah t'kah ta he ts'ot.
114	Fire................	Oo che reh.
115	Water...............	Ah wunh.
116	Ice.................	Oo we seh.
117	Earth, land...........	Ah wunh reh.
118	Sea................	Kahn yah ta reyu.
119	Lake...............	Hahn yah ta reh.
120	River...............	Ke nunh.

121 Stream .... Hah s'nunh yeuh tih.
122 Valley .... Ah wunh rah stroh kenh.
123 Hill................ Yu nunh t'heh.
124 Mountain .... Yu nunh yeuh tih.
125 Plain............... Wah keuh nah yeuh.
126 Forest .... Ooh r'hah nah keuhf.
127 Meadow.............. Ya ha re oh toh.
128 Bog .... Yu teh'r enh t'sah ne reuh.
129 Island.............. Yuh weh nooh.
130 Stone .... Oo reuh neh.
131 Rock................ Oo steuh reh.
132 Silver............... Kah kwis tah no reuh.
133 Copper.............. Kwa nis nees.
134 Iron................. Oo wa nunh.
135 Lead................. Nah wah c'steh.
136 Maize............... Oo nunh heh.
137 Wheat .... Oo toos.
138 Oats .... O'ch.
139 Potatoe .... Oo nunh tseh.
140 Turnip .... Oo che kwah.
141 Tree................. Oo reuh eh.
142 Wood................ Oo yeuh kwe reh.
143 Pine................. Hoh teh.
144 Oak................. Rah rooh.
145 Ash................. Whoh't.
146 Elm................. Kah rah t'kwoh.
147 Basswood .... Oo hoo stroh.
148 Shrub............... Kwe roh keuh.
149 Leaf .... Oo euh reh.
150 Bark................ Skeuh noh reh.
151 Grass............... Yu ha ruh kweh.
152 Nettles.............. Yah koo ha roh roh'r.
153 Thistle .... Oo ne keh weh.
154 Weed............... Chu wa kah ha rah ka.
155 Flower.............. Oo che che streh.
156 Bread............... Oo tah nah reh.
157 Indian meal.......... Oo nuh heh.
158 Flour .... Oo teh c'hrah.
159 Meat................ Wah reh.
160 Beaver.............. Chu noh keuh.
161 Deer................ Ah kweh.
162 Bison or buffalo....... Chu ta kre yoh keuh.
163 Bear................ Oo che reuh.
164 Otter .... Che ah ka we nuh.
Grey fox red fox.
165 Fox................. Che chuh.—Skeuh nahx seuh.
166 Wolf................ Skwah re nunh.
167 Dog................. Chee'sr.
168 Squirrel .... Thah'st.
169 Hare............ ... Kwa ruh.

170 Lynx................ (No name.)
171 Panther .... T'keuh na nih.
172 Muskrat.............. Ah nuh kwinh.
173 Polecat.............. (No name.)
174 Hog.................. Kwis kwis.
175 Horse .... Hah hahts.
176 Cow .... Oo na rah saht.
177 Sheep .... Wa rak seuh.
178 Turtle................ Che koo wa.
179 Toad........,........ Roo nunh skwah reuh.
180 Insect .... Chick euh woh'r.
181 Snake .... Oo skwah na.
182 Bird .... Che nunh.
183 Egg .... Ooh heuh seh.
184 Feather .... Oo snoo kre.
185 Claw .... Oo sheuh kah reh.
186 Beak................. Tuh cheuh seh.
187 Wing .... Oo yeuh we ts'neh.
188 Goose .... Kah tuh'ts euh.
189 Partridge............ Oo kwa'ts euh.
190 Duck .... Ts'uh yeuh.
191 Pigeon .... Oo re neh.
192 Plover .... (No name.)
193 Turkey............... Keuh nuh.
194 Crow .... Ah ah.
195 Eagle .... Suh kwe ah.
196 Hawk .... Ne yeuh ne yeuh.
197 Snipe .... Tah wis ta wis.
198 Owl .... Oo wah.
199 Woodpecker .... Nah rah'r.
200 Robin .... Roo skooh kooh.
201 Fish .... Keuh chink.
202 Trout .... Ruh te ohk teuh.
203 Bass .... Keuh che ah heuh s'che.
204 Pike .... Koo wahk.
205 Sturgeon .... Hah rah.
206 Sunfish .... Nah reh reh.
207 Eel .... Keuh neh.
208 Fin .... Oo too neh.
209 Scale .... Oo s'neh.
210 Roe .... Ta reh.
211 White .... Oo whah re ah keuh.
212 Black .... Kah hunh s'ehe.
213 Blue .... Oo tih heuh re eh.
214 Yellow .... Tih kah che t'kah nahyeuh.
215 Green .... Oo ha reh.
216 Great .... We yu.
217 Small .... Wast teuh.
218 Strong .... Oo te reuh.
219 Old...... .... Oo nunh hah ah.

220 Young .... Oo't oh.
221 Good .... Wah kwast.
222 Bad .... Wah sunh.
223 Handsome .... Yu yah tah yeuh snuh.
224 Ugly................ Koh seuh.
225 Alive .... Wunh heh.
226 Dead .... Yah wunh ha yeuh.
227 Life .... Na yah wunh t'kwah.
228 Death .... Keuh ha yeuh.
229 Cold .... Ah t'huh.
230 Hot................ Yuh nah re hin.
231 Sour .... Na yuh che ra noh neh.
232 Sweet .... Yah wa kenh.
233 Bitter .... Yu che wah kenh.
234 I .... E.
235 Thou .... Ets.
236 He .... Trah ya nueh teh.
237 She .... A ya nueh teh.
238 We................ E ah kwah ya sunh teh.
239 You, ye .... Thwah ya sunh teh.
240 They .... Kah ya yeh sunh teh.
241 This .... Keh'n nuh.
242 That................ Ha nuh.
243 All .... T'wa'hn.
244 Part .... Wa yu rah kwuhn.
245. Many .... Yuh neh'r kenh hu hu.
246 Nothing .... Tsah wunh teh.
247 Who .... Koh na.
248 Near .... Noos keuh.
249 Far off .... E nuh.
250 To-day................ Kah wunh yuh'r heuk enh.
251 Yesterday................ Teh nuh.
252 To-morrow .... Euh yuh'r heuh.
253 Yes................ Euh heuh.
254 No .... Kwuhs.
255 Perhaps................ Ah reuh kweh te.
256 Above .... Strah kwe.
257 Under................ Euh toh kenh'f
258 Within .... Oo nuh skeuh.
259 Without .... Th' neh teh.
260 On .... Hoh heh'n.
261 Something .... Sto e keuh.
262 In the tree .... Ooreuh oh kenk'f.
263 On the rock .... Koh heh'r oo steuh roh keh.
264 By the shore .... Oo che ah tah'qt.
265 On the table .... Na kwah roh kwah keh.
266 In the book .... Oo yah teuh strah keuh'f.
267 Now .... Ka wunh.
268 Never................ Sa nunh.
269 By and by.......... Ka wuh thenh ruh.

270	One	Euh che.
271	Two	Nak te.
272	Three	Ah sunk.
273	Four	Kunh toh.
274	Five	Weesk.
275	Six	Ooh yok.
276	Seven	Che oh noh.
277	Eight	Na kreuh.
278	Nine	Ne reuh.
279	Ten	Wah th'sunk.
280	Eleven	Euh che skah hah.
281	Twelve	Nah tih skah hah.
282	Thirteen	Ah sunk " "
283	Fourteen	Hunh toh " "
284	Fifteen	Weesk " "
285	Sixteen	Ooh yok " "
286	Seventeen	Ohe oh noh " "
287	Eighteen	Na kreuh " "
288	Nineteen	Ne reuh " "
289	Twenty	Na wah th'sunh.
290	Thirty	Ah sunh te wah th'sunk.
291	Forty	Hunh toh te " "
292	Fifty	Weest te " "
293	Sixty	Ooh yok te " "
294	Seventy	Che oh noh te " "
295	Eighty	Na kreuh te " "
296	Ninety	Ne reuh te " "
297	One hundred	Hah yok stre.
298	Two hundred	Nah kah " "
299	One thousand	Euh che oo yoh stre.
300	Two thousand	Nak tih " " "
301	Ten thousand	Wak th'sunk noh oo yoh stre.
302	Ten million	Kah yoh stre te kah yoh stre nah oo. Yoh stre keuh hoh nuh.
303	To eat*	Ah reuh chu reek.
304	To drink	Ah'r weh'r reuhk.
305	To run	Ah kah te ah sr'hink.
306	To walk	Ah reuh ra kwunk.
307	To dance	Nah reuh't t'kwunk.
308	To laugh	Ah kah yeuh skwak.
309	To cry	Nah reuh snah rahk.
310	To burn	Ya choh roh nah re hin.
311	To love	Ah kah no reuh kwunk.
312	To go	Nah reut tah hah kink.
313	To strike	Ah kah keuh kwah re ts'enk.
314	To kill	Ah rah kwunk nahk.
315	To sing	Ah reuh uwunh a renhk.
316	To sleep	Ah kenht oo euhk.

* If there is no infinitive, insert the form, he eats, &c.

317 To die	Ah wunh ha yeuhk.
318 To speak	Ah kah weh reuhk.
319 To see	Ah kah keuhk.
320 To hear	Ah kah koo hunh sh'henhk.
321 To think	Ah kah kah wunh te keuhnunh te enhk.
322 To shout	Ah kah koo hunh renhk.
323 To advance	Ah kah koo ra kwah nunhk
324 To retreat	Ah kah yenh swah nih.
325 To give	Ah kah yenh nah nunh.
326 To carry	Ah kah hahk.
327 To tie	Ah kah treh'nk.
328 Walking	E weh, (he walks, &c.)
329 Singing	Roh uwunh a renk.
330 Dancing	Na nah t'kah.
331 Crying	Na rats nah.
332 Man lives	Euh queh, yah kenh hek 'gh.
333 God exists	Ya wunh ne yuh, yah kenh hek 'gh.
334 Fishes swim	Kenk chinh, keuh hoh nuk, wah nah wuhn's.
335 Birds fly	Che nunh, keuh hoh neuh, na yuh nunh hah n'yeh.
336 A fish swims	Skenh che aht, wah nah wuhn's.
337 A bird flies	Skah che nunh e'shrah.
338 One man	Enh che, a ne hah.
339 Twenty men	Na wah th'sunh, kah ya ne hah.
340 A little man	Renh thras s'tenh, a ne hah.
341 A little dog	A re's.
342 A good man	Renh kweh, strah kwah'st.
343 A bad man	Renh kweh, struh k'senh.
344 A good bow	Wah nah kwah'st.
345 A bad bow	Wah nah k'senh.
346 Good	Kah re whah ya nih.
347 Evil	Kah re whah k'senh.
348 Blessedness	Kah yenh wah nunk.
349 Mankind	Eh noo kenh'f.
350 The world	Wah'f nah kwa kenh.

NOTE.—As the above is intended to be used merely for comparing one Iroquois dialect with another, I desire that our alphabet may be used with the common English powers. If not, and you use a particular system, please to state what sounds it expresses.

H. R. S.

There is nothing answering to the infinitive and participle. I have therefore used the present indicative in the translation. I have divided the words into syllables, whether they are simple or compound. Where two or more words occur in the translation of a phrase, I have separated them by a comma. I have used the English alphabet with natural powers so far as Tuscarora sounds could be indicated by them. It is impossible to give, in many cases, a correct sound. A alone, has the sound of *a* in hate. Ah, like our interjection ah. The sound I intend to indicate by sunh, keuh, heuh, would be given, very nearly, by the Seneca alphabet used by Mr. Wright, thus: s*a*h, k*a*h, or kah, h*a*. The emphasis is, almost invariably, on the penultimate. Often a slight emphasis on some others. There is also often a prolongation of sound not indicated by any mark, as I supposed you would not need it.

I have not been able to finish this translation until now, (Oct. 20,) as I was absent, or otherwise engaged for some time after you had left; and when finally I was ready, Mr. Chew was not, until recently. I hope it has not been too long delayed.

I received your letter from New-York, of Sept. 16th. Nicholas Cusick, the father of James and David, was about 82 when he died. I have not been able to learn where he was born. He died at this place October, 1840. I do not know that there was anything very peculiar about him. He never was a "priest or juggler in his earlier days," that I can learn.

Yours, truly,
GILBERT ROCKWOOD.

Inquiries.

There are several words in your vocabulary of the Tuscarora, in which the sound of F is used, always, however, as a terminal sound, as in "Eh noo keuh'f," mankind.

Is this to be understood as denoting the ordinary sound of the letter?

Does it occur in other positions in words?

What is to be understood by the comma, which is invariably put before it?

H. R. S.

Tuscarora Mission, *Dec.* 6*th*, 1845.

Dear Sir—Your letter of December 1st is this day received. In reference to the vocabulary of Indian words we furnished you, I have further to remark, that the language having never been reduced to writing, each individual undertaking to reduce any portion of it, will have a system in part, at least, of his own. I have tried three different ways myself. It is difficult, if not impossible, to represent all the Tuscarora sounds by any combination of the English alphabet. I presume a stranger to the language would not, with the use of the vocabulary we have furnished you, give the correct sound in many instances.

The letter *f* terminating a word, has the sound of *f* in *chief*. I do not know as the comma before it, as in the word Eh noo keuh'f, is of any use. In common conversation, or at any time when they speak rapidly, the sound of *f* is not distinguished, as a general thing. Yet when they speak a word entire, there is this *f* sound, slowly and distinctly; it seems to be a distinct sound, or very nearly so. It appears to be a little separated from the main part of the syllable, as though another syllable was to follow immediately beginning with f; but as soon as the sound of *f*, as in find, is given, the person stops short. Thus instead of Eh noo keuh find, (I use the English word *find*, because the power of *f* in this word is the power of the letter intended in the Indian word given,) we say Eh noo keuhf, breaking off when you have given the sound of f, without proceeding to give the sound of *ind*. Perhaps if a comma is used at all, it would be more proper to place it *after* the *f*, thus : f' ; or the *f* might join the syllable, thus : Keuhf.

I do not recollect that the sound of *f* is heard in any other part of a word than as a terminating sound.

Sometimes an *r* occurs separated, you will observe, by a comma from the rest of the syllable. It matters not much whether the *r* is joined to the preceding or following syllable. There is the sound of an *r* between them when the word is spoken. I have been puzzled to know where to place it. It seems to answer either way. Thus, in the word for to-morrow: Euh yuh'r heuh ; or Euh yuh' rheuh. If joined to the syllable *yuh*, without being separated by the comma, you would pronounce it very nearly like the English word *your*. As it is, thus, yuh'r, its sound is very nearly like the English word *use*, and I am not sure but that would be a preferable way of writing it, thus : Euh use heuh ; yet there is a twirl or *r* sound you do not get as in the other mode of writing it. R terminating a word has much the same sound.

Instead of using the word *find* above, I might have used any other word beginning with f. It has its ordinary sound.

Any other information you may wish, if in my power to give it, you may be free to ask. Yours, truly,

G. ROCKWOOD.

(I.)

Letter from Rev. Asher Bliss to Henry R. Schoolcraft.

Cattaraugus Mission, Sept. 4th, 1845.

DEAR SIR—Agreeably to your request I forward you some facts in regard to the establishment and progress of the gospel among the natives of this reservation. The Cattaraugus Mission Church was organized July 8th, 1827, (which is a little more than 18 years.) It consisted of Mr. Wm. A. Thayer, the teacher, his wife, and 12 native members. There have been additions to it from time to time, until the whole number who have held a connection with this church is one hundred and eighteen. Thirteen of these have been white persons and most of them connected with the mission family. Of the one hundred and five native members seven or eight have come by letter from other reservations, so that the number who have united on profession of faith is a little short of one hundred. Twenty-five of these have gone to their final account. Some have died in the triumphs of faith, and we humbly hope and trust that they are among the blessed, in the kingdom of our common Father. A number (as it was natural to expect from converts out of heathenish darkness) have apostatized from Christianity, and returned to their former courses. The proportion of these is not probably more than one in ten. Between sixty and seventy are now connected with some of the mission churches. A few only have removed to Allegany, Tuscarora, while the remainder still live on this reservation.

The effect of the gospel in promoting morality and civilization, may be learned in part from the fact that the public worship of God has been steadily maintained ever since the organization of the church, with members ranging from fifty to one hundred, and sometimes one hundred and fifty and two hundred as regular hearers of the word. A Sabbath school has been sustained a considerable share of the time. Many copies of the Holy Scriptures, and the New Testament, together with tracts, Sabbath school books, temperance papers, and religious periodicals, have been circulated among the children and youth. Temperance societies have been patronized by nearly all the chiefs and leading men on the reservation. Pledges have been circulated and received the signatures of a large majority of the population, of all parties, on the Washingtonian plan.

Day schools for teaching the English language have been kept in operation almost without interruption for more than twenty years, under the patronage of the A. B. C. F. M.

During the thirteen years that I have superintended these schools, nearly thirty different persons have engaged for a longer or shorter time, as teachers. For the past year there have been four schools under the patronage of the American Board, and one under the Society of Friends. The whole number who have been instructed in the five schools is probably not far from one hundred and twenty-five. The attendance of a part has been very irregular, sometimes shifting from one school to another, and sometimes attending no school at all. Several of the early pupils in the mission schools are now heads of families, well informed, industrious, temperate and religious, and in good circumstances. Some are interpreters, some teachers of schools, and others engaged in transacting the business of the nation.

You can, sir, best judge of the influence of the gospel in promoting worldly prosperity, when you have fully completed the census which is now being taken. When you count up the framed houses and barns, the horses, cattle, sheep and hogs, the acres of improved land, with the wagons, buggies and sleighs, clocks and watches, and the various productions of agriculture, you can easily conceive the difference between the present, and thirty years ago. I suppose there was not then a framed building of any description, and scarcely a log house, properly so called, no teams, no roads, no ploughed land, and but small patches of corn, beans and squashes. What an astonishing change!

As to the capacity of Indian children for improvement, my own impression is that there is no essential difference between them and white children. The fact that Indian children usually make slow progress in studying English books, can be accounted for in three ways: 1. They generally have little or no assistance from their parents at home. 2. They are irregular in their attendance on schools, for want of order and discipline on the part of parents. 3. Being ignorant of the English language, it is a long time before they comprehend fully the instruction of their teachers.

These circumstances operate to make the school room a very dull and uninteresting place to the scholar, and the reflex influence gives the scholar the same appearanee. When they can once rise above these circumstances, and overcome these obstacles, they make good proficiency in their studies.

Believing that these statements cover the ground of your inquiries, I subscribe myself, dear sir,

Respectfully and truly yours,

ASHER BLISS.

P. S. Should you desire further information on any of these points, or upon others, which have been omitted, please state your questions definitely, in writing. Yours, &c., A. B.

(K.)

Letter from Rev. William Hall to Henry R. School-craft.

Allegany Mission, Sept. 8th, 1845.

Dear Sir :—Your inquiries in relation to the state of religion, education, &c., among the Indians of this reservation, if I rightly understand them, are briefly answered as follows :

Christianity very much prospered here during the four years next preceding the past.

The number of church members during that period, was nearly tripled, and very encouraging additions were made to their knowledge and zeal. But the past year has been one of stupidity and drought.

There has, however, been four additions from the Indians, made to the church, by profession of faith, and two whites.

The present number of Indian members is about one hundred and fifteen. The number of whites is eight. Seven of the Indian members are under censure.

I have sustained three schools during the past summer, in which about eighty Indian children have been more or less taught. One of these schools, whose whole number is only about thirty, gives an average attendance of nearly twenty-five. In this neighborhood the population is sufficiently compact for a farming community, and the younger parents are partially educated.

In the other neighborhoods, the population is very sparse, and the parents very ignorant. The consequence is, that the daily attendance falls short of one half the whole number of scholars, and cannot be called regular at that. Many do not get to school earlier than half past eleven, and very few earlier than ten, and half past ten. Those who attend regularly, evince a capacity to acquire knowledge, equaling the whites, and one of our schools will suffer nothing, in comparison with common country schools.

I am, dear sir,

Yours &c.,

WILLIAM HALL.

(L.)

Letter from Rev. Wm. McMurray to H. R. Schoolcraft.

Dundas, *November* 11*th*, 1845.

MY DEAR SIR—I have just received the vocabularies, with the Indian words, from the Rev. Adam Elliot, of Tuscarora, to whom I sent them for the translation. The cause of the delay was his severe illness, and the difficulty of getting suitable persons to give him the Indian. He says, before you publish, if you will send him, through me, the proof sheets, he will have them corrected for you, and forwarded without delay. He is an amiable and most excellent man.

Yours, most faithfully,
WILLIAM McMURRAY.

MOHAWK.

1 God .... Niyoh
2 Devil .... Onesohrono
3 Man .... Rongwe
4 Woman .... Yongwe
5 Boy .... Raxaa
6 Girl .... Kaxaa
7 Child .... Exaa
8 Infant.............. Owiraa
9 Father (my).... .... Rakeniha
10 Mother " .... Isteaha
11 Husband " .... Teyakenitero
12 Wife " .... Teyakenitero
13 Son " .... Iyeaha
14 Daughter " .... Keyeaha
15 Brother " .... Akyatatekeaha
16 Sister " .... Akyatatoseaha
17 An Indian .... Ongwehowe
18 Head .... Onontsi
19 Hair .... Ononkwis
20 Face................ Okonsa
21 Scalp .... Onora
22 Ear................. Ohonta
23 Eye .... Okara
24 Nose................ Onyohsa
25 Mouth .... Jirasakaronte
26 Tongue .... Aweanaghsa

27 Tooth................ Onawi
28 Beard................ Okeasteara
29 Neck .... Onyara
30 Arm .... Onontsa
31 Shoulder .... Oghneahsa
32 Back .... Oghnagea
33 Hand .... Osnosa
34 Finger .... Osnosa
35 Nail .... Ojiera
36 Breast .... Aonskwena
37 Body . ... Oyeronta
38 Leg .... Oghsina
39 Navel .... Oneritsta
40 Thigh................ Oghnitsa
41 Knee .... Okwitsa
42 Foot................. Oghsita
43 Toe .... Oghyakwe
44 Heel................. Orata
45 Bone .... Ostiea
46 Heart .... Aweri
47 Liver .... Otweahsa
48 Windpipe............. Ratoryehta
49 Stomach.............. Onekereanta
50 Bladder .... Oninheaghhata
51 Blood................ Onegweasa
52 Vein................. Oginohyaghtough
53 Sinew................ Oginohyaghtough
54 Flesh .... Owarough
55 Skin .... Oghna
56 Seat .... Onitskwara
57 Ankle................ Osinegota
58 Town................. Kanata
59 House .... Kanosa
60 Door .... Kanhoha
61 Lodge .... Teyetasta
62 Chief .... Rakowana
63 Warrior .... Roskeahragehte
64 Friend .... Atearosera
65 Enemy................ Shagoswease
66 Kettle .... Onta
67 Arrow .... Kayonkwere
68 Bow.................. Aeana
69 War club............. Yeanteriyohta kanyoh
70 Spear .... Aghsikwe
71 Axe .... Atokea
72 Gun .... Kaghore
73 Knife .... Asare
74 Flint .... Kahnhia
75 Boat................. Kahoweya
76 Ship .... Kahoweyakowa

77	Shoe................	Aghta
78	Legging	Karis
79	Coat................	Atyatawit
80	Shirt................	Onyataraa atyatawit
81	Breechcloth	Kakare
82	Sash	Atyatanha
83	Head dress...........	Onowarori
84	Pipe	Kanonawea
85	Wampum............	Onegorha
86	Tobacco.............	Oyeangwa
87	Sky	Otshata
88	Heaven	Karonghyage
89	Sun	Karaghkwa
90	Moon	Eghnita
91	Star	Ogistok
92	Day	Eghnisera
93	Night	Aghseanteane
94	Light	Teyoswathe
95	Darkness	Tyokaras
96	Morning............	Ohrhonkene
97	Evening............	Yokoraskha
98	Spring	Keankwetene
99	Summer	Akeanhage
100	Autumn	Kanonage
101	Winter..	Koghserage
102	Wind	Owera
103	Lightning	Teweanerekarawas
104	Thunder	Kaweras
105	Rain................	Yokeanorough
106	Snow	Oniyehte
107	Hail	Yoisontie
108	Fire	Yotekha
109	Water	Oghnekanos
110	Ice................	Oise
111	Earth : land	Owhensia
112	Sea................	Kanyaterakekowa
113	Lake	Kanyatare
114	River	Kaihoghha
115	Spring	Yohnaweronte
116	Stream	Yohyohonto
117	Valley	Teyohrowe
118	Hill	Yononte
119	Mountain..........	Yonontekowa
120	Plain	Kaheanta
121	Forest	Karhago
122	Meadow............	Yeheantyakta
123	Bog	Yonanawea
124	Island..............	Kawenote
125	Stone	Oneaya
126	Rock	Otsteara

127	Silver	Karistanoro
128	Copper	Oginigwar karistaji
129	Iron	Karistaji
130	Lead	Kawistanawis
131	Maize	Oneasti
132	Wheat	Eanekeri
133	Oats	Yonohonte
134	Potatoe	Oghneanata
135	Turnep	Ojikwa
136	Tree	Kherhite
137	Wood	Oyeante
138	Pine	Oghnehta
139	Oak	Tokeaha
140	Ash	Eghsa
141	Elm	Akaraji
142	Basswood	Ohosera
143	Shrub	Nikakwerasa
144	Leaf	Oneraghte
145	Bark	Owajiste
146	Grass	Ohonte
147	Nettle	Ohrhes
148	Weed	Kahontaxa
149	Flower	Ojijia
150	Bread	Kanatarok
151	Indian meal	Oneasti othesera
152	Flour	Othesera
153	Meat	Owarough
154	Fat	Yoresea
155	Beaver	Jonitough
156	Deer	Oskoneantea
157	Bison	
158	Bear	Oghkwari
159	Otter	Tawine
160	Fox	Jitsho
161	Wolf	Okwaho
162	Dog	Ehrhar
163	Squirrel	Arosea
164	Hare	Tahontanegea
165	Lynx	
166	Panther	
167	Muskrat	Anokyea
168	Polecat	Takoskowa
169	Hog	Kwiskwis
170	Horse	Yagosateas
171	Cow	Canonta
172	Sheep	Teyotinakarontoha
173	Turtle	Anowara
174	Toad	Jighnanatak
175	Insect	Otsenown
176	Snake	Onyare

177	Bird	Jiteaha
178	Egg	Onhonsa
179	Feather	Ostosera
180	Claw	Otjiera
181	Beak	Ojikeweyeanta
182	Wing	Oweya
183	Goose	Onasakeara
184	Partridge	Oghkwesea
185	Duck	Sora
186	Pigeon	Orite
187	Plover	
188	Turkey	Skawerowane
189	Crow	Jokawe
190	Robin	Jiskoko
191	Eagle	Oteanyea
192	Hawk	Karhakoha
193	Snipe	Tawistawis
194	Owl	Ohowa
195	Woodpecker	Kwarare
196	Fish	Keantsiea
197	Trout	Tyotyaktea
198	Bass	Ojikakwara
199	Pike	Jikonsis
200	Sturgeon	Nikeanjiakowa
201	Sunfish	Karaghkwakeanjiea
202	Fin	Odare
203	Scale	Otsta
204	White	Kearakea
205	Black	Kahonji
206	Red	Onegweantara
207	Blue	Oronya
208	Yellow	Oginigwur
209	Green	Ohonte
210	Great	Kowanea
211	Small	Niwaa
212	Strong	Kashatste
213	Weak	Yoyatakeaheyea
214	Old	Oksteaha
215	Young	Nityoyeaha
216	Good	Yoyawere
217	Bad	Wahetkea
218	Handsome	Yorase
219	Ugly	Wahetkea
220	Alive	Yonhe
221	Dead	Yaweaheyea
222	Life	Yonhe
223	Death	Keaheyea
224	Cold	Yotore
225	Hot	Yotarihea
226	Sour	Teyohyojis

227 Sweet.............. Yaweko
228 Bitter.............. Yotskara
229 I.................... Iih
230 Thou................ Ise
231 He.................. Raonha
232 She................. Aonha
233 They................ Rononha
234 You, Ye............ Jiyoha
235 We.................. Onkyoha
236 This................ Keaikea
237 That................ Toikea
238 All................. Agwegon
239 Part................ Otyake
240 Who................. Onka
241 Near................ Niyorea
242 Far off............. Ino
243 To-day.............. Keaweante
244 Yesterday........... Teteare
245 To-morrow........... Eayhorheane
246 By and by........... Owagehaseaha
247 Yes................. Ea
248 No.................. Yahtea
249 Perhaps............. Tokul
250 Above............... Enegea
251 Under............... Onagon
252 Within.............. Onagounonga
253 Without............. Atstenongati
254 On.................. Ethogh
255 Somethlng........... Onheno
256 Nothing............. Yaghotheno
257 One................. Easka
258 Two................. Tekeni
259 Three............... Aghsea
260 Four................ Kieri
261 Five................ Wisk
262 Six................. Yayak
263 Seven............... Jatak
264 Eight............... Satego
265 Nine................ Tiyohto
266 Ten................. Oyeri
267 Eleven.............. Easkayaweare
268 Twelve.............. Tekniyaweare
269 Thirteen............ Aghseayaweare
270 Fourteen............ Kaiyeriyaweare
271 Fifteen............. Wiskyaweare
272 Sixteen............. Yayakyaweare
273 Seventeen........... Jatakyaweare
274 Eighteen............ Sategoyaweare
275 Nineteen............ Tiyohtoyaweare
276 Twenty.............. Tewasea
277 Thirty.............. Aghseaniwaghsea

278 Forty .... Kaieriniwaghsea
279 Fifty................ Wiskniwaghsea
280 Sixty................ Yayakniwaghsea
231 Seventy .... Jatakniwaghsea
282 Eighty .... Sategoniwaghsea
283 Ninety .... Tiyohtoniwaghsea
284 One hundred .... Easkateweanyawe
285 Two hundred.......... Tekeniteweanyawe
286 One thousand......... Oyeriteweanyawe
287 Two thousand .... Teweayawe eghtseraghsea
288 One million ....
289 To eat*.............. Teayontskahou
290 To drink............. Eayehnekira
291 To run .... Teayoraghtate
292 To walk.............. Eayonteanti
293 To dance............. Teayenonyakwe
294 To Fly............... Teankatea
295 To laugh .... Eayakoyeshough
296 To cry .... Teayoseanthough
297 To burn.............. Eawatsha
298 To love .... Eayontatenoronkwe
299 To go................ Eayonteanti
300 To strike .... Eayeyeanti
301 To kill.............. Eayontateriyo
302 To sing.............. Eayontereanotea
303 To sleep............. Eayakotawe
304 To speak .... Eayontati
305 To die .... Eayaighheye
306 To see............... Eayontkaghtho
307 To hear .... Eayoronkhe
308 To think............. Eayonontonyeawe
309 War cry.............. Waontskwararonyea
310 Retreat cry.......... Tontatsyatonek
311 To give .... Eayontatea
312 To carry............. Eayehhawe
313 To tie............... Eayenereanke
214 Walking.............. Yagohteantyohatyea
215 Singing.............. Yereanote
216 Dancing.............. Teyakononyakwea
217 Crying .... Teyoseanthous
218 To be, or exist...... Eghnoyotea
219 He is .... Raonhase
220 I am .... Iighse.

* If there is no infinitive, insert verbs in their original form, as, He eats, &c.

CAYUGA.

1	God	Niyoh
2	Devil	Onesoono
3	Man	Najina
4	Woman	Konheghtie
5	Boy	Aksaa
6	Girl	Exaa
7	Child	Exaa
8	Infant	Onoskwataa
9	Father (my)	Ihani
10	Mother "	Iknoha
11	Husband "	Ionkniniago
12	Wife "	Iongiahisko
13	Son "	Ihihawog
14	Daughter "	Ikhehawog
15	Brother "	Itekyatehnonte
16	Sister "	Kekeaha
17	An Indian	Ongwehowe
18	Head	Onowaa
19	Hair	Ononkia
20	Face	Okonsa
21	Scalp	Onoha
22	Ear	Honta
23	Eye	Okaghha
24	Nose	Onyohsia
25	Mouth	Sishakaent
26	Tongue	Aweanaghsa
27	Tooth	Onojia
28	Beard	Okosteaa
29	Neck	Onyaa
30	Arm	Oneantsa
31	Shoulder	Oghnesia
32	Back	Eshoghne
33	Hand	Eshoghtage
34	Finger	Onia
35	Nail	Ojeighta
36	Breast	Oahsia
37	Body	Oyeonta
38	Leg	Oghsena
39	Navel	Kotshetot
40	Thigh	Onhoska
41	Knee	Okontsha
42	Foot	Oshita
43	Toe	Oghyakwea
44	Heel	Iyatage
45	Bone	Ostienda
46	Heart	Kawiaghsa
47	Liver	Gotwesia
48	Windpipe	Ohowa
49	Stomach	Onekreanda

50 Bladder .... Onheha
51 Blood.............. Otgweasa
52 Vein............... Ojinohyada
53 Sinew.............. Ojinohyada
54 Flesh.............. Owaho
55 Skin............... Ogoneghwa
56 Seat............... Ondiadakwa
57 Ankle.............. Ojihougwa
58 Town............... Kanatae
59 House.............. Kanosiod
60 Door............... Kanhoha
61 Lodge.............. Teyetasta
62 Chief.............. Aghseanewane
63 Warrior............ Osgeagehta
64 Friend............. Aterotsera
65 Enemy.............. Ondateswaes
66 Kettle............. Kanadsia
67 Arrow.............. Kanoh
68 Bow................ Adota
69 War Club........... Kajihwaodriohta
70 Spear.............. Kaghsigwa
71 Axe................ Atokea
72 Gun................ Kaota
73 Knife.............. Kainatra
74 Flint.............. Atrakwenda
75 Boat............... Kaowa
76 Ship............... Kaowagowa
77 Shoe............... Ataghkwa
78 Legging............ Kaisra
79 Coat............... Atyatawitra
80 Shirt.............. Nikaheha
81 Breechcloth........ Katrotaa
82 Sash............... Teatniagwistrista
83 Headdress.......... Tiodnaawonhasta
84 Pipe............... Atsiokwaghta
85 Wampum............. Otkoa
86 Tobacco............ Oyeangwa
87 Sky................ Otshata
88 Heaven............. Kaohyage
89 Sun................ Kaaghkwa
90 Moon............... Soheghkakaaghkwa
91 Star............... Ojishonda
92 Day................ Onisrate
93 Night.............. Asohe
94 Light.............. Teyohate
95 Darkness........... Tiyotasontage
96 Morning............ Sedetsiha
97 Evening............ Okaasa
98 Spring............. Kagwetijiha
99 Summer............. Kakenhage

100 Autumn.............. Kananagene
101 Winter.............. Kohsreghne
102 Wind................ Kawaondes
103 Lightning .... Teweanihos
104 Thunder............. Kaweanotatias
105 Rain................ Ostaondion
106 Snow .... Onieye
107 Hail................ Oidriondio
108 Fire................ Ojista
109 Water .... Onikanos
110 Ice................. Oitre
111 Earth—Land .... Oeanja
112 Sea................. Kanyateowaneghne
113 Lake .... Kanyataeni
114 River............... Kihade
115 Spring .... Oghnawaot
116 Stream.............. Oghyeanto
117 Valley .... Teyostowento
118 Hill................ Onontae
119 Mountain............ Onontowanea
120 Plain .... Kaheantae
121 Forest .... Kahago
122 Meadow.............. Ustondriakta
123 Bog .... Oweanjanawe
124 Island .... Kaweghnod
125 Stone............... Kaskwa
126 Rock .... Osteaha
127 Silver.............. Kawistanoo
128 Copper.............. Ogwenida
129 Iron .... Kaniawasa
130 Lead................ Kanikanawis
131 Maize............... Oneha
132 Wheat............... Onajia
133 Oats........ ...... Oats
134 Potatoe .... Onata
135 Turnip.............. Okteha
136 Tree................ Krael
137 Wood................ Oyeanda
138 Pine................ Ostaa
139 Oak .... Kakata
140 Ash .... Kahoweya
141 Elm .... Oshkra
142 Basswood............ Ohotra
143 Shrub .... Ohonda
144 Leaf .... Ouraghta
145 Bark................ Owajista
146 Grass .... Owenoghkra
147 Nettle .... Owhesra
148 Weed................ Owenokrasod
149 Flower.............. Oweha

150 Bread................ Onada
151 Indian Meal.......... Oneha otetra
152 Flour................ Otetra
153 Meat................. Owahon
154 Fat.................. Osea
155 Beaver............... Akaniago
156 Deer................. Wahontes
157 Bison................
158 Bear................. Yekwai
159 Otter................ Jutedro
160 Fox.................. Ishaie
161 Wolf................. Tahioni
162 Dog.................. Shoas
163 Squirrel............. Joniskro
164 Hare................. Toutaend
165 Lynx.................
166 Panther..............
167 Muskrat.............. Te out
168 Polecat.............. Kanewageha
169 Hog.................. Kwiskwis
170 Horse................ Kaondanenkwi
171 Cow.................. Tidoskwaout
172 Sheep................ Teyodinekaondoa
173 Turtle............... Kaniaghtengowa
174 Toad................. Naskwagaonta
175 Insect............... Otsinowa
176 Snake................ Osaista
177 Bird................. Jiteae
178 Egg.................. Onhosia
179 Feather.............. Ostotra
180 Claw................. Otsiouhta
181 Beak................. Kaniantasa
182 Wing................. Kawaontes
183 Goose................ Honkak
184 Patridge............. Kawesea
185 Duck................. Oheao
286 Pigeon............... Jakowa
187 Plover...............
188 Turkey............... Sohout
180 Crow................. Kaghka
190 Robin................ Jiskoko
191 Eagle................ Nataongowa
192 Hawk................. Tekayatakwa
193 Snipe................ Tawistewi
194 Owl.................. Owa
195 Woodpecker........... Kwaa
196 Fish................. Otsionda
197 Trout................ Tiadatsea
198 Bass................. Onoksa
199 Pike................. Jikonsis

200	Sturgeon	Kajhista
201	Sunfish	Oaghkwaonio
202	Fin	Owaia
203	Scale	Otsta
204	White	Keaankea
205	Black	Sweandaea
206	Red	Otkwenjia
207	Blue	Drinaea
208	Yellow	Jitkwa
209	Creen	Drahtaea
210	Great	Kowanea
211	Small	Niwaa
212	Strong	Kashatste
213	Weak	Oyatakeaheyo
214	Old	Ostea
215	Young	Ongwetasea
216	Good	Oyanri
217	Bad	Waetgea
218	Handsome	Oyanri
219	Ugly	Waetkea
220	Alive	Onhe
221	Dead	Aweaheyea
222	Life	Onhe
223	Death	Keaheyea
224	Cold	Otowi
225	Hot	Otaiho
226	Sour	Teyohyojis
227	Sweet	Okao
228	Bitter	Odjiwagea
229	I	I
230	Thou	Ise
231	He	Aoha
232	She	Kaoha
233	They	Onoha
234	You Ye	Johha
235	We	Oukyoha
236	This	Neangea
237	That	Shigea
238	All	Gwegon
239	Part	Tewadisto
240	Who	Sonaot
241	Near	Niyoea
242	Far off	Ino
243	To-day	Wanewanisade
244	Yesterday	Tedea
245	To-morow	Iyohea
246	By and by	Swegeha
247	Yes	Eghea
248	No	Teah
249	Perhaps	Tokatgisa

250	Above	Hetgea
251	Under	Nagon
252	Within	Nagongwadi
253	Without	Atstegwadi
254	On	Ethogh
255	Something	Tikaweaniyoh
256	Nothing	Teaskoutea
257	One	Skat
258	Two	Tekni
259	Three	Segh
260	Four	Kei
261	Five	Wis
262	Six	Yei
263	Seven	Jatak
264	Eight	Tekro
265	Nine	Tyohto
266	Ten	Waghsea
267	Eleven	Skatskaie
268	Twelve	Tekniskaie
269	Thirteen	Aghseghskaie
270	Fourteen	Keiskaie
271	Fifteen	Wiskaie
272	Sixteen	Yeiskaie
273	Seventeen	Jatakskaie
274	Eighteen	Tikroskaie
275	Nineteen	Tyohtoskaie
276	Twenty	Tewaghsea
277	Thirty	Seniwaghsea
278	Forty	Keiniwaghsea
279	Fifty	Wisniwaghsea
280	Sixty	Yeiniwaghsea
281	Seventy	Jatakniwaghsea
282	Eighty	Tekroniwagshea
283	Ninety	Tyohtoniwagshea
284	One hundred	Skateweaniawe
285	Two hundred	Tekniteweaniawe
286	One thousand	Waghseanateweaniawe
287	Two thousand	Teweaniaweetsaghsea
288	One million	
289	To eat	Eyondikoni
290	To drink	Eyehnikiha
291	To run	Tesental
292	To walk	Eyohteanti
293	To dance	Teyontkwa
294	To fly	Teankate
295	To laugh	Iyakoyonde
296	To cry	Teyoseanthou
297	To burn	Ewatsia
298	To love	Teyondatnoonk
299	To go	Eyonteandi

300 To stride .... Eyegoheg
301 To kill............. Eyondatriyo
302 To sing .... Eyontreanote
303 To sleep .... Jakota
304 To speak .... Iyeghtaea
305 To die .... Iyaihhe
306 To see .... Iyontkaghto
307 To hear .... Ayohonk
308 To think*............ Ayonontonio
309 War cry .... Yontskwaeonio
310 Retreat cry........... Jatego
311 To give .... Eayontatea
312 To carry .... Eyeha
313 To tie .... Ayeshaondak
314 Walking .... Goghteandiahandia
315 Singing .... Eeanot
316 Dancing............. Teyagotkwea
317 Crying.............. Teyoseantwas
318 To be, or exist .... Nethonanyohtohaag
319 He is .... Aohase
320 I am................ Ii

---

* If there is no infinitive, insert verbs in their simplest concrete form, i. e., indicative mood, present tense, first person, singular, as, he thinks, &c.

(M.)

Letter from Mr. Richard U. Shearman to Henry R. Schoolcraft.

Vernon, October 4th, 1845.

SIR: I completed the enumeration of the Oneida Indians some days ago, but delayed sending a return to you to ascertain the Indian names. It doubtless contains all the information you require at this particular time. Several families are included in the marshal's enumeration of the inhabitants of the town of Vernon. The remainder reside in Madison county.

The houses of these Indians are generally much better than the *log* houses of the whites, being constructed of hewn, even jointed logs, with shingle roofs and good windows. There are three good frame houses belonging to them;—one of these is a very handsome one, belonging to Skenado. I noticed in it some tasty fringed window curtains and good carpets. The Indians whom you met at Oneida were the *flower* of the tribe, being mostly farmers, who raise a sufficiency of produce for their comfortable support. There are several heads of families in my list, who cultivate no land of their own, but gain a subsistence by chopping wood and performing farm labor for others.

The whole number of families, I make, as you will perceive, 31. The whole number of houses I believe is but 28, but in each of these houses I found two families. The number of persons is 157. The count of last winter, which made 180 souls, was made with reference to retaining a certain amount of missionary funds, and Mr. Stafford, the Indian attorney, tells me it was made too high. Skenado says the tribe in this State numbers just 200 souls, of whom 40 are with the Onondagas.

Vernon, December 16th, 1845.

"I have filled up your Indian vocabulary to-day. I wrote down the words as they were given to me by one Johnson, a pretty intelligent man, who sometimes acts as interpreter. My orthography may be somewhat at fault, owing to my limited knowledge of the Indian manner of sounding the letters of the English alphabet. In general, I have endeavored to spell the words according to their sound in English, though the letter *a* is used often as in the English, and often to express the sound of *ah!* With this exception, and the use of *hon*, *han* and *hun*, to express a sound of which nothing in the English can convey an accurate impression, the spelling accords with the pronunciation. The Indian from whom I obtained the information informs me he knows of no words in his language to express such large numbers as *thousands* and *millions*. I have, therefore, in the cases of those numbers, filled the blanks with the Indian for *ten hundred* and *ten hundred thousand*; that is, in the latter case, *ten hundred ten hundreds*.

"I hope the table will be satisfactory, and that it may be of aid to you in making the comparison between the languages which you desire.

"Believe me, your friend, &c.

"RICHARD U. SHEARMAN."

ONEIDA.

223		
224	Alive	Loon ha.
225	Dead	La wan ha yun.
226	Life	Yun ha.
227	Death	Ya wu ha yah.
228	Cold	Yut ho lah.
229	Hot	Yu ta le han.
130	Sour	Ta yo yo gis.
231	Sweet	Ya wa gon.
232	Bitter	Yut ska lot.
233	I	Ee.
234	Thou	Eesa.
		He *she.*
235	He or she	La oon ha—a oon ha.
236	We	Tat ne jah loo
237	You	Eesa.
238	They	Lo no hah.
239	This	Kah e kah.
240	That	To e kuh.
241	All	A qua kòn.
242	Part	Ta kah ha sioun.
243	Many	A so.
244	Who	Hon ka.
245	Near	Ac tah.
246	Far-off	E non.
247	To-day	Ka wan da.
248	Yesterday	Ta tan.
249	To-morrow	A yul ha na.
250	Yes	Ha.
251	No	Yah ten.
252	Perhaps	To ga no nah.
253	Above	A nah kan.
254	Wonder	An ta ka.
255	Within	Na gon.
256	Without	Ats ta.
257	On	Ka ha le.

258 Something........... Ot hok no ho ta.
259 Nothing............. Ya ha ta non.
260 One................. Ans cot.
261 Two...........,..... Da ga nee.
262 Three............... Ha son.
263 Four................ Ki ya lee.
264 Five................ Wisk.
265 Six................. Yah yak.
266 Seven............... Ja dak.
267 Eight............... Ta ka lon.
268 Nine................ Wa tlon.
269 Ten................. O ya lee.
270 Eleven.............. Ans cot ya wa la.
271 Twelve.............. Da ga na ya wa la.
272 Thirteen............ Ha son ya wa la.
273 Fourteen............ Ki ya lu ya wa la.
274 Fifteen............. Wisk ya wa la.
275 Sixteen............. Ya yah ya wa la.
276 Seventeen........... Ja dak ya wa la.
277 Eighteen............ Ta ka lon ya wa la.
278 Nineteen............ Wa tlon ya wa la.
279 Twenty.............. Ta was hon.
280 Thirty.............. Ha son ne was hon.
281 Forty............... Ki ya lu ne was.
282 Fifty............... Wisk ne was.
283 Sixty............... Yah yak ne was.
283 Seventy............. Ja dak ne was.
284 Eighty.............. Ta ka lon ne was.
285 Ninety.............. Wa tlon ne was
286 One hundred......... Ans cot ta wa ne a wa.
287 Two hundred......... Da ga na ta wa ne a wa.
288 One thousand........ O ya lee ta wa ne a wa.
289 Two thousand........ Ta was ha ta wa ne a wa.
290 Million............. O ya lu ta wa ne a wa-o ya lee ta wa ne a wa.
291 To eat.............. Yon take hon ne.
292 To drink............ Yah na kee lah.
293 To run.............. Yah dak ha.
294
295 To walk............. Ee yun.
296
297 To dance............ Ta yunt qua.
298 To laugh............ Yah go yas hon.
299 To cry.............. Da yon unt os.
300 To burn....,........ U dek ha.
301 To love............. Ee no lon qua.
302 To go............... Wa hon ta de.
303 To strike........... Wa a gon lek.
304 To kill............. Wa gon wa lew.

305	To sing	Ka lon no ta.
306	To sleep	Ya go tas.
307	To die	Wa a ee ha ya.
308	To sit	Ya day lon.
309	To speak	Ya god ha la.
410	To see	Wa ont kot.
311	To hear	Yah got hon day.
312	To think	Yonnon ton nion ha.
313	To shout	Tay ya go hon let.
314	The war cry	At lee yos la tay ya go hon let.
315	To shout	Ta ya go hon let.
316	The retreat	Wa ha day go.
317	To give	Wa han da don.
318	To carry	Yay ha we.
319	To tie	Ka warn.
320	Walking	Ee yen.
321	Singing	Ka lon no ta.
322	Dancing	Ta hat qua.
323	Crying	Das yon unt os.
324	To exist	Ya gon ha.
325	I am	E gon ha.

The preceding part of this vocabulary, taken by myself, together with the entire vocabularies of the Onondaga and the Seneca, which are necessary to render the comparison complete, are omitted.

(N.)

Letter from Mr. D. E. Walker to Henry R, Schoolcraft.

Batavia, July 26th, 1845.

MR. SCHOOLCRAFT: I have visited the mound on Dr. Noltan's farm. Nothing of great importance can be learned from it. I should think it about fifty rods from the creek, and elevated, perhaps, some eight feet above the general level of the ground.

A similar one is also found about two miles south of this, and, as is this, it is on high ground, of circular form, and with a radius of about one rod. They were discovered about thirty or thirty-five years since. Nothing has been found in them, save human bones. The first, some nine or ten years since, was nearly all ploughed up and scraped into the road.

It is said that "sculls, arms and legs were seen on fences, stumps and the high-way for a long time after they were drawn into the road."

On, some two miles beyond the second was discovered a burial-ground. At that place were ploughed up shell, bone, or quill-beads. Near this place was found a brown earthen pot, standing between the roots of a large tree, (maple, they think) and with a small sapling grown in it, to some six inches in diameter. Beads of shell, bone or porcupine quills have often been found. I would have remarked, that on the first mound stood a hickory-tree some two feet through. There is also a ridge at the termination of high ground; I say a ridge, it appeared to me to be a regular fortification. It is, I should judge from thirty to forty feet in length. It would appear that the ground was dug down from some distance back, and wheeled to the termination of high ground, until a bank is thrown up to a height of some fifteen or twenty feet. This ridge, some think to be natural; others, from the fact that a smooth stone, about the size and shape of a pestle, was found in it, think it to be artificial. Perhaps other relics may have been found in it that would show it to be an artificial formation. All I could learn (and I rode about seven miles out of my way to converse with an old inhabitant) was, that this pestle was found in the ridge, and within three or four feet of its surface.

We may, perhaps, infer something from the size of an underjaw found here, *which is said to have been so large as to much more than equal that of the largest face in the country.*

Respectfully,

D. E. WALKER.

(O.)

Letter from H. C. Van Schaack, Esq. to Henry R. Schoolcraft.

Manlius, July 18th, 1845.

Dear Sir: Yours of yesterday from Jamesville is received. Its enclosure is the first intimation I have of having been chosen a corresponding member of the N. Y. Historical Society. I shall be happy to advance the objects of the Society.

I regret that you have not found it convenint to call, I hope you will still conclude to come. In the interim, I am convinced that Mr. C. can advance your objects better than I can; he has read several addresses on these subjects before the Literary Associations here and at Syracuse within two years past.

I have a collection of interesting papers (found among my father's papers at Kinderhook) relating chiefly to Indian affairs during the first half of the last century in the colony of New-York. These I am arranging, at my leisure, for the purpose of presentation to the N.Y. H. Society. I hope also to be able to send some papers of my father's which will advance the object of the society in rescuing the Indian names on the east banks of the Hudson from oblivion, and which last I had intended to forward to the Society through you. But I must take my time to effect those objects.

Excuse the haste with which this letter is written, as I have only this moment received your letter, and I do not wish to lose a mail.

Respectfully yours.

Manlius, Nov. 22nd, 1845.

Dear Sir: I forwarded to Mr. Gibbs, the librarian, a few days ago a volume containing various MSS. selected from my father's papers, relating chiefly to our aboriginal history, and about which I wrote you some time ago. You will find among them the journal of Conrad Weiser, Indian interpreter, giving an account of a visit to the Six Nations in 1745, at which time he accompanied the Senecas to Oswego, on their way to pay a visit to the Governor of Canada. You will also find among the papers, the original minutes of the Grand Council at Albany, in 1745, at which were present commissioners from Massachusetts, Connecticut, Pennsylvania, and New-York, with Governors from several of those States and the Sachems of the Six Nations. I think you will be interested in some of the papers. When I visit Kinderhook again, I hope to be able to make some additions to the contribution I have made to the Society. Many of the old papers relating to land trials, contain matter throwing light upon Indian names of objects and places. I, however, despair of ever seeing anything like a completeness of that description.

Respectfully yours,

H. C. VAN SCHAACK.

(P)

Letter from L. T. Morgan, Esq., to H. R. Schoolcraft.

Rochester, October 7, 1845.

SIR—You have doubtless seen a notice of the great council of the Six Nations, recently held at Tonawanda. We call it great, because we never saw any thing of the kind before, and perhaps never will again. Three of us started in season, and spent the whole of last week in attendance, and were also joined by Mr. Hurd, a delegate from Cayuga. We were there before the council opened, and left after the fire was raked up. Our budget of information is large, and overthrows some of our past knowledge, and on the whole, enlarges our ideas of the vastness and complexity of this Indian fabric. We are a great way from the bottom yet; we may never reach it, but what we do bring up to the surface, remunerates richly for the search.

We learn that at the establishment of the confederacy, fifty sachemships were founded, and a name assigned to each, which they are still known by, and which names every sachem of the several sachemdoms, from the beginning to the present time, has borne. There were also fifty sub-sachems, or aids; that is, to every sachem was given a sub-sachem to stand behind him—in a word, to do his bidding. These sachemships are still confined to the five nations; the Tuscaroras were never permitted to have any. They are unequally divided among the five nations, the Onondagas having as many as fourteen. The eight original tribes or families still hold to be correct, as we had it, but each tribe did not have a sachem. In some of the tribes were two or three, in others none. As the English would say the Howard family had a peerage in it, so would the Indians say that a certain tribe or clan had one or two or no sachemships running in it. The idea seems to be that the sachem did not preside over a tribe, as that would leave some tribes destitute; but the nine Oneida sachems, for instance, ruled the Oneida nation conjointly, and when the nations met in council, would represent it. The fifty sachems were the only official characters known at the councils of the confederacy. The sub-sachems and chiefs had nothing to say. And unanimity, as in the Polish diet, was always necessary. Over this council, the Tha-do-da-hoh, or great sachem of the confederacy, presided. He was always taken from the Onondagas, as we heretofore supposed; but what is very important, it is denied that there was any such officer as a Tokarihogea, or military chieftain over the confederacy. They recognize no such office, and deny that Brant was any thing but a chief, or an officer of the third and lowest class. I sifted this matter thoroughly, in conversations with Blacksmith, La Fort, Capt. Frost, and Dr. Wilson, a Cayuga, and am satisfied that the Tha-do-da-hoh* was the chief ruler of the Iroquois, and that they had no other. We fell into this error by following Stone, who in the Life of Brant, pretends to establish in him the title of war chieftain or Tokarihogea of the confederacy In relation to the head warriors or military leaders of the nations, there is still some obscurity. The Seneca nation has two, but the other nations none. The truth is, the learning, if we may so call it, of the Iroquois is in the hands of a few, and it is very difficult to reach it, as those who are the most learned are the most inveterate Indians, and the least communicative.

Their laws of descent are quite intricate. They follow the female line, and as the children always follow the tribe of the mother, and the man never is allowed to marry in his own tribe, it follows that the father and son are never of the same tribe, and hence the son can never succeed the father, because the sachemship runs in the tribe of the father. It really is quite surprising to find such permanent original institutions among the Iroquois, and still more surprising that these institutions have never seen the light. If I can construct a table of descents with any approach to accuracy, I will send it down to the Historical Society. The idea at the foundation of their law of descent, is quite a comment upon human nature. The child must be the son of the mother, though he may not be of his mother's husband—quite and absolutely an original code.

The object of this council was to "raise up sachems" in the place of those who had died. It would require more room than twenty letters would furnish to explain what we saw and heard—the mode of election and deposition—the lament for the dead—the wampum—the two sides of the council fire, &c. &c., and the other ceremonies connected with raising up sachems; also the dances, the preaching, the feast.

We were well received by the Indians, and they seemed disposed to give us whatever information we desired on the religious system of the Iroquois, their marriage and burial rites, &c. Faithfully,

L. T. MORGAN.

---

* This is a Seneca pronunciation of the name written ATOTARHO, by Cusick, and Tatotarho, by another and older authority. For a figure of this noted primary ruler, as it is given in Iroquois picture writing, see page 132. H. R. S.

NOTE.

In Mr. Cusick's statement of his labors, he states that he has been instrumental in forming *three* churches, consisting of *two hundred members;* but he omits noticing the locality and separate number of these churches. The church over which he presides, at Tuscarora, constitutes a part, but I am not able to say what part of the number. He probably includes the Tonewanda church in the estimate; but, from this uncertainty, it was impossible to bring either definitely into the column of "church members." A reference in the appropriate column of the returns from Buffalo, denotes this church also to be "incomplete," as no return from the missionary, Mr. Wright, has been received, and the interpreter, Mr. Pierce, who filled up the returns for that station, dropped this colnmn, after inserting *five* names, under the belief that the information would be given, and better given, by the missionary himself.

Mr. Hall, of Alleghany, returns one more *school* than appears in the column of schools, an error which was not detected till the proof sheets had been returned; nor is it known whether this includes the schools kept by the Society of Frieuds on that reservation, no information having been received from their local teacher, who was, however, verbally requested to state the number of his pupils.

In the pamphlet of this Society, on Seneca affairs, issued at Baltimore, in 1845, the number of pupils under their charge, on the Cattaraugus reservation, is stated at 107, and it is added, that an incipient boarding school for girls had been attempted.

It is not known whether, in the four schools reported by Mr. Bliss, at this reservation, the teachers and labors of the Society of Friends are included.

Mr. Rockwood, of Tuscarora, states that there is but *one* school on that reservation.

In the column of octogenarians, a typographical error gives the Tonewandas twenty-five instead of *ten persons* who had reached that age.

In filling up the column headed "persons who adhere to the native religion," the rule was to deduct from the total population, all who were reported as members of any Christian denomination.

Errata in the text, typographical and critical, which it was impossible to avoid, in the haste of a legislative publication, made in due course, there has been no opportunity to notice here, and it is hoped the proper consideration will be made.